Typographic Design:
Form and Communication

Fourth Edition

Saint Barbara. Polychromed walnut sculpture, fifteenth-century German or French. The Virginia Museum of Fine Arts.

Typographic Design:
Form and Communication

Fourth Edition

ABCD**EFGHIJ**K**LM**NOPQRSTUVWXYZ0123456789&

Rob Carter
Ben Day
Philip Meggs

1807 WILEY 2007
BICENTENNIAL

JOHN WILEY & SONS, INC.

Published by John Wiley & Sons, Inc., Hoboken, New Jersey
Published simultaneously in Canada

For general information on our other products and services or for
technical support, please contact our Customer Care Department
within the United States at (800) 762-2974, outside the United
States at (317) 572-3993 or fax (317) 572-4002.

Wiley also publishes its books in a variety of electronic formats.
Some content that appears in print may not be available in
electronic books.

Library of Congress Cataloging-in-Publication Data

Carter, Rob.
    Typographic design: form and communication / Rob Carter,
Ben Day, Philip Meggs. — 4th ed.
        p. cm.
    Includes bibliographical references and index.
    ISBN 0-471-78390-0 (pbk. : acid-free paper)
    1. Graphic design (Typography)
    I. Meggs, Philip B. II. Day, Ben. III. Title.
    Z246.C217 2006
    686.2'24—dc22
                                            2006045788
Printed in the United States of America

10 9 8 7 6 5 4 3 2

Typographic Design: Form and Communication,
Fourth Edition, is dedicated to Philip B. Meggs.
His scholarship, wisdom, humor, and passion
guide and teach us always. Thanks, Phil.

"The whole duty of typography,
as with calligraphy,
is to communicate to the imagination,
without loss by the way,
the thought or image
intended to be communicated
by the Author."

Thomas James Cobden-Sanderson

Contents

Typography has undergone continuous change over the past six decades. It is the authors' intention to provide a concise yet comprehensive overview of the fundamental information necessary for effective typographic-design practice. A knowledge of form and communication encompasses a range of subjects, including our typographic heritage, letterform anatomy, visual organization, and the interface between form and meaning.

In addition to these fundamentals, this volume presents other topics critical to informed design practice. Recent research provides the designer with an expanded awareness of legibility factors, enabling increased communicative clarity. Technological complexity requires comprehension of earlier and current typesetting processes, for both affect the language of typography. Theoretical and structural problem-solving approaches, evolved by design educators, reveal underlying concepts. Case studies in applied problem solving demonstrate a knowledge of typographic form and communication. A chapter devoted to typographic design process reveals traditional as well as non-traditional methods and practice. An understanding of typographic classification and form subtlety is gained from the study of type specimens.

Through the eleven chapters of this book, the authors share a compilation of information and examples with practitioners and students. It yields both insights and inspiration, bringing order to the complex and diversified subject of typographic design.

Typography is an intensely visual form of communication. Because this visible language communicates thoughts and information through human sight, its history is presented here in chronological visual form on four timelines. This evolution is shown in the context of world events, architectural development, and art history.

The first timeline predates typography. It begins with the invention of writing over five thousand years ago and ends with the invention of movable type in Europe during the middle of the fifteenth century. The second timeline covers the long era of the handpress and handset metal types. This period, from Gutenberg's invention of movable type to the end of the eighteenth century, lasted about three hundred and fifty years. In the third timeline, the Industrial Revolution and nineteenth century are revealed as an era of technological innovation and an outpouring of new typographic forms. The fourth timeline begins with the year 1900 and covers the twentieth century, when type was shaped by the aesthetic concerns of modernism, the need for functional communication, and technological progress. In the late twentieth century, the digital revolution in typography occurred, followed by the dawning of a new century and millennium.

**From the origins
of writing
to Gutenberg's
invention of
movable type:
3150 B.C.–A.D. 1450**

Note: Picture credits and
further descriptive
information for timeline
illustrations start on
page 302.

1.
c. 3150 B.C.: The earliest
written documents are
impressed clay tablets from
Sumer. The signs represent
clay tokens, which were used
for record keeping before the
invention of writing.

2.
c. 3000 B.C.: Cuneiform, a
very early writing system,
consisting of wedge-shaped
marks on clay tablets, was
invented by the Sumerians.

2500 B.C.: Egyptians begin to
make papyrus, a new writing
material derived from the
stems of the papyrus plant.

3.
c. 2600 B.C.: Completion of
the pyramids at Giza, Egypt.

4.
c. 2400 B.C.: False-door stele
inscribed with hieroglyphic
writing, from Old Kingdom
Egypt.

5.
c. 2100 B.C.: Cuneiform tablet
listing expenditures of grain
and animals.

6.
c. 1800–1400 B.C.:
Stonehenge, a megalithic
monument of thirty-foot-
tall stones set into circular
patterns.

7.
c. 1570–1349 B.C.:
Polychromed wood sculpture
from New Kingdom Egypt,
with hieroglyphic inscriptions.

8.
c. 1450 B.C.: Detail, *The Book
of the Dead* of Tuthmosis III,
hieroglyphic writing on
papyrus.

c. 3150 B.C.

1.

2.

4.

3.

7.

5.

8.

6.

2

9.

c. 1500 B.C.: The twenty-two characters of the Phoenician alphabet.

c. 800 B.C.: Homer writes the *Iliad* and *Odyssey*.

540 B.C.: The first public library is established in Athens, Greece.

10.

389 B.C.: Inscription in the Phoenician alphabet on a fragment of a marble bowl.

11.

Fourth century B.C.: Greek manuscript writing.

12.

448–432 B.C.: The Parthenon, temple of the goddess Athena, on the Acropolis in Athens, Greece.

13.

414–413 B.C.: Fragment of a Greek record of sale, carved on stone.

c. 160 B.C.: Parchment, a new writing material made from animal skins, is developed in the Greek state of Pergamum.

44 B.C.: Julius Caesar is murdered.

14.

c. 50 B C.–A.D. 500: Roman square capitals *(capitalis quadrata)* were carefully written with a flat pen.

c. A.D. 33: Crucifixion of Christ.

15.

c. 79: Brush writing from a wall at Pompeii, preserved by the volcanic eruption of Vesuvius.

105: Ts'ai Lun invents paper in China.

150: The Roman codex, with folded pages, begins to be used alongside the rolled scroll.

16.

c. 100–600: Roman rustic writing *(capitalis rustica)* conserved space by using more condensed letters written with a flat pen held in an almost vertical position.

c. 1500 B.C.

9.

11.

13.

12.

10.

MARTISQ·DOLO

14.

15.

CONNERIANTPRIA
SINMANIBUSUESTRI
VITROASIAMMACNO

16.

17.
118–25: The Pantheon, Rome.
18.
Undated: The fluid gestural quality, harmonious proportions, and beautiful forms of Roman writing are effectively translated into the permanent stone carving of monumental capitals *(capitalis monumentalis).*

19.
312–315: Arch of Constantine, Rome. Carved into marble, monumental Roman capitals survived the thousand-year Dark Ages.

325: Emperor Constantine adopts Christianity as the state religion of the Roman Empire.

c. 400–1400: During the thousand-year medieval era, knowledge and learning are kept alive in the Christian monastery, where manuscript books are lettered in the scriptoria.

452: Attila the Hun invades and ravages northern Italy.

476: Emperor Romulus Augustulus, last ruler of the western Roman Empire, is deposed by the Ostrogoths.
20.
533–49: Church of Sant' Apollinare in Classe, Ravenna.
21.
Third–sixth centuries: Uncials are rounded, freely drawn majuscule letters, first used by the Greeks as early as the third century B.C.

22.
Third–ninth centuries: Half-uncials, a lettering style of the Christian Church, introduces pronounced ascenders and descenders.
23.
Sixth–ninth centuries: Insular majuscules, a formal style with exaggerated serifs, was developed by Irish monks from the half-uncials.

A.D. 118

17.

19.

18.

20.

musadquequamuisconsci
mitatisnostraetrepidatio
mur tamenfideixestuincit
21.

morzuautscm
22.

magnum quod erit
23.

732: The Battle of Tours ends the Muslim advance into Europe.

800: Charlemagne is crowned emperor of the Holy Roman Empire by Pope Leo III.

24.
c. 800: Portrait of Christ from *The Book of Kells,* a Celtic manuscript.

868: The earliest extant printed manuscript, the *Diamond Sutra,* is printed in China.

25.
Tenth century: High Cross at Kells, Meath County, Ireland.

26.
c. Eleventh century: Round tower on the Rock of Cashel, Tipperary County, Ireland, a lookout and refuge against Viking invaders.

27.
Eighth–twelfth centuries: Caroline minuscules became the standard throughout Europe after Charlemagne issued his reform decree of 796, calling for a uniform writing style.

1034: Pi Sheng invents movable type in China.

1096–1099: The First Crusade.

28.
1163–1250: Construction of Notre Dame Cathedral, Paris.

29.
Eleventh–twelfth centuries: Early Gothic lettering, a transitional style between Caroline minuscules and Textura, has an increased vertical emphasis.

30.
Twelfth century: Bronze and copper crucifix from northern Italy.

1215: The Magna Carta grants constitutional liberties in England.

31.
Thirteenth–fifteenth centuries: Gothic Textura Quadrata, or Textura, the late Gothic style with rigorous verticality and compressed forms.

1347–1351: First wave of the Black Death, a plague that decimates the European population.

32.
Thirteenth century: Byzantine School, *Madonna and Child on a Curved Throne.*

A.D. 732

24.

25.

31.

27.

29.

26.

30.

28.

32.

33.

Thirteenth–fifteenth centuries: Rotunda, a more rounded Gothic letter, flourished in southern Europe.

34.

Fourteenth century: Lippo Memmi, *Saint John the Baptist.*

35.

1420–36: Filippo Brunelleschi, dome of Florence Cathedral.

1431: Jeanne d'Arc is burned at the stake.

36.

Fifteenth century: First page of a block-book, *Apocalypse.* Woodblock printing probably appeared in Europe before 1400.

37.

1440–45: Fra Filippo Lippi, *Madonna and Child.*

c. 1450: Johann Gutenberg invents movable type in Mainz, Germany.

38.

c. 1450–55: Page from Gutenberg's 42-line Bible, the first European typographic book.

39.

Woodblock print of the hand-printing press, with compositors setting type from a typecase in the background.

40.

The cathedral in the medieval city of Mainz, Germany.

c. 1200

34.

37.

35.

38.

33.

36.

39.

40.

Typography from Gutenberg to the nineteenth century: A.D. 1450–1800

The humanist philosophy that flowered during the Renaissance embraced the study of classical literature, a belief in human dignity and worth, a spirit of individualism, and a shift from religious to secular concerns.

41.
1450–1500: Books printed in the first half-century of typographic printing are called Incunabula.

41.
1465: Sweynheym and Pannartz, the first type designed in Italy. It had some Roman features.

42.
1467: Sweynheym and Pannartz, the first Roman-style type, influenced by Roman inscriptional capitals and manuscripts written in Caroline minuscules.

43.
1470: Nicolas Jenson, early Venetian roman typeface.

44.
1475: William Caxton, typography from the first book printed in the English language.

45.
c. 1485: Filippino Lippi, *Portrait of a Youth*.

46.
1486: Erhard Ratdolt, the earliest known specimen sheet of printing types.

1492: Christopher Columbus lands in America.

47.
c. 1494: Scholar and printer Aldus Manutius established the Aldine Press in Venice to publish works by the great Greek and Roman thinkers.

48.
1495: Francesco Griffo (punch cutter for Aldus Manutius), roman type first used in *De aetna* by Pietro Bembo.

1450

bat ille ihefus:q quom p̄mū aufes uocaret̄ moifes figurā p̄fentiens tuffit eū ihefum uocari: ut dux militię delectus effet aduerfus amalech qui oppugnabant filios ifrabel: et aduerfariū debellaret p nois figuram: et populū m̄
41.

effe fenfum femitaf queritur. tanq̄ illi ad cogitandum rheda & quadrigif opuf eēt. Democrituf quafi in puteo quodam fic alto ut funduffit nulluf: ueritatem iacere demerfam nimirum ftulte
42.

ab omnipotenti dèo miffus deus uerbum quafi lucis ifi cunctis annũciat. Non hinc aut alrunde:fed undiq̄ cun ad deum uerum:græcos fimul et barbaros omnem fexū
43.

In the tyme of p̄ troublous worldz/ and of the fone Beyng and regnyng as well in the top englondz andz fraunce as in all other places vn
44.

45.

47.

 ue maria gf̄a plena dominus tecū benedicta tu in mulierib' et benedictus fruct' uentris tui: ihefus chriftus amen.

Glozia laudis refonet in oze omniũ Patri genitoq̄s proli fpiritu fancto pariter Refultet laude perhenni Laboribus dei uendunt nobis omnia bona. lauf:honoz: virtuf potétia:ꝛ gratiaꝛ actio tibi chrifte. Amen.

Hinc deũ fic ꝛ uincet per fecula cuncta. Prouidet ꝛ tribuit deus omnia nobis. Proficit abfque deo null'in ozbe labor. Illa placet tell' in qua res parua beati. Me facit ꝛ tenuief luxuriantur opes.

Si foztuna volef fieri derberoz conful. Si volet hec eadem fiet de cófule beroz. Quicquid amoz iuffit nó eft cótédere nitü Regnat et in dominos ius habet ille fuos. Aſſa data ꝛ uēda data ꝛ fine fenere nobis Mutua: nec certa perfoluenda die.

Ufus ꝛ ars docuit quod fapit omnis homo Ars animos frangit ꝛ firmas diruit vrbes Arte cadunt turres arte levantur onus Arribus ingenuis queſita eſt gloria multis Principio obſta fero medicina paratur Cum mala per longas conualuere mozas Qui non eſt hodie cras minus aptus erit.

Non bene pzo toto libertas venditur auro Hoc cœleſte bonum præterit orbis opes Pæcunia auido al'bonis veneranda liberu Serenitos ſemper cauete quoq; delpicito Summa petit livoz perflant altiſsima venti Summa petunt dextra fulmina miſſa iove In loca incraenum hy ſieria ſecreta gladio De grege currens ſtuttic mram aquila

Iudicis characteꝛ diuerfaꝛ maneꝛ rerū imprefſioni paratarū: Finis.

Erbardi Ratdolt Auguſtenſis viri folertiſſimi:præclaro ingenio ꝛ miri fica arte:qua olim Veneiijs excelluit celebratiſſimus. In imperiali nunc vrbe Auguſte vindelicoꝛ laudatiſſi me imprefſioni dedit. Annoq̄s ſalutis. M.CCCC.LXXXVI.Calē. Aprilis Sidere felici complevit.
46.

lud admirari ,quod uulgus folet:magnu effe fcilicet tantas flammas ,tam immen fos ignes poft hominum memoriam fem
48.

49.
1501: Francesco Griffo, the first italic typeface, based on chancery script handwriting.

50.
Home of Albrecht Dürer, Nuremberg, Germany.

51.
Woodblock initial by Geoffroy Tory, who returned to France from study in Italy in 1505, inspired by roman letterforms and Renaissance design ideals.

52.
1523: Lodovico Arrighi, an Italian writing master, introduces his formal chancery italic type.

53.
1517: Martin Luther posts his ninety-five theses on the door of Wittenberg Palace Church, launching the Reformation.

53.
1525: Albrecht Dürer, construction of the letter *B*.

54.
1529: Geoffroy Tory, construction of the letter *B*.

55.
1519–47: Pierre Nepveu, Chateau of Chambord, France.

56.
c. 1480–1561: Claude Garamond, outstanding designer of Old Style typefaces during the French Renaissance.

1501

50.

51.

53.

54.

55.

Claude Garamont.

56.

P·O·N·IN PRIMVM GEORGICORVM,
ARGVMENTVM·

Quid faciat lætas segetes, quæ sydera seruet
Agricola, ut facilem terram proscindat aratris,
Semina quo iacienda modo, cultus'q; locorum
Edocuit, messes magno olim fœnore reddi.

P·V·M·GEORGICORVM LIBER PRI
MVS AD MOECENATEM·

Vid faciat lætas segetes, quo sydere
terram,
Vertere Mœcenas, ulmis'q; adiun
gere uites,
Conueniat, quæ cura boum, quis
cultus habendo
Sit pecori, atq; apibus quanta experientia parcis,
Hinc canere incipiam. Vos o clarissima mundi
Lumina, labentem cœlo quæ ducitis annum
Liber, et almæ Ceres, uestro si munere tellus
Chaoniam pingui glandem mutauit arista,
Poculaq; inuentis Acheloia miscuit uuis,
Et uos agrestum præsentia numina Fauni,
Ferte simul, Fauni'q; pedem, Dryades'q; puellæ,
Munera uestra cano, tu'q; o cui prima frementem
Fudit equum magno tellus percussa tridenti
Neptune, et cultor nemorum, cui pinguia Cææ
Tercentum niuei tondent dumeta iuuenci,
Ipse nemus liquens patrium, saltus'q; Licæi

c

49.

Dele uarie sorti de littere poi, che in questo Tratta-
tello trouerai, se io ti uolessi ad una per una descriuere **52.**

57.

c. 1540: Titian, *Portrait of Cardinal Pietro Bembo.*

1543: Copernicus publishes his theory of the heliocentric solar system.

58.

1544: Simone de Colines, title page with woodcut border.

59.

1546: Jacques Kerver, typography, illustration, and decorative initials, which were combined into a rare elegance during the French Renaissance.

60.

After 1577: El Greco, *Saint Martin and the Beggar.*

1582: Pope Gregory XIII initiates the Gregorian Calendar, which is still in use.

1584: Sir Walter Raleigh discovers and annexes Virginia.

61.

1595: Johann Theodor de Bry, illustrative initial *E.*

1603: Shakespeare writes *Hamlet.*

62.

1607: Carlo Maderna, façade of St. Peter's, the Vatican.

1609: Regular weekly newspapers appear in Strasbourg, Germany.

63.

1621: Jean Jannon, typefaces upon which twentieth-century Garamonds are based.

64.

1628: The Vatican Press, specimen of roman capitals.

---

c. 1540

58.

60.

57.

F R A N C I S C V S

64.

LIVRE PREMIER DE

Poliphile racompte comme il luy fut aduis en songe qu'il dormoit, & en dormant se trouuoit en une uallee fermee d'une grand closture en forme de pyramide, sur laquelle estoit assis un obelisque de merueilleuse haulteur, qu'il regarda songneusement, & par grande admiration.

A forest espouentable aiant esté par moy passée, & apres auoir delaisse ceste premiere region par le doulx sommeil qui m'auoit lors espris, ie me trouuay tout de nouueau en vn lieu beaucoup plus delectable que ie premier, car il estoit bordé & enuironné de plaisans cotaulx verdoians, & peuplez de diuerses manieres d'arbres, comme chesnes, faux, planes, ormes, fraisnes, charmes, tilleulz, & autres, plantez selon l'aspect du lieu. & abas atrauers la plaine, y auoit de petitz buyssons d'arbrisseaux sauluaiges, côme genestz, geneuriers, bruyeres, & tamarins, chargez de fleurs. parmy les prez croissoient les herbes medicinales, a scauoir les trois consolides, enule, cheurefeuil, branque vrsine, liuesche, persil de macedoine, piuoyne, guymauues, plantain, betoyne, & autres simples de toutes sortes & especes, plusieurs desquelles m'estoient incôgneues. Vn peu plus auant que le mylieu de ceste plaine, y auoit vne sablonniere meslée de petites mottes verdes, & pleine d'herbe menuette, & vn petit boys de palmiers, esquelz les Egyptiés cueillent pain, vin, huille, vestement, & mesrain pour bastir. leurs fueilles sembloient lames d'espees, & estoiét chargées de fruict. il y en auoit de grandes, moiennes, & petites, & leur ont les anciens donnéce

59.

61.

La crainte de l'Eternel est le chef de science: mais les fols mesprisent sapiéce &

63.

62.

65.
1632–43: The Taj Mahal, India.
66.
c. 1630: Sir Anthony van Dyck, portrait of *Henri II de Lorraine.*

1639: The first printing press in the British Colonies is established in Massachusetts.

1657: First fountain pen is manufactured, in Paris.
67.
c. 1664: Jan Vermeer, *Woman Holding a Balance.*

1666: The great fire of London.

1667: Milton publishes *Paradise Lost.*

68.
c. 1670: Christoffel van Dyck, Dutch Old Style type.

1686: Sir Isaac Newton sets forth his law of gravity.
69.
1675–1710: Sir Christopher Wren, St. Paul's Cathedral, London.

During the eighteenth century, type design went through a gradual transition from Old Style to Modern Style fonts designed late in the century.

1700: The emergence of the Rococo Style.
70.
1702: Philippe Grandjean (punch cutter), Romain du Roi, the first transitional face.

71.
1709: Matthaus Poppelmann, Zwinger Palace, Dresden.

1709: England adopts the first modern copyright law.
72.
1720: William Caslon, Caslon Old Style types, which from this date were used throughout the British Empire.

1632

65.

66.

Ad me profeſtam eſſe aiebant. D. quid
Quæſo, igitur commorabare, ubi id

68.

69.

sa doctrine et de ses lois. Après, il nous fait voir tous
les hommes renfermés en un seul homme, et sa femme
même tirée de lui ; la concorde des mariages et la

70.

ABCDEFGHIKLMN
OPQRSTUVWXYZJ
Quouſque tandem abutere,
Catilina, patientia noſtra ? qu
Quouſque tandem abutere, Ca-
tilina, patientia noſtra? quam-

This new Foundery was begun in the Year 1720,
and finiſh'd 1763; and will (with God's leave) be
carried on, improved, and inlarged, by WILLIAM
CASLON and Son, Letter-Founders in LONDON.

72.

71.

67.

73.

1722: Castletown, near Dublin, Ireland.

1738: First spinning machines are patented in England.

74.

1744: Benjamin Franklin, title page using Caslon type.

75.

1750: François Boucher, *The Love Letter*.

76.

1750s: John Baskerville creates extraordinary transitional typefaces.

77.

1765: Thomas Cottrell introduces display types two inches tall (shown actual size).

78.

1768: Pierre Simon Fournier le Jeune, ornamented types.

79.

1773: Johann David Steingruber, letter *A* from *Architectonishes Alphabet*.

80.

1774: John Holt, broadside of the American revolutionary era, using Caslon type.

1775: James Watt constructs the first efficient steam engine.

1776: American Declaration of Independence is signed.

81.

1784: François Ambroise Didot, the first true Modern Style typeface.

1789: The fall of the Bastille launches the French Revolution.

82.

1791: Giambattista Bodoni, Modern Style typefaces of geometric construction, with hairline serifs.

1791: American Bill of Rights

guarantees freedoms of religion, speech, and the press.

1793: French King Louis XVI and Marie Antoinette are sent to the guillotine.

1796: Aloys Senefelder invents lithography.

1799: Nicolas-Louis Robert invents the papermaking machine.

1722

73.

M. T. CICERO's

CATO MAJOR,

OR HIS

DISCOURSE

OF

OLD-AGE:

With Explanatory NOTES.

PHILADELPHIA:
Printed and Sold by B. FRANKLIN,
MDCCXLIV.

74.

77.

LA
DIVINA
COMMEDIA
DI
DANTE ALIGHIERI
CON
ILLUSTRAZIONI

TOMO I.

PISA
DALLA TIPOGRAFIA
DELLA SOCIETÀ LETTERARIA
MDCCCIV.

82.

75.

76.

HISTOIRE
DE
LOUIS DE BOURBON,
SECOND DU NOM,
PRINCE
DE CONDÉ,
PREMIER PRINCE DU SANG,
Surnommé *LE GRAND.*

LIVRE PREMIER.
1621-1643.

LOUIS DE BOURBON, fecond du nom, naquit à Paris 1621, le 7 Septembre 1621 ; il fut titré *Duc d'Enguien*, nom heureux qui rappelloit la mémoire du vain-

78.

79.

80.

lumes in-4° sur papier-vélin de la fabrique de messieurs Matthieu Johannot pere et fils, d'Annonai, premiers fabricants de cette sorte de papiers en

81.

11

The nineteenth century and the Industrial Revolution: A.D. 1800–1899

The Industrial Revolution had a dramatic impact upon typography and the graphic arts. New technology radically altered printing, and designers responded with an outpouring of new forms and images.

83.
c. 1803: Robert Thorne designs the first Fat Face.

1804: Napoleon Bonaparte crowned Emperor of France.

1808: Beethoven composes his Fifth Symphony.
84.
1812: Jacques-Louis David, *Napoleon in His Study* (detail).

1814: Friedrich Koenig invents the steam-powered printing press.

85.
1815: Vincent Figgins shows the first Egyptian (slab-serif) typefaces.
86.
1815: Vincent Figgins shows the earliest shaded type.

87.
1816: William Caslon IV introduces the first sans serif type.
88.
1818: Page from *Manuale Tipographico,* which presented the lifework of Giambattista Bodoni.
89.
1821: Robert Thorne, Tuscan styles with splayed serifs.

1800

84.

83.

85.
ABCDEFGHIJK

86.
ABCDEFGHIKM

87.
LETTERFOUNDER

89.
Manchester

PARANGONE

Quousque tandem abutêre, Catilina, patientiâ nostrâ? quamdiu etiam furor iste tuus nos eludet? quem ad finem sese effrenata jactabit audacia? nihilne te nocturnum præsidium Palatii, nihil urbis vigiliæ, nihil timor populi, nihil concursus bonorum omnium, nihil hic munitissimus habendi se-

MARCUS TULL. CICERO

ORATOR ATQUE PHILOSOPHUS.

CHERASCO

88.

90.

1822: Thomas Jefferson, Rotunda of the University of Virginia in the neoclassical style based on Greek and Roman architecture.

1822: Joseph Niepce produces the first photographic printing plate.

91.

c. 1826: Bower, Bacon and Bower, early reversed type entitled White.

1826: Joseph Niepce takes the first photograph from nature.

92.

1827: Darius Wells invents the mechanical router, making the manufacture of large display wood types possible.

93.

1833: Vincent Figgins introduces outline types.

94.

1836: Davy and Berry, poster printed with wood type.

1830s–80s: Wood-type posters and broadsides flourished in America and Europe.

95.

1836: Vincent Figgins, perspective type.

96.

1837: Handbill set in Fat Face.

1837: Victoria crowned queen of England.

1822

STOCKS

91.

DARIUS WELLS.

92.

95.

90.

THEATRE-ROYAL, NORWICH.

FOR THE BENEFIT OF

R. Battley,

FRUITERER.

On THURSDAY, 12th May, 1836,

Will be performed the POPULAR PLAY, of The

CASTLE SPECTRE.

Earl Osmond....Mr. MADDOCKS
Reginald .....Mr. HAMERTON | Kenric....Mr. G. SMITH
Earl Percy....Mr. NICHOLS | Saib....Mr. HARRISON
Father Philip..Mr. GRAY | Muley....Mr. BRYAN
Motley ......Mr. GILL | Hassan,...Mr. NANTZ.

Angela ....Mrs. G. SMITH
Alice ..... Mrs. WATKINSON | Evelina ....Miss HONEY.

END OF THE PLAY,

A COMIC SONG

BY MR. MARTIN.

To conclude with the NAUTICAL DRAMA, of The

PILOT,

OR, A

STORM AT SEA!

The Pilot, Mr. MADDOCKS
Barnstable, Mr. G. SMITH—Captain Boroughcliffe, (a regular Yankee), Mr. GILL
Long Tom Coffin, Mr. NANTZ
Captain of the Alacrity, Mr. HAMERTON—Colonel Howard Mr. GRAY
Lieutenant Griffith, Mr. TAYLOR—Serjeant Drill, Mr. NICHOLS.

Sailors, Soldiers, &c.
Kate Plowden, Mrs. PLUMER—Cecilia, Miss HONEY
Irish Woman, Mrs. WATKINSON.

DAVY & BERRY, PRINTERS, ALBION OFFICE.

94.

HOUSEHOLD FURNITURE, PLATE, CHINA-WARE, JEWELS, WATCHES

93.

Working Men, Attention!!

Globe Office
Saturday, November
20. 1837

It is your imperious duty to drop your *Hammers and Sledges!* one and all, to your post repair, *THIS AFTERNOON,* at *FIVE* o'clock P. M. and attend the

GREAT MEETING

called by the papers of this morning, to be held at the CITY HALL, then and there to co-operate with such as have the GREAT GOOD OF ALL THEIR *FELLOW CITIZENS at Heart.* Your liberty! yea, your *LABOUR!!* is the subject of the call: who that values the services of HEROES of the *Revolution* whose blood achieved our Independence as a Nation, will for a moment doubt he owes a few hours this afternoon to his wife and children?

HANCOCK.

96.

97.

c. 1840–52: Sir Charles Barry and A. W. N. Pugin, Houses of Parliament, inspiration for the Gothic Revival.

98.

c. 1841: Wood and Sharwoods, ornamental type.

During the 1840s, ornamented type becomes increasingly important.

99.

1845: Robert Besley, the first Clarendon style.

1848: The California gold rush begins.

1851: Joseph Paxton designs the Crystal Palace.

100.

1853: Handbill combining Egyptian, outline, and decorative types.

101.

1854: Broadside using elongated Fat Face fonts.

1854: The United States makes its first treaty with Japan.

1856: Sir Henry Bessemer develops process for converting iron to steel.

102.

1859: William H. Page and Company, Ornamented Clarendons.

1859: Charles Darwin publishes *Origin of Species by Means of Natural Selection*.

c. 1840

97.

100.

101.

98.

audacia tua? nihilne te noc
dium palatii, nihil urbis vigi

99.

102.

103.

1860: *Charleston Mercury,* broadsheet announcing the dissolution of the Union.

1861–65: American Civil War.

1863: Abraham Lincoln signs the Emancipation Proclamation.

104.

c. 1865: Honoré Daumier: *The Third-Class Carriage.*

1866: The first successful transatlantic cable is laid.

1867: Alfred Nobel invents dynamite.

1867: Christopher Sholes constructs the first practical typewriter.

105.

1868: Currier and Ives, *American Homestead Winter.*

106.

c. 1875: J. Ottmann, chromolithographic card for Mrs. Winslow's Soothing Syrup.

1876: Alexander Graham Bell invents the telephone.

1877: Thomas Edison invents the phonograph.

1879: Thomas Edison invents the electric lightbulb.

107.

1883: The Brooklyn Bridge is opened to traffic.

1883: William Jenney designs the first skyscraper, a ten-story metal frame building in Chicago.

108.

c. 1885: Maverick & Wissinger, engraved business card.

109.

c. 1880s: Lettering printed by chromolithography.

110.

1886: Ottmar Mergenthaler invents the Linotype, the first keyboard typesetting machine.

1861

105.

107.

106.

109.

110.

103.

108.

104.

111.
1887: Advertisement for Estey
Organs.

1887: Tolbert Lanston invents
the monotype.

112.
1889: Alexandre Gustave
Eiffel, the Eiffel Tower.
113.
c. 1890s: Coca-Cola syrup jug.
114.
1892: Paul Gauguin, *By the
Sea.*

115.
William Morris' typeface
designs: 1890, Golden; 1892,
Troy; 1893, Chaucer.

116.
1891–98: William Morris'
Kelmscott Press launches
a revival of printing and
typography.
117.
1892: William Morris, page
from *News from Nowhere.*

1887

111.

112.

113.

114.

This is the Golden type.
This is the Troy type.
This is the Chaucer type.
115.

116.

Afloat again CHAPTER XXIV. UP THE THAMES. THE SECOND DAY.

HEY were not slow to take my hint; & indeed, as to the mere time of day, it was best for us to be off, as it was past seven o'clock, & the day promised to be very hot. So we got up and went down to our boat; Ellen thoughtful and abstracted; the old man very kind and courteous, as if to make up for his crabbedness of opinion. Clara was cheerful & natural, but a little subdued, I thought; and she at least was not sorry to be gone, and often looked shyly and timidly at Ellen and her strange wild beauty. So we got into the boat, Dick saying as he took his place, "Well, it is a fine day!" and the old man answering "What! you like that, do you?" once more; and presently Dick was sending the bows swiftly through the slow weed-checked stream. I turned round as we got into mid-stream, and waving my hand to our hosts, saw Ellen leaning on the old man's shoulder, and caressing his healthy apple-red cheek, and quite a keen pang smote me as I thought how I should never see the beautiful girl again. Presently I insisted on taking the sculls, and I rowed a good deal that day; which no doubt accounts for the fact that we got very late

230

117.

118.

1893: Henri van de Velde, title page for *Van Nu en Straks.*

1895: The Lumièire brothers give the first motion-picture presentation.

119.

1897: Edmond Deman, title page in the curvilinear Art Nouveau style.

120.

1890s–1940s: Inspired by Kelmscott, Americans Frederick Goudy and Bruce Rogers bring renewed excellence to book and typeface design.

121.

1897: Will Bradley, title page in his "Chap Book" style, reviving Caslon type and colonial woodcut techniques.

1898: Zeppelin invents his airship.

122.

1899: Josef Hoffmann, catalogue cover for a Vienna Secession exhibition.

123.

1898–1902: Hector Guimard, entrance to Paris Metro Station.

1893

118.

122.

119.

120.

121.

123.

Typography in the twentieth century: 1900–2000.

The twentieth century was a period of incredible ferment and change. Unprecedented advances in science and technology, and revolutionary developments in art and design have left their marks on typography.

124.
1900: Peter Behrens, dedication page from *Feste des Lebens und der Künst.*

1903: The Wright brothers succeed in the first powered flight.

1905: Einstein proposes his theory of relativity.

125.
1909: Filippo Marinetti founds Futurism, experimentation with typographic form and syntax.

126.
c. 1910: German sans-serif "block style."

127.
1913: Wassily Kandinsky, *Improvisation 31 (Sea Battle).*

1914–18: World War I.

c. 1915: Kasimir Malevich, Suprematist painting shown at the *0.10* group exhibition launching Suprematism.

128.
c. 1916: Bert Thomas, British war bonds poster.

1917–22: The Dada movement protests the war and conventional art.

129.
1917: John Heartfield, Dadaist advertisement.

130.
1917: Vilmos Huszar, De Stijl magazine cover.

1918: Czar Nicholas II and his family are executed.

131.
1919: Raoul Hausmann, Dada poem.

1900

124.

126.

127.

129.

128.

130.

131.

1920: Women's suffrage is granted in the United States.

1920: Bolsheviks triumph in the Russian Revolution.

132.
1921–25: Piet Mondrian, *Diamond Painting in Red, Yellow, and Blue.*

133.
c. 1923: Alexander Rodchenko, Russian Constructivist poster.

1924: Surrealist manifesto.

134.
1924: Gerrit Rietveld, Schroeder house.

135.
1925: El Lissitzky, title page.

136.
1925: Herbert Bayer, universal alphabet.

137.
1925: Constantin Brancusi, *Bird in Space.*

138.
1925: Jan Tschichold, title page for his article "Elementary Typography."

139.
1926: Piet Zwart, advertisement.

1927: Charles Lindbergh makes the first solo Atlantic flight.

140.
1928: Piet Zwart, advertisement.

1920

132.

134.

140.

133.

135.

137.

138.

bauhaus

136.

139.

1929: The New York Stock Market collapses, and the Great Depression begins.
141.
1930: Paul Renner, prospectus for Futura.

142.
1930: Chrysler Building, an example of Art Deco decorative geometric style.
143.
1931: Max Bill, exhibition poster.
144.
c. 1932: Alexey Brodovitch, exhibition poster.

1933: Adolf Hitler becomes chancellor of Germany.
145.
1936: Walker Evans, photograph of sharecropper family.

1939: Germany invades Poland; World War II begins.
146.
1942: Jean Carlu, advertisement.
147.
1944: Max Bill, exhibition poster.

1945: Atomic bombs destroy Hiroshima and Nagasaki; World War II ends.
148.
1948: Paul Rand, title page.

1929

FUTURA
DIE
SICH DIE WELT
EROBERTE

MAPPE

141.

konkrete kunst

147.

negerkunst
prähistorische felsbilder südafrikas
kunstgewerbemuseum zürich
ausstellung 2.—30. august 1931
geöffnet   10—12 14—18 uhr
sonntag   —17 uhr
montag   geschlossen
eintritt —.50
nachmittag und sonntag frei

143.

DESIGN FOR THE MACHINE
PENNSYLVANIA MUSEUM OF ART PHILA
OPEN ON : MON . WED . SAT . SUN .

144.

a   r
      p

148.

145.

146.

142.

20

149.
1948: Willem de Kooning, *Painting.*

150.
1950: Ladislav Sutnar, book cover.

1950: North Korea invades South Korea.

151.
1950–55: Le Corbusier, Notre Dame de Haut.

1952: School segregation is declared unconstitutional by the Supreme Court.

152.
1952: Henri Matisse, *Woman with Amphora and Pomegranates.*

153.
1955: Josef Muller-Brockmann, concert poster.

154.
1956: Saul Bass, advertisement.

155.
1956: Willem Sandberg, book cover.

1957: Russia launches Sputnik I, the first Earth satellite.

156.
1959: Saul Bass, film title.

157.
1959: Frank Lloyd Wright, the Guggenheim Museum, New York.

158.
1958: Carlo L. Vivarelli, magazine cover.

1948

149.

158.

153.

152.

151.

157.

150.

155.

154.

156.

159.
1959: Henry Wolf, magazine cover.
160.
c. 1959: Gerald Holton, "peace symbol."

161.
1959: Otto Storch, figurative typography.
162.
1960: Karl Gerstner, advertisement.
163.
c. 1960: Herb Lubalin, advertisement.

164.
c. 1961: George Lois, pharmaceutical advertisement.
165.
1962: Eero Saarinen, Dulles International Airport.

1963: President John F. Kennedy is assassinated.
166.
1965: Seymour Chwast and Milton Glaser, poster.

1965: The U.S. Marines land in force in Vietnam.
167.
1966: George Lois, magazine cover.

1959

159.

160.

DIVINE TO EAT, EASY TO MAKE, AND BEAUTIFUL TO LOOK ON: ELEGANT PARFAITS. THERE ARE TWO TYPES: THE FRENCH, WHICH IS A CREAMY, DELICATE, COOL (BUT NOT ICY) MIXTURE WITH A BASE OF SUGAR, EGGS, CREAM, FRUIT AND/OR FLAVORINGS; AND THE AMERICAN, MADE WITH COMMERCIAL ICE CREAMS OR SHERBETS OR BOTH WITH A SURPRISE INGREDIENT, SUCH AS FRUITS, CORDIALS, COGNAC, NUTS, SAUCES (SEE McCALL'S FINE SAUCE RECIPES ON PAGE 00). WITH AMERICAN PARFAITS, YOUR IMAGINATION CAN HAVE FREE REIN. WITH THE FRENCH, HOWEVER, YOU MUST FOLLOW RECIPE DIRECTIONS TO THE LETTER. PARFAIT MEANS, OF COURSE, PERFECT, AND WE CAN IMAGINE FEW MORE PERFECT DESSERTS, ESPECIALLY IF YOU WANT TO SHOW OFF. FOR THESE ARE TRULY SHOWOFF RECIPES! FROM THE COOK'S STANDPOINT, THERE IS A REAL ADVANTAGE IN SERVING FROZEN DESSERTS. FOR THE OBVIOUS REASON, THEY MUST BE MADE WELL AHEAD AND REFRIGERATED. THUS, THE BIG DESSERT PROBLEM IS OUT OF THE WAY WHEN IT'S TIME TO PREPARE THE MAIN PART OF THE MEAL. AT FAR RIGHT, YOU SEE AN AMERICAN PARFAIT, VANILLA ICE CREAM LAYERED WITH PISTACHIO AND TOPPED WITH WALNUTS AND WHIPPED CREAM. THE STRAWBERRY AND APRICOT PARFAITS ARE BOTH CLASSIC FRENCH. FOR THE RECIPES, TURN TO PAGE 00, WHERE YOU WILL FIND THE FRENCH AS WELL AS GOOD VARIATIONS OF THE QUICK AND POPULAR AMERICAN PARFAITS. THEN, PLAN A PARTY.

161.

ugh!'ly?

Ugliness, like beauty, is in the eye of the beholder. It is a value imposed upon a thing which, properly used, might well be called beautiful. At S H & L we try to avoid misleading labels. Our business is to design for advertising. Typography is one of our essential tools. If what we do with it is effective, we don't care if it is called pretty, ugly, or pretty ugly. If you think as we do, we ought to get together. Call Herb Lubalin at Plaza 1-1250, where we take the ugh! out of ugly.

ugh!'ly?

163.

allergic
SWELLING
Dimetane works

164.

167.

165.

162.

166.

168.
c. 1968: Seymour Chwast and Milton Glaser, poster.

169.
1968: R. Buckminster Fuller, American Pavilion, Montreal World's Fair.

170.
c. 1967: Symbol for the environmental movement.

171.
1969: First Moon walk.

172.
1972: Wolfgang Weingart, typographic interpretation of a poem.

173.
1974: Herb Lubalin, newspaper cover.

174.
1974: Cook and Shanosky, standard symbol signs.

1975: The Vietnam War ends.

175.
1976: American bicentennial, symbol design by Bruce Blackburn.

1968

168.

169.

170.

171.

172.

173.

174.

175.

176.
1977: Pompidou National Center of Arts and Culture, Paris.

177.
1977: Bill Bonnell, RyderTypes trademark.

178.
1978: Willi Kunz, poster design.

179.
1979: Richard Greenberg, film titles.

1979: Soviet troops invade Afganistan.

1980s: Digital typography and computer technology impact typographic design, leading to electronic page design by the end of the decade.

180.
1981: Bitstream founded; first independent digital type foundry.

1982: Pat Gorman and Frank Olinsky, Manhattan Design, MTV logo.

181.
1983: Michael Graves, Portland, Oregon, city hall.

182.
1984: Warren Lehrer, page from *French Fries.*

1984: Apple Macintosh computer, first laser printer, and PageMaker page layout software are introduced.

183.
1985: Zuzana Licko, Emperor, early bitmapped typeface designs.

1986: Fontographer software makes possible high-resolution font design on desktop computers.

1988: Tiananmen Square massacre.

1977

176.

MUSIC TELEVISION

180.

182.

177.

179.

181.

Fredrich **Cantor**

178.

Emperor 8
Emperor 10
Emperor 15
Emperor 19

183.

184.
1990: David Carson, page from *Beach Culture.*

185.
1991: Ted Mader + Associates, book jacket.

Experimental digital typefaces:
186.
1990: Barry Deck, Template Gothic (Emigre).
187.
c. 1991: Jonathan Barnbrook, Exocet Heavy (Emigre).
188.
1993: Jonathan Hoefler, HTF Fetish No. 338.

1990: Reunification of Germany.
189.
1991: Erik Spiekermann, Meta (FontShop).

1991: Persian Gulf War.

1991: Fall of Communism in

Russia; apartheid ends in South Africa.
190.
1992: Robert Slimbach and Carol Twombley, Myriad, Adobe's first Multiple Master typeface.
191.
1992: Ron Kellum, Topix logo.

192.
1993: James Victore, Racism poster.
193.
1994: Netscape founded, early Web browser.

1990

184.

185.

186.
ABCDEFGHIJK

187.
ABCDEFGMOL

188.
EXCESSIVE?

189.
MetaMeta**MetaMeta**

190.

191.

193.

192.

194.
1994: Matthew Carter, Walker typeface with "snap-on" serifs.

195.
1995: Landor Associates, Xerox /The Document Company logo.

196.
1996: Stefan Sagmeister, poster.

197.
1997: Frank Gehry, Guggenheim Museum, Bilbao, Spain.

198.
1997: Dolly the sheep, first adult animal clone.

198.
1997: Paula Scher and Keith Daigle, book jacket.

Digital versions of classical typefaces:

199.
1989: Robert Slimback, Adobe Garamond.

200.
1994–95: Janice Fishman, Holly Goldsmith, Jim Parkinson, and Sumner Stone, ITC Bodoni.

201.
c. 1996: Zuzana Licko, Mrs. Eaves roman.

202.
1998: Neville Brody, conference poster.

1994

194.

197.

202.

198.

195.

Adobe Garamond
199.

ITC Bodoni Roman
200.

Mrs. Eaves Roman
201.

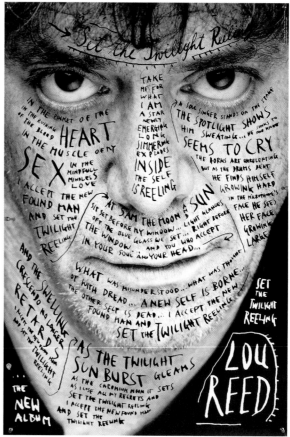

196.

A new century and millennium begin: 2000

203.
2000: Wolfgang Weingart, book cover.

2001: Terrorists attack the World Trade Center towers and Pentagon.

204.
2001: Jennifer Sterling, calendar page (detail).

205.
2001: Mirko Ilić Corp., cover for *Antiwall: Calendar of the New Art and Contemporary Life.*

206.
2001: Jim Sherraden, book cover for Hatch Show Print.

207.
2002: Irma Boom, telephone card.

2003: The United States invades Iraq.

208.
2003: Philippe Apeloig, poster.

2004: A powerful earthquake in Southeast Asia causes a tsunami, killing tens of thousands of people in nearly a dozen countries.

2000

203.

204.

205.

207.

206.

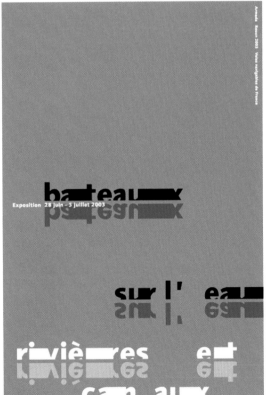

208.

209.
2003: Max Kisman, typeface poster.

210.
2004: Jianping He, Page from Hesign International, GmbH, website

211.
2005: Lawrence Weiner, typographic installation.

212.
2005: Mevis & Van Deursen, book cover.

213.
2005: Jean-Benoît Lévy, Swiss Einstein stamp.

2004

209.

210.

211.

212.

213.

Typographic design is a complex area of human activity, requiring a broad background for informed practice. This chapter explores the basic language of typography. Letterforms, the fundamental components of all typographic communications, are carefully examined. Nomenclature, measurement, and the nature of typographic font and family are presented.

The alphabet is a series of elemental visual signs in a fixed sequence, representing spoken sounds. Each letter signifies only one thing: its elementary sound or name. The twenty-six characters of our alphabet can be combined into thousands of words, creating a visual record of the spoken language. This is the magic of writing and typography, which have been called "thoughts-made-visible" and "frozen sounds."

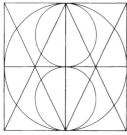

1.
Strokes written with the reed
pen (top), and brush (middle),
and carved with a chisel
(bottom).

2.

3.
Capital and lowercase
letterform construction.

The four timelines in chapter one graphically present the evolution of letterforms and typographic design from the beginning of writing to the present. Our contemporary typographic forms have been forged by this historical evolution. Typography evolved from handwriting, which is created by making a series of marks by hand; therefore, the fundamental element constructing a letterform is the linear stroke. Each letter of our alphabet developed as a simple mark whose visual characteristics clearly separated it from all the others.

The marking properties of brush, reed pen, and stone engraver's chisel influenced the early form of the alphabet (Fig. **1**). The reed pen, used in ancient Rome and the medieval monastery, was held at an angle, called a cant, to the page. This produced a pattern of thick and thin strokes. Since the time of the ancient Greeks, capital letterforms have consisted of simple geometric forms based on the square, circle, and triangle. The basic shape of each capital letter can be extracted from the structure in Figure **2**, which is composed of a bisected square, a circle, a triangle, an inverted triangle, and two smaller circles.

The resulting vocabulary of forms, however, lacks several important attributes: optically adjusted proportions, expressive design properties, and maximum legibility and readability. The transition from rudimentary mark to letterforms with graphic clarity and precision is a matter of design.

Because early capital letters were cut into stone, these letters developed with a minimum number of curved lines, for curved strokes were difficult to cut (Fig. **3**). Lowercase letters evolved as reed-pen writing. Curved strokes could be written quickly and were used to reduce the number of strokes needed to write many characters.

The parts of letterforms
Over the centuries, a nomenclature has evolved that identifies the various components of individual letterforms. By learning this vocabulary, designers and typographers can develop a greater understanding and sensitivity to the visual harmony and complexity of the alphabet. The

following list (Fig. **4**) identifies the major components of letterform construction. In medieval times, horizontal guidelines were drawn to contain and align each line of lettering. Today, letterforms and their parts are drawn on imaginary guidelines to bring uniformity to typography.

Baseline: An imaginary line upon which the base of each capital rests.

Beard line: An imaginary line that runs along the bottoms of descenders.

Capline: An imaginary line that runs along the tops of the capital letters.

Meanline: An imaginary line that establishes the height of the body of lowercase letters.

x-height: The distance from the baseline to the meanline. Typically, this is the height of lowercase letters and is most easily measured on the lowercase *x.*

All characters align *optically* on the baseline. The body height of lowercase characters align optically at the x-height, and the tops of capitals align optically along the capline. To achieve precise alignments, the typeface designer makes optical adjustments.

Apex: The peak of the triangle of an uppercase *A.*

Arm: A projecting horizontal stroke that is unattached on one or both ends, as in the letters *T* and *E.*

Ascender: A stroke on a lowercase letter that rises above the meanline.

Bowl: A curved stroke enclosing the counterform of a letter. An exception is the bottom form of the lowercase roman *g,* which is called a loop.

Counter: The negative space that is fully or partially enclosed by a letterform.

Crossbar: The horizontal stroke connecting two sides of the letterform (as in *e, A,* and *H*) or bisecting the main stroke (as in *f* and *t*).

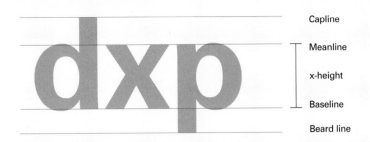

Capline

Meanline

x-height

Baseline

Beard line

Descender: A stroke on a lowercase letterform that falls below the baseline.

Ear: A small stroke that projects from the upper right side of the bowl of the lowercase roman *g.*

Eye: The enclosed part of the lowercase *e.*

Fillet: The contoured edge that connects the serif and stem in bracketed serifs. (Bracketed serifs are connected to the main stroke by this curved edge; unbracketed serifs connect to the main stroke with an abrupt angle without this contoured transition.)

Hairline: The thinnest stroke within a typeface that has strokes of varying weights.

Leg: The lower diagonal stroke on the letter *k.*

Link: The stroke that connects the bowl and the loop of a lowercase roman *g.*

Loop: See *Bowl.*

Serifs: Short strokes that extend from and at an angle to the upper and lower ends of the major strokes of a letterform.

Shoulder: A curved stroke projecting from a stem.

Spine: The central curved stroke of the letter *S.*

Spur: A projection – smaller than a serif – that reinforces the point at the end of a curved stroke, as in the letter *G.*

Stem: A major vertical or diagonal stroke in the letterform.

Stroke: Any of the linear elements within a letterform; originally, any mark or dash made by the movement of a pen or brush in writing.

Tail: A diagonal stroke or loop at the end of a letter, as in *R* or *j.*

Terminal: The end of any stroke that does not terminate with a serif.

Arm

Stem

Terminal

Shoulder

Stroke

Tail

Ascender

Leg

Eye

Spine

Apex

Hairline

Fillet

Crossbar

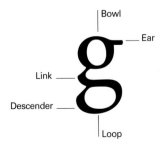

Bowl

Ear

Link

Descender

Loop

Serifs

Counter

Spur

4.

5.

1499 Old Style

1757 Baskerville

1793 Bodoni

1816 First sans serif

c. 1928 Ultra Bodoni

1957 Univers 55

6.

Proportions of the letterform

The proportions of the individual letterform are an important consideration in typography. Four major variables control letterform proportion and have considerable impact upon the visual appearance of a typeface: the ratio of letterform height to stroke width; the variation between the thickest and thinnest strokes of the letterform; the width of the letters; and the relationship of the x-height to the height of capitals, ascenders, and descenders.

The stroke-to-height ratio. The roman letterform, above, has the stroke-width-to-capital-height proportion found on Roman inscriptions (Fig. **5**). Superimposition on a grid demonstrates that the height of the letter is ten times the stroke width. In the adjacent rectangles, the center letter is reduced to one-half the normal stroke width, and the letter on the right has its stroke width expanded to twice the normal width. In both cases, pronounced change in the weight and appearance of the letterform occurs.

Contrast in stroke weight. A change in the contrast between thick and thin strokes can alter the optical qualities of letterforms. The series of *O*s in Figure **6,** shown with the date of each specimen, demonstrates how the development of technology and printing has enabled typeface designers to make thinner strokes.

In the Old Style typography of the Renaissance, designers attempted to capture some of the visual properties of pen writing. Since the writing pens of the period had a flat edge, they created thick and thin strokes. *Stress* is the term to define this

thickening of the strokes, which is particularly pronounced on curves. Note how the placement of weight within the Old Style *O* creates a diagonal axis. As time has passed, type designers have been less influenced by writing.

By the late 1700s, the impact of writing declined, and this axis became completely vertical in many typefaces of that period. In many of the earliest sans-serif typefaces, stress disappeared completely. Some of these typefaces have a monoline stroke that is completely even in weight.

Expanded and condensed styles. The design qualities of the typographic font change dramatically when the widths of the letterforms are expanded or condensed. The word *proportion,* set in two sans-serif typefaces, demonstrates extreme expansion and condensation (Fig. **7**). In the top example, set in Aurora Condensed, the stroke-to height ratio is one to nine. In the bottom example, set in Information, the stroke-to-height ratio is one to two. Although both words are exactly the same height, the condensed typeface takes up far less area on the page.

X-height and proportion. The proportional relationship between the x-height and capital, ascender, and descender heights influences the optical qualities of typography in a significant way. The same characters are set in seventy-two-point type using three typefaces with widely varying x-heights (Fig. **8**). This example demonstrates how these proportional relationships change the appearance of type. The impact of x-height upon legibility will be discussed in chapter four.

8.

On the same-size body (72 point), the x-height variation between three typefaces – Garamond 3, Bodoni, and Univers – is shown. The proportion of the x-height to the point size significantly affects the appearance of type.

72 points

PROPORTION PROPORTION

A font is a set of characters of the same size and style containing all the letters, numbers, and marks needed for typesetting. A typographic font exhibits structural unity when all the characters relate to one another visually. The weights of thick and thin strokes must be consistent, and the optical alignment of letterforms must appear even. The distribution of lights and darks within each character and in the spaces between characters must be carefully controlled to achieve an evenness of tone within the font.

In some display faces, the font might include only the twenty-six capital letters. In a complete font for complex typesetting, such as for textbooks, it is possible to have nearly two hundred characters. The font for Adobe Garamond (Fig. **9**) includes the following types of characters.

Capitals: The set of large letters that is used in the initial position.

Lowercase: The smaller set of letters, so named because in metal typesetting these were stored in the lower part of a type case.

Small caps: A complete set of capital letters that are the same height as the x-height of the lowercase letters. These are often used for abbreviations, cross references, and emphasis.

Lining figures: Numbers that are the same height as the capital letters and sit on the baseline.

Old Style figures: A set of numbers that are compatible with lowercase letters; *1, 2,* and *O* align with the x-height; *6* and *8* have ascenders; and *3, 4, 5, 7,* and *9* have descenders.

Superior and inferior figures: Small numbers, usually slightly smaller than the x-height, used for footnotes and fractions. Superior figures hang from the capline, and inferior figures sit on the baseline.

Fractions: Common mathematical expressions made up of a superior figure, an inferior figure, and a slash mark. These are set as a single type character.

Ligatures: Two or more characters linked together as one unit, such as *ff.* The ampersand is a ligature originating as a letter combination for the French word *et* ("and") in medieval manuscripts.

Digraphs: A ligature composed of two vowels which are used to represent a dipthong (a mono-syllabic speech sound composed of two vowels).

Mathematical signs: Characters used to notate basic mathematical processes.

Punctuation: A system of standard signs used in written and printed matter to structure and separate units and to clarify meaning.

Accented characters: Characters with accents for foreign language typesetting or for indicating pronunciation.

Dingbats: Assorted signs, symbols, reference marks, and ornaments designed for use with a type font.

Monetary symbols: Logograms used to signify monetary systems (U.S. dollar and cent marks, British pound mark, and so on).

7.

abcdefghijklmnopqrstuvwxyz
ABCDEFGHIJKLMNOPQRSTUVWXYZ
ABCDEFGHIJKLMNOPQRSTUVWXYZ
1234567890& 1234567890& 1234567890&
¼½¾ ⅛⅜⅝⅞ ⅓⅔‰ 1234567890/1234567890-

 fffiflffiffl ÆŒßRpæœ√π=±+÷∞°-–—
ÂÅÁÇÍÎÏØÓÒÔÚ(.,;:'"!?^""''"··^˘˜‹›«»`
áéíóú åäëïöüàèìòùâêîôûøÁÉÍÓÚÅÄËÏÖÜ
™©®@#$$$¢¢�ₒ₵£¥%^*
{}[]¡¢§¶•†‡

9.

15.

Optical relationships within a font

Mechanical and mathematical letterform construction can result in serious spatial problems, because diverse forms within an alphabet appear optically incorrect. These letterform combinations show the optical adjustment necessary to achieve visual harmony within a font.

AEVO

10.

Pointed and curved letters (Fig. **10**) have little weight at the top and/or bottom guidelines; this can make them appear too short. To make them appear the same height as letters that terminate squarely with the guidelines, the apexes of pointed letters extend beyond the baseline and capline. Curved letterforms are drawn slightly above and below these lines to prevent them from appearing too small.

HBESKX38

11.

In two-storied capitals and figures (Fig. **11**), the top half appears too large if the form is divided in the mathematical center. To balance these letters optically, the center is slightly above the mathematical center, and the top halves are drawn slightly narrower than the bottom half.

Horizontal strokes (Fig. **12**) are drawn slightly thinner than vertical strokes in both curved and straight letterforms. Otherwise, the horizontals would appear too thick.

Tight junctions where strokes meet (Fig. **13**) are often opened slightly to prevent the appearance of thickening at the joint.

Letters combining diagonal and vertical strokes (Fig. **14**) must be designed to achieve a balance between the top and bottom counterforms. Strokes can be tapered slightly to open up the

spaces, and adjustments in the amount of stroke overlap can achieve a harmony of parts. Letters whose vertical strokes determine their height (Fig. **15**) are drawn slightly taller than letters whose height is determined by a horizontal stroke. Optically, they will appear to be the same height.

MBNB

16.

The stroke weight of compact letterforms (Fig. **16**), such as those with closed counterforms, are drawn slightly smaller than the stroke weight of letterforms having open counterforms. This optically balances the weight.

OHQ

17.

Curved strokes are usually thicker at their midsection than the vertical strokes, to achieve an even appearance (Fig. **17**).

These adjustments are very subtle and are often imperceptible to the reader. However, their overall effect is a more ordered and harmonious visual appearance.

Unity of design in the type font

Tremendous diversity of form exists in the typographic font. Twenty-six capitals, twenty-six lowercase letters, ten numerals, punctuation, and other graphic elements must be integrated into a system that can be successfully combined into innumerable words.

Letterform combinations from the Times Roman Bold font (Fig. **18**) demonstrate visual similarities that bring wholeness to typography. Letterforms share similar parts. A repetition of curves, verticals, horizontals, and serifs are combined to bring variety and unity to typographic designs using this typeface. All well-designed fonts of type display this principle of repetition with the variety that is found in Times Roman Bold.

ETO

12.

M

13.

NK

14.

DCGOQ

The diagonal strokes of the *A* are repeated in *V W M.*

Lowercase letters have common serifs.

AVWM jiru

F E B demonstrates that the more similar letters are, the more common parts they share.

Repetition of the same stroke in *m n h u* creates unity.

Likewise, the letters *b d p q* share parts.

FEB mnhut

bdpq SCGH

Capital serifs recur in similar characters.

BRKPR atfr

ZLE MYX

Subtle optical adjustments can be seen. For example, the bottom strokes of the capital *Z* and *L* have longer serifs than the bottom stroke of the *E*. This change in detail compensates for the larger counterform on the right side of the first two letters.

bq bhlk ceo

18.

An infinite variety of type styles is available today. Digital typography, with its simple and economical introduction of new typefaces, has made the entire array of typefaces developed over the centuries available for contemporary use. Numerous efforts have been made to classify typefaces, with most falling into the following major categories. Some classification systems add a decorative, stylized, or novelty category for the wide range of fanciful type styles that defy categorization. A selection of decorative typefaces appear on pages 302 and 303.

Old Style

Old Style type began with designs of the punchcutter Francesco Griffo, who worked for the famous Venetian scholar-printer Aldus Manutius during the 1490s. Griffo's designs evolved from earlier Italian type designs. His Old Style capitals were influenced by carved Roman capitals; lowercase letters were inspired by fifteenth-century humanistic writing styles, based on the earlier Carolingian minuscules. Old Style letterforms have the weight stress of rounded forms at an angle, as in handwriting. The serifs are bracketed (that is, unified with the stroke by a tapered, curved line). Also, the top serifs on the lowercase letters are at an angle.

Italic

Italic letterforms slant to the right. Today, we use them primarily for emphasis and differentiation. When the first italic appeared in the earliest "pocket book," printed by Aldus Manutius in 1501, it was used as an independent typestyle. The first italic characters were close-set and condensed; therefore, Manutius was able to get more words on each line. Some italic styles are based on handwriting with connected strokes and are called scripts.

Transitional

During the 1700s, typestyles gradually evolved from Old Style to Modern. Typefaces from the middle of the eighteenth century, including those by John Baskerville, are called Transitional. The contrast between thick and thin strokes is greater than in Old Style faces. Lowercase serifs are more horizontal, and the stress within the rounded forms shifts to a less diagonal axis. Transitional characters are usually wider than Old Style characters.

Modern

Late in the 1700s, typefaces termed Modern evolved from Transitional styles. These typefaces have extreme contrasts between thick and thin strokes. Thin strokes are reduced to hairlines. The weight stress of rounded characters is vertical. Serifs are horizontal hairlines that join the stems at a right angle without bracketing. The uppercase width is regularized; wide letters such as M and W are condensed and other letters, including P and T, are expanded. Modern-style typefaces have a strong geometric quality projected by rigorous horizontal, vertical, and circular forms.

Egyptian

In 1815, the English typefounder Vincent Figgins introduced slab-serif typestyles under the name Antique. At the time, there was a mania for ancient Egyptian artifacts, and other typefounders adopted the name Egyptian for their slab-serif designs. These typestyles have heavy square or rectangular serifs that are usually unbracketed. The stress of curved strokes is often minimal. In some slab-serif typefaces, all strokes are the same weight.

Sans Serif

The first sans serif typestyle appeared in an 1816 specimen book of the English typefounder William Caslon IV. The most obvious characteristic of these styles is, as the name implies, the absence of serifs. In many sans serif typefaces, strokes are uniform, with little or no contrast between thick and thin strokes. Stress is almost always vertical. Many sans serif typefaces are geometric in their construction; others combine both organic and geometric qualities.

The development of photo and digital technology has stimulated the design and production of countless new typefaces whose visual characteristics defy standard classification. The visual traits of these "hybrid" forms may fall into more than one of the historical classifications presented on the preceding two pages. The following is a classification system derived from the visual features common to letters throughout the typeface kingdom. It may be used for comparative purposes to pinpoint the most dominant traits of specific typefaces. Type designers use these variations to create a family of typefaces. The type family is discussed on pages 43–46.

Serifs:

Serifs provide some of the most identifiable features of typefaces, and in some cases they reveal clues about their historical evolution. The serifs shown are those that appear most frequently in typefaces.

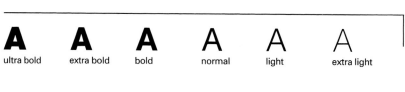

Weight:

This is a feature defined by the ratio between the relative width of the strokes of letterforms and their height. On the average, a letter of normal weight possesses a stroke width of approximately 15% of its height, whereas bold is 20% and light is 10%.

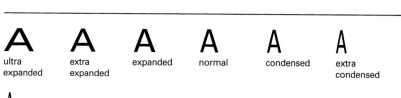

Width:

Width is an expression of the ratio between the black vertical strokes of the letterforms and the intervals of white between them. When white intervals appear larger, letters appear wider. A letter whose width is approximately 80% of its height is considered normal. A condensed letter is 60%, and an expanded letter is 100% of its height.

Posture:

Roman letters that slant to the right but are structurally the same as upright roman letters are referred to as oblique. Italic letters, which are based on handwriting, are structurally different from roman letters of the same type family. Italic letters with connecting strokes are called scripts. The angle of posture varies from typeface to typeface; however, a slant of approximately 12% is considered to be normal.

h italic   *h* oblique   *h* script

Thick/thin contrast:

This visual feature refers to the relationship between the thinnest parts of the strokes in letters and the thickest parts. The varying ratios between these parts produce a wide range of visual textures in text type.

high
contrast

medium
contrast

low contrast

no contrast

x-height:

This proportional characteristic can vary immensely in different typefaces of the same size. Typically, x-heights are considered to be "tall" when they are at least two-thirds the height of capital letters. They are "short" when they measure one-half the height of capital letters.

   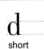

extra tall

tall

medium

short

extra short

Ascenders/descenders:

Ascenders and descenders may appear longer in some typefaces and shorter in others, depending on the relative size of the x-height. Descenders are generally slightly longer than ascenders among letters of the same typeface.

extra long

long

medium

short

extra short

Stress:

The stress of letters, which is a prominent visual axis resulting from the relationships between thick and thin strokes, may be left-angled, vertical, or right-angled in appearance.

left-angled

vertical

right-angled

Typographic measurement

19.

1. Face (printing surface)
2. Counter
3. Beard
4. Shoulder
5. Feet
6. Groove
7. Nick

8. Point size (body size)
9. Type-high (.918″ height)
10. Set width

Our measurement system for typography was originally developed for the handset metal type invented by Johann Gutenberg around 1450. The rectangular metal block of type (Fig. **19**) has a raised letterform on top, which was inked to print the image.

Metal type measurement

The small sizes of text type necessitated the development of a measuring system with extremely fine increments. There were no standards for typographic measurements until the French type designer and founder Pierre Simon Fournier le Jeune introduced his point system of measurement in 1737. The contemporary American measurement system, which was adopted during the 1870s, has two basic units: the point and the pica (Fig. **20**). There are approximately 72 points in an inch (each point is 0.138 inches) and 12 points in a pica. There are about six picas in an inch.

Metal type exists in three dimensions, and an understanding of typographic measurement begins with this early technology. The depth of the type (Fig. **19,** caption 8) is measured in points and is called the point size or body size. All metal type must be the exact same height (Fig. **19,** caption 9), which is called type-high (.918 inch). This uniform height enabled all types to print a uniform impression upon the paper. The width of a piece of type is called the set width (Fig. **19,** caption 10) and varies with the design of each individual letter. The letters *M* and *W* have the widest set width; *i* and *l* have the narrowest. The length of a line of type is the sum of the set width of all the characters and spaces in the line. It is measured in picas.

Before the development of the point and pica system, various sizes of type were identified by names, such as *brevier, long primer,* and *pica;* these became 8-point, 10-point, and 12-point type. The chart in Figure **21,** reproduced from a nineteenth-century printers' magazine, shows the major point sizes of type with their old names.

0				1			2	Inches

| 0 | 1 | 2 | 3 | 4 | 5 | 6 | Picas |
| 0 | 12 | | | 72 Points | | | |

6 Picas = 1 Inch
12 Points = 1 Pica
72 Points = 1 Inch

20.

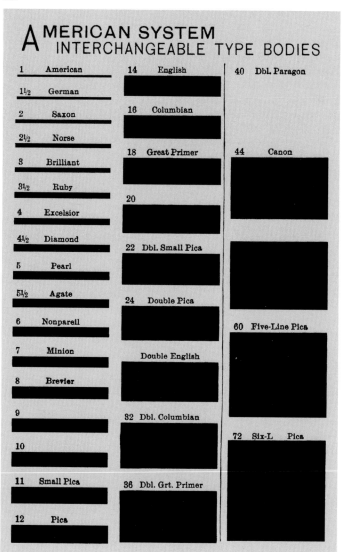

AMERICAN SYSTEM
INTERCHANGEABLE TYPE BODIES

1	American
1½	German
2	Saxon
2½	Norse
3	Brilliant
3½	Ruby
4	Excelsior
4½	Diamond
5	Pearl
5½	Agate
6	Nonpareil
7	Minion
8	Brevier
9	
10	
11	Small Pica
12	Pica

14 English
16 Columbian
18 Great Primer
20
22 Dbl. Small Pica
24 Double Pica
Double English
32 Dbl. Columbian
36 Dbl. Grt. Primer

40 Dbl. Paragon
44 Canon
60 Five-Line Pica
72 Six-L Pica

21.

Reproduced actual size from
The Inland Printer, April 1885.

This line has word spacing with em quads.

This line has word spacing with en quads.

This line has word spacing with thick quads.

This line has word spacing with middle quads.

This line has word spacing with thin quads.

This line has word spacing with hair quads.

Type that is 12 point and under is called text type and is primarily used for body copy. Sizes above 12 point are called display type, and they are used for titles, headlines, signage, and the like.

Traditional metal type had a range of text and display sizes in increments from 5 point to 72 point (Fig. **22**). The measurement of point size is a measurement of the metal block of type including space above and below the letters; therefore, one cannot measure the point size from printed letters themselves. This is sometimes confusing. Refer to the labels for x-height, cap height, and point size on Figure **22** and observe that the point size includes the cap height plus a spatial interval above and below the letters.

Spatial measurement

In addition to measuring type, the designer also measures and specifies the spatial intervals between typographic elements. These intervals are: interletter spacing (traditionally called letterspacing), which is the interval between letters; interword spacing, also called word-spacing, which is the interval between words; and interline spacing, which is the interval between two lines of type. Traditionally, interline space is called leading, because thin strips of lead are placed between lines of metal type to increase the spatial interval between them.

In traditional metal typography, interletter and interword spacing are achieved by inserting metal blocks called quads between the pieces of type. Because these are not as high as the type itself, they do not print. A quad that is a square of the point size is called an *em*. One that is one-half an em quad is called an *en*. In metal type, other smaller divisions of space are fractions of the em (Fig. **23**). These metal spacers are used for letter- and wordspacing, paragraph indentions, and centering or justifying lines of type.

5 Point
6 Point
7 Point
8 Point
9 Point
10 Point
11 Point
12 Point
14 Point
18 Point
24 Point
30 Point
36 Point
42 Point
48 Point
54 Point
60 Point
72 Point

Cap height | Body size

22.

Univers   53 em   55 em   57 em   59 em

24.

This line is set with plus ten units of interletter spacing.
This line is set with normal, unaltered interletter spacing.
This line is set with minus five units of interletter spacing.
This line is set with minus ten units of interletter spacing.
This line is set with minus twenty units of interletter spacing.

26.

For design considerations, the em of a condensed type style can be narrower than a square, and the em of an expanded type size can be wider than a square. This is demonstrated by the em quads from four styles in the Univers family of typefaces (Fig. **24**).

While *em* and *en* are still used as typographic terms, spacing in digital typesetting and desktop publishing is controlled by a computer, using a unit system. The *unit* is a relative measurement determined by dividing the em (that is, the square of the type size) into equal vertical divisions. Different typesetting systems use different numbers of units; sixteen, thirty-two, and sixty-four are common. Some desktop publishing software even permits adjustments as small as twenty-thousandths of an em. The width of each character (Fig. **25**) is measured by its unit value. During typesetting, the character is generated, then the typesetting machine advances the number of units assigned to that character before generating the next character. The unit value includes space on each side of the letter for normal interletter spacing. Adding or subtracting units to expand or contract the space between letters is called *tracking.* Changing the tracking changes the tone of the typography (Fig. **26**). As will be discussed later, tracking influences the aesthetics and legibility of typesetting.

Some letter combinations, such as *TA,* have awkward spatial relationships. An adjustment in the interletter space to make the interval more consistent with other letter combinations is called *kerning.* In metal type, kerning was achieved by sawing notches in the types. Contemporary typesetting software can contain automatic kerning pairs, and the designer can manually change the kerning between characters when these awkward combinations appear.

| 13 Units | 10 Units | 9 Units | 5 Units | 10 Units | 11 Units |

25.
The unit value of each letter in the word *Design* is shown.

In this setting, minus one unit is used for tighter interletter spacing.

In this setting, minus two units is used. The letters touch.

A type family consists of a group of related type-faces, unified by a set of similar design characteristics. Each face in the family is an individual one that has been created by changing visual aspects of the parent font. Early type families consisted of three fonts: the regular roman face, a bolder version, and an italic. The roman, bold, and italic fonts of the Baskerville family (Fig. **27**) demonstrate that a change in stroke weight produces the bold version, and a change in stroke angle creates the italic. The bold font expands typographic possibilities by bringing impact to titles, headings, and display settings. Today, italics are primarily used for emphasis as a variation of roman. In addition to weight and angle changes, additional members of a type family are created by changing proportions or by design elaboration.

Weight changes. By simply changing the stroke width relative to the height of the letters, a whole series of alphabets, ranging from extremely light to very bold, can be produced. In England, a classification standard has been developed that contains eight weights: extralight, light, semilight, medium, semibold, bold, extrabold, and ultrabold. Most type families do not, however, consist of eight weights. Four weights – light, regular or book, medium, and bold – are often sufficient for most purposes. In the Avant Garde family (Fig. **28**), stroke weight is the only aspect that changes in these five fonts.

Proportion. Changing the proportions of a type style by making letterforms wider (expanded) or narrower (condensed), as discussed earlier, is another method for adding typefaces to a type family. Terms used to express changes in proportion include: ultraexpanded, extraexpanded, expanded, regular, condensed, extracondensed, and ultracondensed.

Sometimes confusion results because there is no standardized terminology for discussing the variations in type families. For example, the regular face is sometimes called *normal, roman,* or *book.* Light weights are named *lightline, slim,* and *hairline. Black, elephant, massive, heavy,* and *thick* have been used to designate bold weights. Names given to condensed variations include *narrow, contracted, elongated,* and *compressed.* Expanded faces have been called *extended, wide,* and *stretched.*

27.

Baskerville

Baskerville

Baskerville

AVANT GARDE

AVANT GARDE

AVANT GARDE

AVANT GARDE

AVANT GARDE

28.

Futura Italic

Baskerville Italic

Bodoni Italic
29.

Angle. In our discussion about the basic classification of typefaces, italics were presented as a major independent category. They were first introduced four hundred years ago as a new style. Now italics serve as a member of type families, and they are used for contrast or emphasis. Italic fonts that retain curvilinear strokes inspired by handwriting are called cursives or scripts. In geometric typefaces constructed with drafting instruments, the italic fonts created by slanting the stroke angle are called obliques. Baskerville Italic (Fig. **29**) is a cursive, demonstrating a handwriting influence; Futura Italic is an oblique face; and Bodoni Italic has both cursive and oblique qualities. Although the Bodoni family was constructed with the aid of drafting instruments, details in the italic font (for example, some of the lower serifs) evidence a definite cursive quality.

Elaboration. In design an elaboration is an added complexity, fullness of detail, or ornamentation. Design elaboration can be used to add new typefaces to a type family. These might include outline fonts, three-dimensional effects, and the application of ornaments to letterforms. Some of the variations of Helvetica (Fig. **30**) that are available from the German firm of Dr. Boger Photosatz GmbH include outlines, inlines, perspectives, rounded terminals, and even a chipped antique effect.

While many elaborations are gaudy and interfere with the integrity and legibility of the letterforms, others can be used successfully. Goudy

Handtooled (Fig. **31**) is based on Goudy Bold. A white linear element is placed on each major stroke. Dimensionality is suggested, and the face alludes to incised inscriptional lettering.

Decorative and novelty type styles should be used with great care by the graphic designer. At best, these can express a feeling appropriate to the content and can allow for unique design solutions. Unfortunately, the use of design elaboration is often a mere straining for effect.

The Cheltenham family
One of the most extensive type families is the Cheltenham series of typefaces (Fig. **32**). The first version, Cheltenham Old Style, was initially designed around the turn of the century by architect Bertram G. Goodhue in collaboration with Ingalls Kimball of the Cheltenham Press in New York City. When this typeface went into commercial production at the American Type Founders Company, designer Morris F. Benton supervised its development. Benton designed about eighteen additional typefaces for the Cheltenham family. Variations developed by other typefounders and manufacturers of typesetting equipment expanded this family to more than thirty styles. The design properties linking the Cheltenham family are short, stubby slab serifs with rounded brackets, tall ascenders and long descenders, and a moderate weight differential between thick and thin strokes.

Cheltenham
Cheltenham
Cheltenham
Cheltenham
Cheltenham
Cheltenham
Cheltenham
Cheltenham
Cheltenham
Cheltenham
Cheltenham
Cheltenham
Cheltenham
Cheltenham
Cheltenham
Cheltenham
Cheltenham
Cheltenham
Cheltenham
Cheltenham
Cheltenham

32.

Goudy Handtooled
31.

44

30.
Elaborations of
Helvetica Medium.

39
Univers

45	46		47	48	49
Univers	*Univers*		Univers	*Univers*	Univers

53	55	56	57	58	59
Univers	Univers	*Univers*	Univers	*Univers*	Univers

63	65	66	67	68
Univers	Univers	*Univers*	Univers	*Univers*

73	75	76
Univers	**Univers**	***Univers***

83
Univers

33.

The Univers family

A full range of typographic expression and visual contrast becomes possible when all the major characteristics – weight, proportion, and angle – are orchestrated into a unified family. An exceptional example is the Univers family (Fig. **33**). This family of twenty-one type styles was designed by Adrian Frutiger. Instead of the usual terminology, Frutiger used numerals to designate the typefaces. Univers 55 is the "parent" face; its stroke weight and proportions are the norm from which all the other designs were developed. The black-and-white relationships and proportions of Univers 55 are ideal for text settings. Careful study of Figure **33** reveals that the first digit in each font's number indicates the stroke weight, three being the lightest and eight the heaviest. The second digit indicates expansion and contraction of the spaces within and between the letters,

which results in expanded and condensed styles. Roman fonts are designated with an odd number, and oblique fonts are designated with an even number.

In the design of Univers, Frutiger sparked a trend in type design toward a larger x-height. The lowercase letters are larger relative to ascenders, descenders, and capitals. The size and weight of capitals are closer to the size and weight of lowercase letters, creating increased harmony on the page of text. Because the twenty-one members of the Univers family share the same x-height, capital height, and ascender and descender length and are produced as a system, they can be intermixed and used together without limitation. This gives extraordinary design flexibility to the designer (Fig. **34**).

34.

Typographic interpretation of *The Bells* by Edgar Allan Poe using the Univers family. (Designer: Philip Meggs)

Hear the

sledges with the **Bells**

SILVER Bells- -

What a world of **merriment** their *melody* foretells!

How they *tinkle,*

tinkle,

tinkle, in the icy air of night!

While the stars that

o v e r s p r i n k l e

All the heavens seem to t w i n k l e

With a *crystalline* delight:

Keeping *time, time, time,*

In a sort of Runic rhyme,

To the **tin**tin*nabula*tion that so *musically* wells

From the *bells,* bells, Bells,

Bells,

BELLS, Bells- -

From the *jingling* and the *tingling* of the bells.

Like the anatomy of typography, typographic syntax and communication have a language that must be learned to understand typographic design. Syntax is the connecting of typographic signs to form words and sentences on the page. The elements of design – letter, word, line, column, and margin – are made into a cohesive whole through the use of typographic space, visual hierarchy, ABA form, and grid systems.

Typographic syntax

In grammar, syntax is the manner in which words are combined to form phrases or sentences. We define typographic syntax as the process of arranging elements into a cohesive whole. The study of typographic syntax begins with its basic unit, the letter, and progresses to word, line, column, and margin.

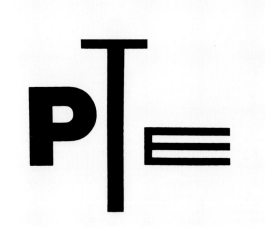

1.

This composition demonstrates contrasting visual characteristics of three letterforms. (Designer: Robert Boyle)

2.

Through precise letterform drawing and carefully considered form-to-counterform interaction, two dissimilar letters form a cohesive sign. (Designer: Gail Collins)

3.

Two letterforms are each broken into two geometric shapes of varying size and density, and the four resulting forms are combined into a delicate, asymmetrically balanced symbol. (Designer: Frank Armstrong)

2.

The letter

Our initial discussion of typographic syntax addresses the intrinsic character of the individual letter. This well-drawn form, exhibiting subtlety and precision, is the unit that distinguishes one family of type from another. It exists in various weights, sizes, and shapes (Fig. **1**).

Although the letter typically functions as part of a word, individual letters are frequently combined into new configurations. As shown in Figures **2** and **3,** combinations of letters *A* and *g* and *P* and *Q* are unified to create a stable gestalt. In the illustrated examples, there is an expressiveness and boldness to the individual letters. The syntax displayed here is an example of letter combinations acting as signs, extracted from a larger system of signs.

A typographic sign is visually dynamic because of its interaction with the surrounding white space or void – the white of the paper. This form-to-void relationship is inherent in the totality of typographic expression. The repetition of the letter *T* in Figure **4** is balanced and complemented by its white space. In the title page for Hans Arp's book *On My Way,* the visual interplay between the three letterforms animates the page (Fig. **5**). This equilibrium and spatial interaction and the manner in which it is achieved will be discussed further in our study of typographic space.

Contemplating this ability of space to define form, Amos Chang observed, ". . . it is the existence of intangible elements, the negative, in architectonic forms which makes them come alive, become human, naturally harmonize with one another, and enable us to experience them with human sensibility."

4.
It is the figure/ground reversal in the repetition of the letter *T* that creates a balanced and expressive poster. (Designer: Willi Kunz)

5.
A dynamic composition is formed by the precise spatial location of the letterforms *a, r,* and *p,* which also spell the author's name. (Designer: Paul Rand)

4.

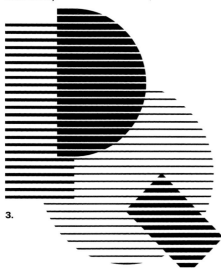

3.

5.

10.

Of all the achievements of the human mind, the birth of the alphabet is the most momentous.

11.

13.

10.
Symmetrical placement produces a quiet, balanced configuration.
11.
Asymmetrical placement achieves a dynamic division of space on the page. (Designer: Ivy Li)

The line

Words are joined to form verbal sentences and typographic lines. The configuration and placement of lines of type are significant structural concerns. In its most basic form, a line of type consists of a single point size and a single weight extended horizontally over a specific line width.

Lines of type can be arranged symmetrically (Fig. **10**), or asymmetrically (Fig. **11**). The viewer/reader must sense a clearly established relationship between individual lines of type and the surrounding space (Fig. **12**).

The smallest change in point size, weight, or line length controls the overall emphasis given to a line of type. The designer or typographer must determine when the overall effect is balanced and fully integrated. All design considerations – typeface selection, alignments, and spacing – should display connections that are apparent and distinct (Fig. **13**). Jan Tschichold states, "The relationship of the sizes must in any case be clearly visible, its effect must be lively, and it must always follow the sense of the text exactly."

The length of a group of lines of type can be equal (justified), unequal (flush left/ragged right, ragged left/flush right), or centered. The examples in this section illustrate various typographic alignments. Typographic form becomes lively and harmonious through these alignments, which enhance individual lines of type and activate the surrounding space (Figs. **14** and **15**).

The placement of punctuation marks is of special significance to these alignments. In Figure **16** punctuation marks extend into the margin. Slight adjustments and subtle refinements heighten the degree of unity.

Typographic rules are used in conjunction with type and separate one line of type from another or one group of typographic lines from another as in Figure **12**, or in footnotes. Rules are found in a variety of forms (Fig. **17**) and numerous sizes and weights. (The use of visual punctuation, including typographic rules, is detailed in *Visual Hierarchy*.)

Earlier, we discussed kerning and the optical spacing of letterforms. Control of these factors makes possible a judicious use of letterspacing in a line of type. The orientation of lines raises a multiplicity of other spacing concerns; for example, interword spacing, interline spacing, and line-to-page relationships, as well as the establishment of columns and margins.

12.
Type and rules combine to bring a sense of unity to the page. Note the recurrence of similar space intervals and the attention given to individual line breaks (the rhythmic pattern of line endings). (Designer: Cheryl Van Arnam)

13.
This multiple-line composition contains varying line weights, yet expresses wholeness through the careful placement of all elements. It displays the diversity possible in the spacing of lines of type. (Designer: Wolfgang Weingart)

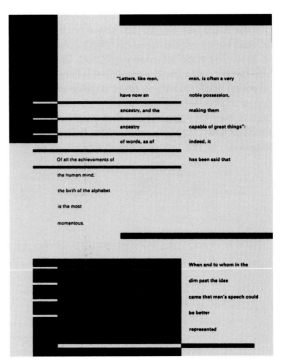

12.

"Bauhaus Masters"
Marcel Breuer
Paul Klee
Herbert Bayer

"Bauhaus Masters"
Marcel Breuer
Paul Klee
Herbert Bayer

16.

14.

14.

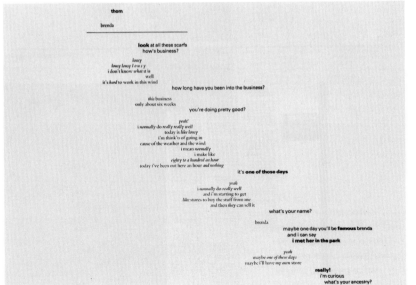

15.

Straight-line rule

Bar rule

Bracket rule

Swelled rule

Oxford rule

Leader

17.

14.
Complex and subtle relationships in interline spacing are achieved here by varying type size, weight, and spatial interval, which separate the statements for the reader. The overall effect is rhythmic and expressive. (Designer: Frank Armstrong)

15.
In this conversation, the placement of lines and intervals reflects the dialogue. (Designer: Warren Lehrer)

16.
In the top setting the lines are flush left, but the edge appears uneven because of the punctuation. In the bottom version, "hanging" the punctuation into the margin is an adjustment resulting in an optically aligned edge.

17.
Hierarchical clarity can be established by using this standard collection of typographic rules to separate, emphasize, and bring order to parts of information.

28.

Spatial elements are balanced through the principle of visual compensation, achieving equilibrium and tension. Elements form relationships with other elements through carefully planned juxtapositions and alignments.

Tension exists between the edge of the composition and adjacent elements. These basic forces affect typographic organization and help achieve dynamic, asymmetrical composition. (Designer: Jean Brueggenjohann)

"Speech proceeds in time and writing proceeds in space." Applying Karl Gerstner's statement to typographic design, typographic space is the rhythmic and dimensional field in which typographic communication exists. This field consists of positive form (the typographic elements) and void (the spatial ground) upon which the elements are arranged. Unity within the space is achieved by visual compensation; that is, the spatial balance and arrangement of typographic elements. Amos Chang, discussing the relationship between compensation and visual dynamics, wrote, "This process of growth from deficiency to compensation brings inherent movement to physical form . . . we may borrow an important rule of balance from the anatomy of a zoological being, man in particular . . . man's body is in a state of balance when his arms and legs are in a position to be moved effectively to compensate for position changes of the body."

Visual compensation is achieved by balancing elements against each other, adjusting their sizes, weights, spatial intervals, and other visual properties until unity and equilibrium are achieved (Figs. **28–30**). In Figure **31,** two contrasting letterform pairs are balanced. The letterform pair *fj* suggests contraction and consonance, while *gv* expresses expansion and dissonance. Consonance is a harmonious relationship between similar or corresponding elements, while dissonance is a discordant relationship between dissimilar elements. In Figure **32,** dissonant elements are combined with consonant form-to-void relationships, resulting in a state of visual balance and unity.

29.

Pictorial and typographic elements are placed in asymmetrical balance. Two pointed arches balance three rounded arches, and the ruled line moving into the margin corresponds to the letterspaced word *Messiah.*

ABC abc abc abc

56.
As typographic joinery becomes more developed, the unity of a mark is enhanced dramatically. (ABC logo, Designer: Paul Rand)

55.

54.
In this poster, a complex system of rules separates, connects, and emphasizes the names of composers, conductors, and other information about numerous events. In the top area of the poster, ruled lines perform a different function: they combine to create a rhythmic visual sign for music. (Designer: Frank Armstrong)

55.
Visual accentuation is demonstrated by this symbol. Striking visual contrast is achieved through the opposition of straight and curved edges and shapes. (Designer: Nick Schrenk)

54.

57.
In this signage for NASA, viewing context determines the visual hierarchy. For example, the size and position of the arrow in the interior directional signage are quite different from the size and position of the roadside signage. (Designer: Danne and Blackburn)

57.

ABA form

59.
Even though the functions of the small text block and the photograph are unrelated, these elements correspond to one another because of their similar sizes.

60.
Letters, when combined together as text, provide a treasury of textural contrasts. Corresponding textures reveal visual links between elements.

61.
When typographic elements possess contrasting tonal qualities, the eye perceives an implied three-dimensionality.

In typographic communication, visual relationships are established through an active dialogue between two fundamental design principles: repetition and contrast. It is through these principles that the typographic designer imbues messages with visual order and rhythmic variety.

Music structure is also based upon repetition and contrast, and because it is linear in nature, a quality that is common also to typography, it provides an excellent model for understanding basic typographic structure. The primary structural pattern of music is the three-part form of statement-departure-return (ABA). The unifying components (the two *A*s) function as repetition, while the middle component (the *B*) functions as contrast. Arnold Schoenberg observed that "the principle function of form is to advance our understanding. It is the organization of a piece which helps the listener to keep the idea in mind, to follow its development, its growth, its elaboration, its fate." This quote also clarifies the mission of typographic form, where relationships between visible typographic elements are guided by the dynamics of ABA form.

The viewer of typographic communication perceives form relationships as being either in opposition or correspondence. This principle suggests that a fully integrated typographic composition depends upon the successful blending of elements of contrast and repetition. The viewer seeks a variety that stimulates both eye and mind, while structuring the communications experience. This is the dual basis of ABA form.

ABA form in typography, as in music, is based

A	B	A	B
The whole duty of typography, as of calligraphy, is to communicate to the imagination, without loss by the way, the thought or image intended to be communicated by the Author. And the whole duty of beautiful typography is not to substitute for the beauty or interest of the thing thought and intended to be	The whole duty of typography, as of calligraphy, is to communicate to the imagination, without loss by the way, the thought or image intended to be communicated by the Author. And the whole duty of beautiful typography is not to substitute for the beauty or interest of the thing thought and intended to be conveyed by the symbol, a beauty or interest of its own, but, on the one hand, to win access for that communication by the clearness and beauty of the vehicle, and on the other hand, to take advantage of every pause or stage in that communication to interpose some characteristic & restful beauty in its own art. We thus have a reason for the clearness and beauty of the text as a whole, for the especial beauty of the first or introductory page and of the title, and for the especial beauty of the headings of chapters, capital or initial letters, and so on, and an opening for the illustrator as we shall see by and by. Further, in the case of Poetry, verse, in my opinion, appears by its form to the eye, as well as to the ear, and should be placed on the page so that its structure may be taken in at a glance and distinctively appreciated, &	The whole duty of typography, as of calligraphy, is to communicate to the imagination, without loss by the way, the thought or image intended to be communicated by the Author. And the whole duty of beautiful typography is not to substitute for the beauty or interest of the thing thought and intended to be	The whole duty of typography, as of calligraphy, is to communicate to the imagination, without loss by the way, the thought or image intended to be communicated by the Author. And the whole duty of beautiful typography is not to substitute for the beauty or interest of the thing thought and intended to be conveyed by the symbol, a beauty or interest of its own, but, on the one hand, to win access for that communication by the clearness and beauty of the vehicle, and on the other hand, to take advantage of every pause or stage in that communication to interpose some characteristic & restful beauty in its own art. We thus have a reason for the clearness and beauty of the text as a whole, for the especial beauty of the first or introductory page and of the title, and for the especial beauty of the headings of chapters, capital or initial letters, and so on, and an opening for the illustrator as we shall see by and by. Further, in the case of Poetry, verse, in my opinion, appears by its form ro the

59.

A	B	A	B
The whole duty of typography, as of calligraphy, is to communicate to the imagination, without loss by the way, the thought or image intended to be communicated by the Author. And the whole duty of beautiful typography is not to substitute for the beauty or interest of the thing thought and intended to be conveyed by the symbol, a beauty or	*The whole duty of typography, as of calligraphy, is to communicate to the imagination, without loss by the way, the thought or image intended to be communicated by the Author. And the whole duty of beautiful typography is not to substitute for the beauty or interest of the thing thought and intended to be conveyed by the symbol, a beauty or interest of its own, but, on the one hand, to win access for that communication by the clearness and beauty of the vehicle, and on the other hand, to take advantage of every pause or stage in that communication to interpose some characteristic & restful beauty in its own art. We thus have a reason for the clearness and beauty of the text as a whole, for the especial beauty of the first or introductory page and of the title, and for the especial beauty of the headings of chapters, capital or initial letters, and so on, and an opening for the illustrator as*	The whole duty of typography, as of calligraphy, is to communicate to the imagination, without loss by the way, the thought or image intended to be communicated by the Author. And the whole duty of beautiful typography is not to substitute for the beauty or interest of the thing	*The whole duty of typography, as of calligraphy, is to communicate to the imagination, without loss by the way, the thought or image intended to be communicated by the Author. And the whole duty of beautiful typography is not to substitute for the beauty or interest of the thing thought and intended to be conveyed by the symbol, a beauty or interest of its own, but, on the one hand, to win access for that communication by the clearness and beauty of the vehicle, and on the other hand, to take advantage of every pause or stage in that communication to interpose some characteristic & restful beauty in its own art. We thus have a reason for the clearness and beauty of the text as a whole, for the especial beauty of the first or introductory page and of the title, and for the especial beauty of the headings of chapters, capital or initial letters, and so on, and an opening for the illustrator as we shall see by and by. Further, in the case of Poetry, verse, in*

60.

A	B	A	B
The whole duty of typography, as of calligraphy, is to communicate to the imagination, without loss by the way, the thought or image intended to be communicated by the Author. And the whole duty of beautiful typography is not to substitute for the beauty or interest of the thing thought and intended to be	The whole duty of typography, as of calligraphy, is to communicate to the imagination, without loss by the way, the thought or image intended to be communicated by the Author. And the whole duty of beautiful typography is not to substitute for the beauty or interest of the thing thought and intended to be conveyed by the symbol, a beauty or interest of its own, but, on the one hand, to win access for that communication by the clearness and beauty of the vehicle, and on the other hand, to take advantage of every pause or stage in that communication to interpose some characteristic, & restful beauty in its own art. We thus have a reason for the clearness and beauty of the first or introductory page and of the title, and for the especial beauty of the headings of chapters, capital or initial letters, and so on, and an opening for the illustrator as we shall see by and by. Further, in the case of Poetry, verse, in my opinion, appears by its form to the eye, as well as to the ear, and should be placed on the page so that its structure may be taken in at a glance and distinctively appreciated, & anything	**The whole duty of typography, as of calligraphy, is to communicate to the imagination, without loss by the way, the thought or image intended to be communicated by the Author. And the whole duty of beautiful typography is not to substitute**	The whole duty of typography, as of calligraphy, is to communicate to the imagination, without loss by the way, the thought or image intended to be communicated by the Author. And the whole duty of beautiful typography is not to substitute for the beauty or interest of the thing thought and intended to be conveyed by the symbol, a beauty or interest of its own, but, on the one hand, to win access for that communication by the clearness and beauty of the vehicle, and on the other hand, to take advantage of every pause or stage in that communication to interpose some characteristic, & restful beauty in its own art. We thus have a reason for the clearness and beauty of the first or introductory page and of the title, and for the especial beauty of the headings of chapters, capital or initial letters, and so on, and an opening for the illustrator as we shall see by and by. Further, in the case of Poetry, verse, in my opinion, appears by its form to the eye, as

61.

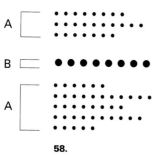

58.

upon a fundamental three-part structure where two *repeating* parts are in correspondence, and a third *contrasting* part stands in opposition (Fig. **58**). This fundamental structure, however, may be found in abundant variation. This is true because contrasting and repeating typographic elements within a composition are governed by the dynamic principles of proportion and rhythm. It is via these principles that ABA form grows in complexity and diversity. By definition, proportion in ABA form is the ratio determined by the quantity, size, weight, texture, tone, shape, color (or other syntactic quality) of similar and dissimilar typographic elements (A**A**BA**A**BA**A**). Rhythm is established in the intervals of space separating these elements (A**A** . B . A**A** . B . A**A**). The following examples illustrate this idea:

When typographic elements are similar in size to one another, an immediate correspondence between these elements is established (Fig. **59**). This correspondence is heightened because the tonality of the photograph and small text block is darker than the tone of the larger text block. In the middle diagram, the correspondence between the smaller text blocks is also magnified (Fig. **60**). A third variation is created by altering the tone of the elements: a bold typeface is introduced in the smaller text blocks, linking them together. Here, the factors of both scale and tone establish a distinct pattern of repetition and contrast (Fig. **61**). In an applied example – the design of a concert poster – the recurrence and contrast of typographic tone and texture are demonstrated (Fig. **62**).

Further variations in ABA form are discovered when elaborations (ABa, ABAb or AbAc) of corresponding elements occur to establish subtle contrasts (Fig. **63**), or when primary and secondary relationships occur in compositions

62.
This poster is zoned into three spatial corridors: two columns of text, finely textured and light in tonal value, flank a dynamic arrangement of music-related visual signs, coarser in texture and darker in tone. (Designer: Ben Day)

simultaneously (Fig. **64**). The foregoing examples show the influence of proportion upon the relationships between typographic elements. The rhythmic patterns in each of these examples are identical, with equal or nearly equal intervals of space separating the elements. In a detail of the concert poster (Fig. **65**), a distinct rhythm composed of unequal spatial intervals between typographic elements can be observed. This rhythmic pattern may be viewed on two levels: the major group (A . B . A), and the minor group (**a** . bb . . **a** . b . . **a** . bb . . **a,** etc.). The intervals between these elements facilitate the functional grouping of the parts of the message: the "instruments" are separated from the "performers" by a "1X" interval of space, and each of these groupings is separated one from another by a "2X" interval of space. Other syntactic traits bind and isolate the parts: the "instruments" are bold in typographic weight, linking them together, while the "performers" are light in weight. At the same time, all these typographic elements share the same type size to distinguish them from the location of the event, which is presented in a larger, italic, all-capitals typeface.

In this example, it is also possible to observe a phenomenon that appears at first as a contradiction in terms, but nonetheless is a condition in typographic design: perceiving typographic forms that are *simultaneously* in correspondence and opposition. This is a concept that is linked to a fundamental design notion: achieving unity within diversity (Fig. **66**). ABA form variations are capable of unifying diverse forms through visual correspondence while at the same time bringing variety to similar forms through opposition. The skilled designer manipulates typographic elements to achieve this essential balance.

64.

The relationships established by the three vertical columns of equal width (ABA) achieve visual dominance over the three horizontal bands (aba). The small column of text (c), which departs from the visual pattern of the main unit in position and type weight, provides an additional variation.

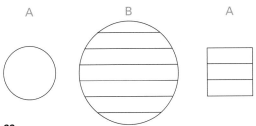

A   B   A

66.
Shape relates the first and
middle forms; texture relates
the middle and right forms;
and size relates the left and
right forms.

ABA form is composed of both simple and
complex patterns that give order and emphasis
to the visual linking of typographic elements.
These are not fixed systems but are a way of
understanding the interrelationships of
typographic form. About music Joseph Machlis
stated, "The forms . . . are not fixed molds into
which the composer pours his material. What
gives a piece of music its aliveness is the fact that
it adapts a general plan to its own requirements."

a	**Bass**
b	Thomas Coleman
b	Anthony Beadle
a	**Flute**
b	Elinor Preble
a	**Oboe**
b	Peggy Pearson
b	Raymond Toubman
a	**Clarinet**

A

S Y M P H O N Y

H A L L

B

a	**Bassoon**
b	Francis Nizzari
b	Ronald Haroutunian
a	**French Horn**
b	Oaneka Oaujub

A

65.

Typographic legibility is widely misunderstood and often neglected by designers. Yet it is a subject that requires careful study and constant evaluation. Legibility is achieved by controlling the qualities and attributes inherent in typography that make type readable. These attributes make it possible for a reader to comprehend typographic forms with the least amount of difficulty.

Typographers and designers have a definite responsibility to their readers to communicate as clearly and appropriately as possible. This responsibility is suggested by Henry David Thoreau in *Walden:* "A written word is the choicest of relics. It is something at once more intimate with us and more universal than any other work of art."

a a d d d d

1.

As the top stroke of the letter *a* rises to become the ascender of the *d,* the intermediate forms are not easily deciphered by the reader.

As signs representing sounds in spoken language, letters are basic to legible typography. The primary purpose of a letterform is to convey a recognizable meaning to the mind. Therefore, letterforms must be designed with clarity, each being distinct within the alphabet. The contrast among individual characters makes it possible for the reader to decipher written information without confusion.

The most legible typefaces are those timeless examples characterized by three qualities upon which legibility is dependent: contrast, simplicity, and proportion. These typefaces exemplify beautiful and functional letterforms. A close look at typefaces such as Garamond, Baskerville, and Bodoni will reveal why their forms are as vital now as when they were first designed. (See the type specimens in Chapter Eleven.) The use of well-designed typefaces, however, is no guarantee that typography will be legible. Effective typography depends upon such factors as the communications context and the subtle adjustment of letterforms and their spatial relationships, each of which may have an effect upon how easily typography is read. Making type legible is a masterful achievement, requiring a process of intelligent decision making.

In the strictest sense, legible typography is a means of communicating information objectively. However, typographic designers sometimes bend the traditional criterion of legibility for expressive purposes. Designers, with their instinctive curiosity, have experimented with typography, playing with forms, imposing new meaning, and changing the standards of typographic communication. Innovative typography always poses fresh questions, challenges edicts of the past, and redefines the concepts of legibility and functionality.

This chapter approaches legibility as an art of spatial synthesis. As an art, it is not absolute. Therefore, information derived from legibility research should be considered only a guideline. The knowledge designers have of legibility is based upon a legacy of typographic history and a keen awareness of the visible world. This knowledge will continually evolve, creating new standards for readability and functional typography.

Distinguishing characteristics of letters

The alphabet consists of twenty-six letters, each of which has evolved over the centuries to a unique place within this system of signs. This evolution has occurred gradually. It is no accident that the individual shapes of letterforms have developed out of a need to improve the communication process. As the alphabet has evolved, it has become a flexible system of signs in which all letters are distinct, yet all work together harmoniously as visible language.

In spite of the innumerable variations of size, proportion, weight, and elaboration in letterform design, the basic structure of each letterform must remain the same. For example, the capital *A* always consists of two oblique strokes joined at the top and connected by a horizontal stroke at their midsection. Sufficient contrast must exist between the letters in a font so that they can be easily distinguished (Fig. **1**).

2.

Four groupings show the structural relationships of all letters in the alphabet. The divisions are based upon the dominant strokes of each letter.

il
acegos
bdfhjmnpqrtu
kvwxyz

EFHILT
COQS
BDGJPRU
AKMNVWXYZ

Letters can be clustered into four groups, according to their contrasting properties. These are letterforms with strokes that are vertical, curved, a combination of vertical and curved, or oblique (Fig. **2**). From these groupings, one notices that letters are not only similar in many ways but that there are also some important differences. Obviously, letters with similar characteristics are more likely to be confused, while letters with distinct qualities provide contrast within a word. Letters within a word are most legible when they are taken, in equal number, from each group.

A closer look at the alphabet reveals additional characteristics distinguishing letters. The upper halves of letters provide more visual cues for letter recognition than the lower halves (Fig. **3**). Likewise, the right halves of letters are more recognizable than the left halves (Fig. **4**). Dominant letters within the alphabet that aid in word recognition are those that have either ascenders or descenders. Through tests, researchers have contributed valuable information about the comparative legibility of each letter in the alphabet. Findings vary only slightly. Lowercase letters can be rank ordered according to their distinctiveness as follows: *d k m g h b p w u l j t v z r o f n a x y e i q c s.* This varies, however, with different typefaces.

The most frequently used letters, such as the vowels *a e i o u,* are among the most illegible, and *c g s x* are easily missed in reading. Other letters that often cause confusion and are mistaken for one another are *f i j l t.* For example, the words *fail, tail,* and *jail* each begin with letters of similar shape and could easily be misread. The eye could possibly perceive *f* as *t,* or *t* as *j* (Fig. **5**). The designer should carefully study the words in display typography to identify such potential problems in legibility.

fail
tail
jail

6–7.
As with the changing position
of the dancer, subtle changes
in the drawing of the forms
and counterforms significantly
affect perception.

6.

7.

DANCER
DANCER
DANCER

G
DANCER
DANGER
G

shape

SHAPE

8.
Word recognition is based on
word structure, a combination
of word shape (defined by the
contours of the letters) and
internal word pattern. The
word set in lowercase letters is
more distinct than the word
set in all capitals, because its
irregular word shape makes it
more recognizable.

The perception of a letter is based upon the form/counterform relationship. Counterforms are as significant to legibility as the shapes of the letters themselves. This principle relates to all aspects of visual phenomena. A dancer manipulates space with the body, "making shape," defining, and redefining space (Fig. **6**). If the shape of a letter is changed, so is the way in which that letter is perceived. Letter shapes are cues that distinguish one letter in the alphabet from another (Fig. **7**).

Much controversy has surrounded the issue of the comparative legibility of serif and sans-serif typefaces. One argument claims that serif text type is more readable because the serifs reinforce the horizontal flow of each line. Serif typefaces also offer more character definition: for example, the serif on the bottom horizontal stroke of a capital *E* accentuates the difference between it and a capital *F*. However, the relative legibility between serif and sans-serif typefaces is negligible. Reader familiarity and the control of other legibility factors (to be discussed later) are far more significant than the selection of a serif or sans-serif typeface. (See the text-type specimens in Chapter 11 to compare the legibility of serif and sans-serif type.)

The nature of words
While individual letters as discrete units, affecting all other spatial and aesthetic considerations, are the basis for a discussion of legibility, one reads and perceives words and groups of words and not just letters. In discussing typographic legibility, Frederic Goudy observed that "a letter may not be considered apart from its kinsmen; it is a mere abstract and arbitrary form far remote from the original picture or symbol out of which it grew, and has no particular significance until it is employed to form part of a word."

There are two important factors involved in the reading process: word shape and internal pattern. Words are identified by their distinctive word shapes, strings of letters that are instantaneously perceived, permitting the reader to grasp content easily (Fig. **8**). Counterforms create internal word patterns that provide cues for word recognition.

```
O R D W
R D W O
D W O R
R O W D
W O R D
O W R D
```
9.

When these internal spaces are altered sufficiently, the perceptual clarity of a word may also be altered. The weight of letters is vital to word recognition and influences an adequate internal pattern. The combination of word shape and internal pattern creates a word structure, an all-inclusive term describing the unique composition of each word (Fig. **9**).

Capital and lowercase letters
If a text is set entirely in capital letters, it suffers a loss of legibility and the reader is placed at a significant disadvantage. Type set in this manner severely retards reading – more so than any other legibility factor. Figure **8** demonstrates that a word set in all capital letters is characterized by a straight horizontal alignment, creating an even word outline with letters of similar shape and size. A reader is not provided with the necessary visual cues that make words recognizable.

TEXT SET IN ALL CAPITAL LETTERS ALSO USES A SIGNIFICANTLY GREATER AMOUNT OF SPACE THAN TEXT SET IN LOWERCASE LETTERS OF THE SAME SIZE. AS MUCH AS 35 PERCENT MORE SPACE CAN BE CONSUMED WHEN USING ALL CAPITAL LETTERS.

On the other hand, text set in lowercase letters forms words that are distinct, based upon their irregular word shape and internal pattern. A variety of letter shapes, ascenders, and descenders provides rich contrasts that assure satisfactory perception. Once a specific word shape is perceived, it is stored in the reader's memory until the eye confronts it again while reading. A reader can become confused if a word takes on an appearance that differs from the originally learned word shape.

Interletter and interword spacing
The spacing of letterforms has a significant impact on legibility. Most readers are unaware of the typographic designer's attention to this detail. Minute spatial relationships are controlled to create not only readable but beautiful and harmonious typographic communication. It takes great skill to specify spaces between letters and

words, determining proper spatial relationships. Letters must flow rhythmically and gracefully into words, and words into lines.

Typographic texture and tone are affected by the spacing of letters, words, and lines. When the texture and the spatial intervals between typographic elements are consistent, the result is an easily readable text. Texture is also affected by qualities unique to the design of specific typefaces. Sometimes designers arrange type for specific spatial effects, sensitively balancing norms of legibility with graphic impact. (See the text-type specimens in Chapter Eleven.)

Too much or too little space between letters and words destroys the normal texture intended by the typeface designer. As you read this sentence, notice that the narrow letter and word spacing causes words to merge together visually. L i k e w i s e , t h e e x t r e m e l y w i d e l e t t e r s p a c i n g o f t h i s s e n t e n c e i s a l s o d i s r u p t i v e f o r t h e r e a d e r.

There is often a danger of misfit letter combinations, which, in earlier typesetting systems such as Linotype, could not be easily corrected. (If the type size is small and evenly textured, this is a minor problem.) With phototypesetting and digital typesetting, these details can be corrected easily. The kerning of specific letter combinations can be programmed into the typesetting system. As type is set, appropriate letterspacing appears automatically (Fig. **10**).

SPACING
SPACING

9.
Letters can be grouped in myriad combinations. Words that are perceived as having meaning are those with which we have become familiar over time. They form a distinct and familiar shape.

Reading is disrupted by inappropriate wordspacing.

10.
Misfit letter combinations and irregular spacing can be a problem, particularly for display type. Optical adjustments should be made to achieve spatial consistency between elements.

EdwardoJohnston,oaocalligrapher,
advocatedoaowordospaceoequaloto
aolowercaseoo.

11.

AaronrBurns,ranrinfluential
typographer,rsuggestedrwordrspacing
equalrtorarlowercaserr.

Space between letters and words should be proportional to the width of letters. This proportion is often open to personal judgment (Fig. **11**). With experience and practice comes an understanding of the spacing that is suitable to a particular design project.

Type size, line length, and interline spacing
Critical to spatial harmony and legibility is an understanding of the triadic relationship of type size, line length, and interline spacing. When properly employed, these variables can improve the legibility of even poorly designed letterforms or enhance the legibility of those forms considered highly legible.

It is difficult to generalize about which sizes of type should be used, how long lines should be, or how much space should be inserted between lines. These decisions are based upon comparative judgments. The guidelines discussed in this section can never replace the type designer's sensitively trained eye for typographic detail. The normal reading distance for most printed matter is from twelve to fourteen inches, a fact to be kept in mind when making decisions about type size, since it affects the way in which a specific type size is perceived.

Text type that is too small or too large makes reading difficult. Small type reduces visibility by destroying counterforms, which affect word recognition, while large type can force a reader to perceive type in sections rather than as a whole. According to legibility research, the most legible sizes of text type at normal reading distances range from 9 to 12 point. This range results from the wide variation of x-height in different typefaces. That is, when typefaces of the same

point size are placed side by side, they may appear to be different sizes, because their x-heights vary radically. This is important to keep in mind when selecting typefaces and sizes.

An interesting comparison is the relationship between Univers 55 and Baskerville. Univers 55 has a very large x-height, with short ascenders and descenders. It appears much larger than Baskerville set in the same size, which has a smaller x-height and large ascenders and descenders. (See text column specimens in Chapter 11.)

Type sizes larger than 12 point may require more fixation pauses, making reading uncomfortable and inefficient. A fixation pause occurs when the eye stops on a line of type during reading, actually perceiving the meaning of groups of words. When there are fewer fixation pauses, there is greater reading efficiency and comprehension. When text type is smaller than 9 point, internal patterns can break down, destroying legibility. The reading audience is also a major consideration. For example, children learning to read need large type sizes in simple formats, as do adults with poor eyesight.

An appropriate line length is essential for achieving a pleasant reading rhythm, allowing a reader to relax and concentrate on the content of the words. Overly short or long lines will tire a reader. Excess energy is expended when reading long lines, and it is difficult to find the next line. A short column measure requires the eye to change lines too often, and there is an inadequate supply of horizontal perceptual cues. Compare the legibility of this paragraph with the legibility of Figures **12** and **13**.

An appropriate line length is essential for achieving a pleasant reading rhythm, allowing a reader to relax and concentrate on the content of the words. Overly short or long lines will tire a reader. Excess energy is expended when reading long lines, and it is difficult to find the next line. A short column measure requires the eye to change lines too often, and there is an inadequate supply of horizontal perceptual cues.

13.

An appropriate line length is essential for achieving a pleasant reading rhythm, allowing a reader to relax and concentrate on the content of the words. Overly short or long lines will tire a reader. Excess energy is expended when reading long lines, and it is difficult to find the next line. A short column measure requires the eye to change lines too often, and there is an inadequate supply of horizontal perceptual cues.

12.

Interline spacing intervals

Interline spacing intervals

14.

Certainly, every typographic problem has its own legibility requirements. The following data can serve as a point of departure in determining how to create legible typography. Line length is dependent upon both the size of type and the amount of space between lines. When working with the optimum sizes of 9-, 10-, 11-, and 12-point text type, a maximum of ten to twelve words (or sixty to seventy characters) per line would be acceptable. This would equal a line length of approximately 18 to 24 picas. An optimum line length for the average 10-point type is 19 picas.

The amount of interline spacing is dependent upon several factors. Generally, lines with no added space between them are read more slowly than lines with added space. Proper interline spacing carries the eye naturally from one line to the next. When there is inadequate space between lines, the eye takes in other lines as well. If lines are too widely spaced, a reader may have trouble locating the next line. As column measure increases, the interline spacing should also increase to maintain a proper ratio of column length to interline spacing.

Typefaces with larger x-heights need more interline spacing than those with smaller x-heights. Also, when working with display types, the frequency with which ascenders and descenders occur makes a difference. They can optically lessen the amount of white space between lines. Optical adjustments in display types should be made when spaces between lines appear inconsistent because of ascenders and descenders (Fig. **14**). Generally, the maximum line length for text type with a small x-height – used without interline spacing – is about sixty-five characters. When text type with a large x-height is used without interline spacing, legibility is diminished when line length exceeds about fifty-two characters.

Research has shown that for the optimum sizes of text type (9, 10, 11, and 12 point), one to four points of interline spacing can be effectively added between lines to increase legibility. Remember, this is not to say that type set outside these optimum specifications will be illegible, for critical judgment can ensure legible typography without inhibiting fresh approaches.

Weight
When considering the legibility of a typeface, the thickness (weight) of the strokes should be examined. A typeface that is too light or too heavy has diminished legibility. Light typefaces cannot be easily distinguished from their background, while a typeface that is too heavy has a tendency to lose its internal pattern of counterforms.

Weight can be used advantageously to provide contrast and clarity between typographic page elements such as titles, headlines, and subheads. A heavier or lighter weight can emphasize one piece of information over another, thereby making information more comprehensible.

Extreme thick and thin strokes within letters of a particular typeface make reading more difficult, preventing smooth transitions from one word or group of words to the next. Thin strokes are less visible, creating confusion with letters of similar shape. When a typeface with extreme contrasts between thick and thin strokes is used in a text setting, a dazzle or sparkle effect is created. The reader begins to have difficulty distinguishing the words, and legibility decreases significantly.

Character Width
The shape and size of the page or column can influence the selection of character width. For example, a condensed typeface might be selected for a narrow page or column, achieving proportional harmony and an adequate number of characters and words to the line.

The width of letters is also an important legibility factor. Generally, condensed type is more difficult to read. A narrower letter changes the form/counterform relation-ship, causing letters to have an extreme vertical posture that can alter eye move-ment and reading patterns, diminishing legibility.

Italics
Similar to other situations where typeforms deviate from a reader's expectations, italics impede reading. An extreme italic slant can slow the reading process and is disliked by many readers. However, italic type can be very effective when used as a means of providing emphasis.

Typefaces of median weight are most legible.

In text type, weight change significantly affects legibility.

In text type, legibility is affected when condensed or expanded typefaces are used.

79

15.

Black type on a white
background and on a light
gray background prove highly
legible. Legibility suffers as the
contrast between type and its
background diminishes. The
color temperature of the paper
upon which type is printed
and the choice of typeface
also have a relative affect
upon legibility.

16.

Legibility is greatly
compromised when type and
background are assigned
complementary colors.
Adjusting the value of either
color improves contrast and
thus legibility. In this example,
the backgrounds of the
complementary colors blue
and orange are lightened,
for improved legibility.

Black type on
a white background

Black type on
a light gray background

White type on
a light gray background

White type on
a dark gray background

White type on
a black background

15.

Blue type on
an orange background

Orange type on
a blue background

Blue type on
a light orange background

Orange type on
a dark blue background

16.

Legibility and color

Incorporating color into type significantly affects
legibility, and the most important consideration
when working with type and color is to achieve an
appropriate contrast between type and its
background. The degree of legibility sought
depends entirely upon the intent of the designer
and the nature of the content.

It has long been considered that black type on a
white background is most legible. While this
combination remains an excellent choice, other
alternatives may offer equal if not improved
legibility due to improved digital and printing
technologies, and the fact that color is a relative
phenomenon (Fig. **15**). When applied to type, color
should be evaluated in relationship to the
conditions in which it is read. In print, for example,
one should consider the specific nature of the
paper. If the paper is white, is it a warm or cool
white? Is the surface of the paper rough or
smooth? Is it coated or uncoated? What typeface is
being considered, and in what size will it appear?

Generally, all legibility guidelines related to
working with color and type in print apply also to
type appearing on a computer screen. However,
the use of color and type on a screen should also
take into consideration the conditions of screen
resolution and luminescence, as well as whether
the type is static or in motion. Digital technologies
have vastly changed the way in which designers
use color and type, making it possible to easily
assign color from palettes containing millions of
colors. Also, the range of typographic applications
continues to expand, with type asserting a role
not only in printed and environmental communications, but also in on-screen media such as
the Internet.

Appropriate contrast between type and its
background requires that designers carefully
weigh the three basic color properties of hue,
value, and saturation. By definition, *hue* and *tone*
are simply more specific names for color. *Value*
refers to the lightness or darkness of a color,
and *saturation* – also called *chroma* or *intensity* –
is the relative brightness of a color.

17.

The analogous hues yellow-green and blue are sufficiently different in value, resulting in an acceptable combination. A moderate adjustment of the yellow-green to a lighter value further improves legibility.

18.

Red and orange hues exist very close to each other on the color wheel, and when used for type and background do not offer sufficient contrast. A tint or shade of one of the colors, however, improves legibility.

19.

By scrutinizing the roles of value and hue contrast, the legibility of most typefaces can be improved. Typefaces that are visually challenging due to extreme proportions (heavy, light, wide, or thin) can be made more legible by assigning appropriate color combinations.

All colors possess characteristics of hue, value, and saturation, and when combining color and type, balancing these properties is a critical legibility concern. For example, the highly saturated, complementary colors blue and orange offer maximum hue contrast, but when applied to type and background the effect is one of vibration that quickly tires the eye. These colors compete in brightness and vie for attention. If the type or background is lightened or darkened by selecting a tint or shade of the hue, legibility is improved (Fig. **16**).

But not all fully saturated hues are of the same value. Two highly saturated, analogous colors, for example, such as blue and green, provide sufficient contrast without a dizzying effect. (Analogous colors are those that appear in close proximity on a color wheel.) Because the green is actually lighter in value and brighter in saturation than the blue, there may be no need for further adjustment (Fig. **17**). However, if analogous colors are too close to each other on the color wheel, adjustments in contrast will be necessary (Fig. **18**).

Of all the contrasts of color, value affects legibility most significantly. Value contrasts effectively preserve the shapes and formal details of letters, thus making them more easily recognizable.

Typefaces possess unique shapes, proportions, and individual characteristics that should be taken into consideration when selecting color. A typeface with fine serifs, ultrathin strokes, small counters, or any number of other visual eccentricities may appear illegible if color is not carefully articulated. By turning value or intensity up or down in these situations, legibility can improve greatly (Fig. **19**).

Blue type on a green background

Blue type on a light green background

17.

Violet type on a blue background

Light violet type on a blue background

18.

Univers 49, an ultracondensed typeface

Univers 49, an ultracondensed typeface

Bauer Bodoni Black, a typeface with extreme thick and thin strokes

Bauer Bodoni Black, a typeface with extreme thick and thin strokes

19.

7-point Minion Regular

The smaller and more delicate the type, the more contrast is needed to ensure adequate legibility.

10-point Minion Regular

The type size is also an important consideration in the planning of color. At smaller sizes, type requires backgrounds that are significantly different in hue and/or value (Fig. **20**).

Whether type is printed on paper or appears on-screen, an optical effect referred to as "typographic color" occurs. Not to be confused with the particular hue of a typographic element, this effect is the result of the visual qualities inherent in individual typefaces and the spacing of letters, words, and lines of type (Fig. **21**). Typographic color is an important tool, for it is an effective means by which hierarchical order and emphasis are achieved between different typographic elements. Also, if a large amount of text is set in an elaborate or unusual color setting, an increase in the space between lines can significantly improve legibility (Fig. **22**).

color color

color color

color color

21.

If you find it necessary to present large amounts of text type in color, try increasing slightly the amount of space between lines. Even an additional point of space can make a significant difference, and a reader might be encouraged to continue rather than stop.

If you find it necessary to present large amounts of text type in color, try increasing slightly the amount of space between lines. Even an additional point of space can make a significant difference, and a reader might be encouraged to continue rather than stop.

22.

The reading process can be severely retarded when reading type on textured or photographic backgrounds, for they potentially interfere with the internal patterns of words and their distinctive word shapes. This problem is further exacerbated when such backgrounds and the type appearing on them are incompatible in color for reasons stated earlier in this discussion.

21.
Words set in various typefaces appear different in "color." As interletter spacing increases, the words also appear lighter in tone.

22.
The illusion of "lighter" or "darker" text is achieved with the introduction of additional interline spacing, and in some situations, legibility is improved.

Compare the legibility of
the justified and unjustified
columns.

Justified and unjustified typography

Traditionally, it was common practice to set type in a justified alignment. This was done for reasons of efficiency; in addition, it was more familiar and was considered to be more refined. In the 1920s, designers began to question this typographic convention and experiment with alternative text-setting styles. Unjustified and asymmetrical typography began to find widespread acceptance. Among experimental typographic designers was Herbert Bayer, who said, "I have long believed that our conventional way of writing and setting type could be improved for easier reading. In my first typographic works in the early twenties, I started to abandon the flush-left-and-right system for short lines of text and have introduced the flush-left system, leaving a ragged-right outline."

There are appropriate reasons for setting either justified or unjustified typography, but type set flush left and ragged right promotes greater legibility. If properly used, flush-left, ragged-right typography provides visual points of reference that guide the eye smoothly down the page from line to line. Because each line is either shorter or longer than the next, the eye is cued from one to another. In a justified setting, all lines are of equal length. Lacking are visual cues that promote easy reading.

With the use of unjustified typography, wordspacing is even, creating a smooth rhythm and a consistent texture. The indiscriminate placement of additional space between words in order to justify lines causes awkward gaps or "rivers" in paragraphs, which are disruptive to reading. Hyphenations at the end of lines should be used – but not overused – whenever possible to keep wordspacing consistent.

When setting ragged-right text, care should be taken not to rag the type too much. Uncontrolled line breaks of erratic rhythm can create awkward spaces that inhibit reading. In ragged-right type, care should be given to the selection of interline spacing, for it influences legibility and appearance. Spatial consistency and rhythmic line breaks result from careful typographical decisions.

The breaking of lines can be determined by the author's meaning rather than by appearance. This method, sometimes referred to as "thought-unit" typography, arranges lines into discrete parts related to the meaning of the text. Ragged-right lines may be of any length, with line breaks that are logical and focus on the intended message of the writer (Fig. **23**).

Paragraphs and indentions

An important goal for a designer is to distinguish typographically one thought from another, clarify content, and increase reader comprehension. Clear separation of paragraphs in a body of text is one way to accomplish this goal.

It is common practice in the design of books, magazines, and newspapers to indent each paragraph, usually with moderate indention of one to three ems. It is also typographic practice not to indent the first paragraph in an article, chapter, or advertisement so that the square corner of the first column can be maintained.

Paragraphs can also be separated by inserting additional space between them. This space should be proportional to the amount of interline spacing, which corresponds to the vertical measurement of the typographic grid. Paragraphs are often separated by one line space. This method should be avoided if the original copy is full of short, choppy paragraphs. Spaces between such paragraphs could be very disturbing, consuming too much space. Indentions and additional linespace are also used to establish order within complex tabular matter, such as financial charts and scientific data.

83

23.

Thought-unit typography from
the Washburn College Bible.
(Designer: Bradbury Thompson)

1:1 In the beginning
God created the heaven and the earth.

2 And the earth was without form, and void;
and darkness was upon the face of the deep.
And the Spirit of God
moved upon the face of the waters.

3 And God said,
Let there be light:
and there was light.

4 And God saw the light, that it was good:
and God divided the light from the darkness.

5 And God called the light Day,
and the darkness he called Night.
And the evening and the morning
were the first day.

6 And God said,
Let there be a firmament
in the midst of the waters,
and let it divide the waters from the waters.

7 And God made the firmament,
and divided the waters
which were under the firmament
from the waters
which were above the firmament:
and it was so.

8 And God called the firmament Heaven.
And the evening and the morning
were the second day.

9 And God said,
Let the waters under the heaven
be gathered together unto one place,
and let the dry land appear:
and it was so.

10 And God called the dry land Earth;
and the gathering together of the waters
called he Seas:
and God saw that it was good.

11 And God said,
Let the earth bring forth grass,
the herb yielding seed,
and the fruit tree yielding fruit after his kind,
whose seed is in itself, upon the earth:
and it was so.

12 And the earth brought forth grass,
and herb yielding seed after his kind,
and the tree yielding fruit,
whose seed was in itself, after his kind:
and God saw that it was good.

This is Garamond
This is Garamond
This is Garamond
24.

a b c d e f g
h i j k l m n
o p q r s t u
v w x y z
25.

Legibility and electronic page design

New legibility issues emerged when the digital revolution occurred in typography and design. This includes concerns relating to software, discussed in this section, and problems related to on-screen display, covered in the following section. Electronic page design offers designers more possibilities for type manipulation than ever before, resulting in an obligation to know more about the cultural and formal evolution of typography than in times past. Without adequate knowledge of typographic legibility, it is easy for designers to blindly follow fads, succumb to common visual clichés provided by software, or thoughtlessly yield to the built-in defaults of a computer application. Legibility is a concern that should be continually addressed as technology changes. Because designers now work at a keyboard, they are directly responsible for composing legible type – a task once accomplished by sending specifications to a compositor at a typesetting firm.

As a result of desktop technology and type-design software, new typefaces and revivals of old typefaces are being released at an unprecedented rate. Some of these are well designed, but others are not. Many different typefaces from various digital foundries have the same name, yet the design of some of these faces is far removed from the original (Fig. **24**). It is not enough to make typeface selections on the basis of a name; designers should make visual comparisons before deciding which typefaces are most suitable.

Well-drawn typefaces possess the following optical characteristics: crisp edges without stair-stepping, no out-of-control pixels, curves with smooth and flowing thick-to-thin transitions, bowls of curved characters that slightly extend beyond the baseline and meanline, form and counterform relationships that provide consistent texture and color, characters that do not "dance" up and down on the baseline, optically equal spacing, and the absence of "black sheep" characters that visually stray from the rest of the letters due to an anomalous shape (Fig. **25**).

Tools available in desktop software enable type to be outlined, stretched, rotated, skewed, mirrored, placed on a curved baseline, and manipulated in innumerable other ways. Upon determining the objectives, requirements, and limitations of the typographic problem at hand, designers can creatively employ these tools while also addressing legibility needs. These tools are best used to express ideas visually, rather than to merely embellish type. When using such tools, it is desirable to make typography as legible as possible by adhering to the legibility factors discussed earlier in this chapter, and to maintain the proportional integrity of letterforms. Even though type set on a curved baseline, for example, is not as legible as type set on a horizontal baseline, it can be made more legible by carefully spacing the letters and choosing a well-designed typeface. Figures **26–28** present a variety of electronic type manipulations with accompanying alterations for improved legibility.

26.

27.

28.
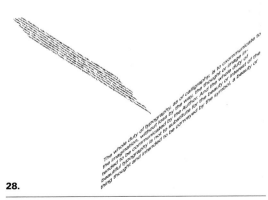

24.
Three typefaces have the same name, but significantly different properties. The size, weight width, and shape of characters differ from one to the other.

25.
The lowercase *i*, *j*, and *l* appear out of place due to the presence of serifs in an otherwise sans-serif typeface. Also, the *m* and *w* appear darker in tone than their neighbors.

26.
Type improperly scaled on a tightly curved baseline causes characters to awkwardly bump into each other (bottom). Smaller type on a similar curve flows smoothly and consistently (top).

27.
Type skewed to the degree that it is no longer readable (top). Type similarly skewed, but word pictures are preserved enough to ensure legibility (bottom).

28.
Several skewed lines of type suggest a textural plane floating in space. Due to the degree of skew and the proximity of the lines one to another, the type is totally unreadable (left). By increasing interline spacing, changing the type weight, and reducing the degree of skew, lines can still be read (right).

EOA EOA
EOA
EOA

29.

31.

a a
32. **33.** **34.**

30.

quote: edward abbey
design: rob carter

29.
When letters are stretched horizontally or vertically on a computer to create condensed and expanded letterforms, their proportions change. The optical relationships of the original typeface design are destroyed.

30.
Experimental typography exploring computer manipulation of type. (Text: Ann Zwinger; Design: Rob Carter)

31.
Digital letterforms have decreasing resolution as the number of pixels is reduced.

32.
This enlargement of an *a,* displayed on a computer screen at a five-pixel height, shows the distortion that resulted. (Designer: Matt Woolman)

33.
Enlargement of a screen display of an *a* shows "the jaggies" caused by pixels. (Designer: Matt Woolman)

34.
Anti-aliasing smooths out the hard, stair-stepped diagonal and curved edges. (Designer: Matt Woolman)

a a a a
a   a   a   a
36 point   24 point   18 point   12 point

35.

Verdana Georgia
Verdana Georgia
Verdana Georgia
Verdana Georgia

36.

Gross distortion of the optical relationships within a font occurs when only one axis, such as its width or height, is changed, as shown in Figure **29**. Adobe introduced its multiple-master font technology around 1992 to address the need to alter letterforms by changing more than one axis while maintaining their design integrity. Multiple-master type is discussed in Chapter 7.

Typographic experimentation on the computer allows designers to probe the relationship between type, space, and expression. Syntactic exploration reveals boundless potential to inform, amuse, and astonish. In recent years designers have extended their range of possibilities by approaching work as play and tools as toys. One example of the expressive potential of computer-manipulated type is seen in a page from a series of experiments created to document wanderings in canyons of the Utah desert (Fig. **30**).

Legibility and the Internet

The Internet is a challenging environment for good typography, especially at text sizes. Its problems are inherent in all on-screen font displays, whether designing typography for a CD-ROM, cell-phone display, interactive kiosk, or Web site. When designing on a computer screen – even when the final production will take another form, such as offset printing – the same legibility issues apply to the on-screen type. Screen fonts are bitmaps, which are digitized images made up of tiny dots. To render a letterform on a computer screen, it must be rasterized, or converted into tiny dots called pixels, which is short for picture elements. The relatively low resolution of many contem-porary computer screens, which typically have a bitmap matrix of 72 or 96 pixels per inch, cannot display the subtle nuances of a beautifully designed font. When type is rendered on a screen, details such as stroke weight, subtle curves, and serif detail are reduced to a coarse approximation of the refined forms found in the original design. This occurs because curved and diagonal edges rendered as pixels on a raster-scan display have a jagged stair-step quality, called "the jaggies." The more pixels used to generate the letterform, the higher the resolution (Fig. **31**). When small type appears on-screen with too few pixels to accurately display the subtle forms of the letter, a

catastrophic decrease in legibility can occur (Fig. **32**). Several methods are used to improve on-screen font display.

Anti-aliasing is a technique used to replace the jagged stair-step edges (Fig. **33**) created by pixels with an illusion of the smooth curves found in a well-designed typeface. Pixels around the edges of curved or angled letterforms are rendered in an intermediate tone or color. These pixels are displayed in a blend of the type color and the background color, resulting in an appearance of smoother, more refined letterforms (Fig. **34**). The drawbacks of anti-aliased type are that it looks fuzzy and it is only effective in larger sizes. When text-size type is anti-aliased, it becomes so fuzzy that legibility is significantly decreased, often to the point of illegibility.

Hinting. A major factor influencing the legibility of on-screen type is resolution. Where fewer pixels are available to describe letters, resolution decreases. To compensate for this problem, type designers reshape the outlines of characters – a process called "hinting"– to create the best possible image at various point sizes. Hints alter the actual outlines of letters by selectively activating pixels, thus improving the legibility of letters on the screen and from low-resolution output devices. An *unhinted* typeface will typically instruct the computer to turn on a pixel if more than half of its area is covered by the letterform. A *hinted* typeface has the pixels activated to display each letter adjusted to more accurately display it at various sizes (Fig. **35**). Hinting information is built into the software that generates the typeface on the screen and automatically occurs when the type is displayed on the screen.

Two widely used on-screen typefaces were specifically created for use as Web-page text. These are Verdana and Georgia (Fig. **36**), designed by Matthew Carter and hinted by Thomas Rickner. Most digital typefaces are designed as outline fonts that are used to generate bitmapped screen fonts. Verdana and Georgia were first designed as bitmaps of pixels (Fig. **37**), *then* they were translated into outline fonts. As a result, they have better on-screen fidelity than most typefaces originally designed for high-resolution output.

35.
Four sizes of a hinted letter *a* are shown enlarged and at on-screen reproduction sizes. (Designer: Matt Woolman)

36.
Verdana (left) and Georgia (right) are shown at 9-, 14-, 24-, and 36-point on-screen sizes. Hinting improves legibility by adjusting the design for each size. Note that the 9-point type is bitmapped, while the computer applied anti-aliasing to the larger sizes. (Font designer: Matthew Carter, hinted by Thomas Rickner)

37.
This screen photograph shows a text-size Georgia *h* as a bitmapped letterform and as an outline letterform. (Photographer: Matthew Carter)

38.

39.

Pixel fonts are typefaces specifically designed as bitmapped type. These are designed to the pixel; for example, the characters in Emperor 15 (Fig. **38**) are exactly 15 pixels high. On a 72-dpi screen, these will be the same height as a 15-point typeface, since there are also 72 points in an inch. On a 96-dpi screen, however, a 15-pixel tall bitmap font will appear smaller, about the size of 11-point type. Pixel fonts can degrade when used at larger or smaller sizes than the size for which they have been designed. Pixel fonts are especially useful for very small on-screen text, as they can be designed to maximize legibility when pixellated. The distinctive appearance of these fonts has led to their occasional use as display fonts because their character is expressive of computer technology.

On-screen typefaces often face the problem of platform inconsistency. People will often view Web pages set in typefaces that are not installed on their computer. This results in a carefully designed Web page being rendered on many viewers' screens in a different font than the one used in the original design. The different set width and letterform designs can totally change the appearance of the page layout and type. Fonts can be imbedded into Web pages, but often these are not downloaded and displayed. Some Web-design software permits a designer to list a string of commonly available fonts (for example, Georgia, Times New Roman, Times) that are frequently installed on computers. The computer will set the text in the first available font from the list.

HTML and CSS are two programming possibilities for generating font and size selection on the Web. HTML (Hyper Text Markup Language) is the primary programming language used to produce Web pages. An HTML designer can only specify general type category and an approximate size measure. Tracking, linespacing (sometimes called line height by Web designers), and wordspacing are usually arbitrary. CSS (Cascading Style Sheets) allow designers to specify exact type size, letter-, line-, and word-spacing. As discussed earlier in this chapter, these characteristics are

major determinates of text type legibility. CCS also have the capability to specify different style sheets for different output devices. For example, one type style can be specified in pixel size for on-screen viewing, while another can be specified in points for printing on a laser printer. When developing a Web site in HTML and CSS, designers do not yet have control over anti-aliasing.

Type as image. Type, especially display type, is often converted to a picture file (for example, a GIF), and downloaded as an image on a Web site (Fig. **39**). The benefits are fidelity to the designer's intent and compatibility with almost all Web-browser software. Since images require more file size than plain text, this slows the downloading of the Web page. If a large number of typographic elements are downloaded as images, this further increases the time required for a browser to display the Web page. Type downloaded as an image is fixed in size and cannot be selected or copied as text. It cannot be scaled or changed in size. Revisions are difficult, because an image, rather than the words in running text, must be revised. When the design of a Web site is changed or updated, each text treated as an image has to be revised individually.

The rapid pace of computer technology holds promise for greater on-screen type resolution, faster download speeds on the Internet, and more sophisticated software. Newer vector-based software (for example, the FLASH plug-in) permits the downloading of a font's outline data, not just the pixels. More accurate letterforms can be downloaded and rendered on-screen.

The legibility problems and design difficulties facing designers creating on-screen graphics are gradually diminishing. The resolution of computer screens and output devices such as printers will continue to improve, and the gap between printed and on-screen type legibility will lessen over time.

38.
Emperor is a pixel font with a different design for display at different point sizes, with each pixel equaling one point. Emperor 19, for example, is nineteen pixels tall. (Designer: Zuzana Licko)

39.
This element from a Web site timeline demonstrates that typography downloaded as an image – rather than as a text file – maintains its fidelity to the original fonts. A detail of the element is reproduced at screen size (above), with the complete element shown below. (Designer: Lois Kim)

Typographic details

In typography, paying attention to detail is a fact of life. Every letter, word, and line of type is a subject of detail, and as such, it is the designer's responsibility to be alert and aware of these details. To those just learning the intricacies of typographic form and nuance, adherence to the following recommendations will be highly beneficial, and practicing them will eventually become second nature. These recommendations apply primarily to normative typography, which supports the idea that "The whole duty of typography, as with calligraphy, is to communicate to the imagination, without loss by the way, the thought or image intended to be communicated by the author." Expressive forms of typography may intelligently ignore these recommendations all together.

	Recommended	Not recommended
When working with typography, begin with the same typeface and type size. Add additional typefaces, sizes and other variations such as type weight only as needed.	The whole duty of typography, as with calligraphy, **is to communicate to the imagination,** without loss by the way, the thought or image intended to be communicated by the author.	The whole duty of typography, as with CALLIGRAPHY, IS TO COMMUNICATE TO THE IMAGINATION, *without* **loss** by the way, the THOUGHT or image intended to be communicated by the author.
Contrast is one of the most important principles in typographic design. Any shift in typeface, type size, or type weight should be emphasized.	The whole duty of typography, as with calligraphy, **is to communicate to the imagination, without loss by the way, the thought or image intended to be communicated by the author.**	The whole duty of typography, as with calligraphy, is to communicate to the imagination, without loss by the way, the thought or image intended to be communicated by the author.
Interletter, interword, and interline spacing should be based on the spatial character of the typeface in use. This applies to both text and display settings.	The whole duty of typography, as with calligraphy, is to communicate to the imagination, without loss by the way, the thought or image intended to be communicated by the author.	The whole duty of typography, as with calligraphy, is to communicate to the imagination, without loss by the way, the thought or image intended to be communicated by the author.
Manually kern and letterspace display type settings. This is always an optical consideration, and the computer is no substitute for the trained eye.	**The whole duty**	**The whole duty**
Never place two word spaces after periods, commas, semicolons, question marks, and exclamation marks.	The whole duty of typography, as with calligraphy, is to communicate to the imagination, without loss by the way, the thought or image intended to be communicated by the author. And the whole duty of beautiful typography is not to substitute for the beauty or interest of the thing thought	The whole duty of typography, as with calligraphy, is to communicate to the imagination, without loss by the way, the thought or image intended to be communicated by the author. And the whole duty of beautiful typography is not to substitute for the beauty or interest of the thing thought
When setting flush-left, ragged-right or flush-right, ragged-left text, the effort to create pleasing, feathered rags will prevent text blocks from acquiring awkward shapes.	The whole duty of typography, as with calligraphy, is to communicate to the imagination, without loss by the way, the thought or image intended to be communicated by the author. And the whole duty of beautiful typography is not to substitute for the beauty or interest of the thing thought and	The whole duty of typography, as with calligraphy, is to communicate to the imagination, without loss by the way, the thought or image intended to be communicated by the author. And the whole duty of beautiful typography is not to substitute for the beauty or interest of the thing

	Recommended	Not recommended
Two forms of dashes are desirable: an en-dash with space before and after, and an em-dash with no space. Never use double dashes, and use an en-dash to connect numbers.	The whole duty of typography – as with calligraphy – is to communicate to the imagination The whole duty of typography—as with calligraphy—is to communicate to the imagination 2006–2010	The whole duty of typography--as with calligraphy--is to communicate to the imagination The whole duty of typography — as with calligraphy — is to communicate to the imagination 2006-2010
Do not use dashes where hyphens are required.	The whole duty of typography, as with calligraphy, is to communicate to the imagination, without loss by the way, the thought or image intended to be communicated by the author.	The whole duty of typography, as with calligraphy, is to communicate to the imagination, without loss by the way, the thought or image intended to be communicated by the author.
A common mistake is to substitute prime marks for quotation marks and apostrophes. Prime marks are used to indicated feet and inches.	The whole duty of typography, as with calligraphy, is to "communicate" to the imagination, without loss by the way, the thought or image intended to be communicated by the author.	The whole duty of typography, as with calligraphy, is to "communicate" to the imagination, without loss by the way, the thought or image intended to be communicated by the author.
To achieve optical alignment, it is desirable to "hang" punctuation at the edge of text blocks.	"The whole duty of typography, as with calligraphy, is to communicate to the imagination, without loss by the way, the thought or image intended to be communicated by the author."	"The whole duty of typography, as with calligraphy, is to communicate to the imagination, without loss by the way, the thought or image intended to be communicated by the author."
It is not necessary to insert an additional word space between initial letters.	**T.M.**	**T. M.**
The periods forming an ellipsis character can be separated by letterspaces, or preferably tracked open to achieve desired spacing. Too much space between the periods should be avoided.	The whole duty of typography…as with calligraphy, is to communicate to the imagination, without loss by the way, the thought or image intended to be communicated by the author.…	The whole duty of typography . . . as with calligraphy, is to communicate to the imagination, without loss by the way, the thought or image intended to be communicated by the author . . . .

A grid is a skeletal framework used by designers to organize information within a spatial field. It is a system characterized by the dualities of freedom and constraint, simplicity and complexity. It provides a strategy for composing text and other visual information in two- and three-dimensional space, including those of printed materials, film, computer screens, built environments, and typographic installations. Grid systems aid designers in making information clear and optimally accessible – highly desirable traits in a world increasingly inundated by visual noise. When used effectively, typographic grids provide form and space with proportional harmony and aesthetic beauty. The final result is clearer and more accessible communication.

1.

In 1925, Jan Tschichold designed this cover for the journal *Typographische Mitteilungen*. His 24-page insert for this journal presented and advocated asymmetrical typography to its readers. This marked a movement toward a new language of typographic form and structure. (Designer: Jan Tschichold)

Background

The grid as we know it today is rooted in the earliest written forms, from columnar cuneiform tablets impressed by the Mesopotamians as early as 3000 B.C., to Hieroglyphic writing on papyrus (see Chapter 1, Figs. **5**, **8**).

The mechanization of printing in Europe during the fifteenth century led to structural conventions and typographic principles that have survived for centuries. The architecture of moveable type and the mechanics of letterpress printing yielded rectilinear structures – text set into blocks framed by margins. Beginning with Gutenberg's 42-line Bible (Europe's first typographic book) other similarly structured books were created during the Renaissance in Germany, France, and Italy (see Chapter 1, Figs. **38**, **49**, and **59**).

The development of the modern grid cannot be attributed to a single individual or to an accidental discovery. It is the result of many pioneering efforts, including experiments by renegade designers associated with the movements of Futurism, Dadaism, Constructivism, and de Stijl, breakthroughs initiated at the Bauhaus, and the functionalist works and writings of Jan Tschichold (Fig. **1**). The grid finally emerged as a programmatic system of mathematical precision in Switzerland during the 1950s. Among others, designer Max Bill embraced absolute order in his work. During the last half of the 20th century, the typographic grid achieved universal acceptance as a visual organizational tool.

Now, grids are ubiquitous carriers of information, to the degree that we are not consciously aware of them on a daily basis. Yet the grid, artifice of time and space, is woven deeply into our subconscience. Grids serve as the underlying structure for modelling and archiving human thought, interactions, and events.

typographische mitteilungen

sonderheft

elementare typographie

zeitschrift des bildungsverbandes der deutschen buchdrucker leipzig ● oktoberheft 1925

natan altman
otto baumberger
herbert bayer
max burchartz
el lissitzky
ladislaus moholy-nagy
molnár f. farkas
johannes molzahn
kurt schwitters
mart stam
ivan tschichold

1.

Structure and space

Space is the common denominator for all typographic communication. When typographic elements are introduced into space, they create subliminal divisions, and these divisions create spatial structure. As typographic elements shift syntactically in size, weight, and position, new structures emerge (Fig. **2**).

Another way of thinking about type and its relationship to space is to imagine a letterform as a point in space, the extension of a point as a line in space (line of text), and the extension of a line

3.

Letterforms gain velocity as
they move towards the edges
of space. Here, submitting to
the force of gravity, the letter
T appears to topple.

T   T   T   ⊤

3.

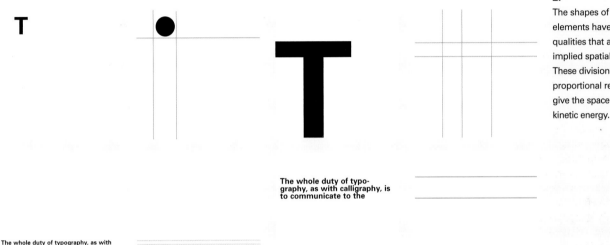

T

2.

The shapes of typographic
elements have directional
qualities that are echoed as
implied spatial corridors.
These divisions establish
proportional relationships, and
give the space movement and
kinetic energy.

**The whole duty of typo-
graphy, as with calligraphy, is
to communicate to the**

The whole duty of typography, as with

The grid is a skeletal framework
used by designers to organize,
relate, and control content within a
spatial field. It is a system
characterized by the dualities of
freedom and constraint, simplicity
and complexity. It provides a stategy
for composing text and other visual
information in two- and three-
dimensional space, including those
of printed materials, film, computer
screen, built environments, and
typographic installations. Grid
systems aid designers in making
information clear and optimally
accessible – highly desirable traits in
a world increasingly inundated by
visual noise. When used effectively,

2.

The grid is a skeletal framework
used by designers to organize,
relate, and control content within
a spatial field. It is a system characterized by the dualities of freedom and constraint, simplicity
and complexity. It provides a
stategy for composing text and
other visual information in two-
and three-dimensional space,

as a plane in space (text block). This analogy
suggests that typographic elements are kinetic in
nature, that they are in perpetual motion.

Consider the single letterform. When centered it
appears motionless. When placed off center, it
appears to move – gaining velocity as it
approaches the outermost boundaries of the
space. Rotate the letter and it appears to tumble.
Lines of type are put into motion – from the
direction of their origin (usually left to right) – at
the moment they are read. They suggest
horizontal movement, unless of course they are

positioned vertically or at an angle in space. The
kinetic possibilities of typographic elements are
potentially endless (Fig. **3**).

Firmly grounded by gravity, we are oriented to
the earth in terms of the horizontal and the
vertical. We perceive the natural world according
to these opposites, and we create the built
environment in relationship to them. We are more
comfortable with the horizontal – in this realm we
feel safe. The vertical dimension is more
challenging – we are afraid of both flying and
of falling.

4.

4.
This exploratory composition exhibits modular relationships among elements. (Designer: Debra Thompson)

5.
Removing the square from a golden rectangle leaves another golden rectangle.

6.
The golden rectangle can be drawn by making a square, dividing it in half, and striking an arc from the half-point of one side of the square to the opposite corner of the square.

7.
Medieval manuscript (Psalterium) from the 12th century. Shown is a page of text with 3-line and 1-line initials proportioned according to the golden ratio.

Proportion

Divided space is perceived as a system of proportional relationships. To work effectively with the typographic grid is to understand that it also is a system of proportions. A grid ratio, which is a mathematical relationship between two or more grid measurements, governs the size and placement of typographic elements. The ratio X:2X (one unit to two units), for example, indicates the basic grid ratio. This stepped progression of X:2X establishes an underlying proportional system among the parts (Fig. **4**)

Designers most often rely upon an innate sense of proportion. But it is helpful also to consider models that have been handed down over centuries. The most familiar of these is the golden section, which is a law of proportionality found frequently in nature, the human body, and used throughout centuries in art, architecture, design, and music. First developed by Vitruvius, the golden section is basically a relationship or ratio between two numbers (or objects) wherein the ratio of the smaller number to the larger number is the same as the sum of both numbers. The algebraic expression of this relationship is a : b = b : (a+b). Stated numerically, the ratio is 1 : 1.618, and stated in percentages the ratio is 38% to 62% (Fig. **5**). The golden section, which can easily be constructed from the square (Fig. **6**), dominated as the proportional system for the design of medieval manuscripts (Fig. **7**).

The Fibonacci sequence is another important proportional model. Closely related to the golden section, this is a mathematical sequence wherein a number is the sum of the two preceding numbers – in other words, you add the two current numbers to get the third number. The progressive series of mathematical relationships found in the Fibonacci sequence can be observed throughout nature, from sea shells and pinecones to the arrangement of seeds on flowering plants (Fig. **8**).

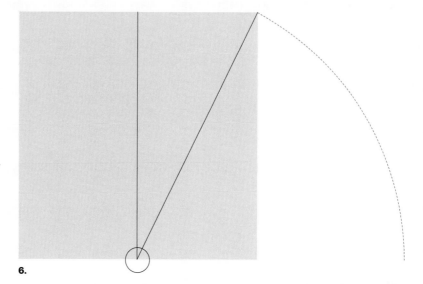

b (62%)

a (38%)

5.

6.

7.

0+1=1	3+5=8	21+34=55
1+1=2	5+8=13	34+55=89
1+2=3	8+13=21	etc.
2+3=5	13+21=34	

The square

A natural division of the golden section is the basic square. This archetypal form has influenced the development of the modern grid perhaps more than any other system of proportion. Squares in combination lend an infinite variety of visual patterns. In Japan, for example, the tatami mat, a straw floor covering based on double square modules, is a system for creating asymmetrical spaces in traditional Japanese homes (Fig. **9**). Paul Rand used squares as metaphorical building blocks, and as an organizational strategy for a book cover. It appears as contemporary today as it was when it was created in 1955 (Fig. **10**). A Web site for the Spanish type foundry Type-o-tones utilizes squares as the navigational system for the site (Fig **11**).

8.

The golden spiral winds through a series of conjoined golden rectangles. The spiral is linked to many forms in nature and is related to the Fibonacci sequence.

8.

9.

10.

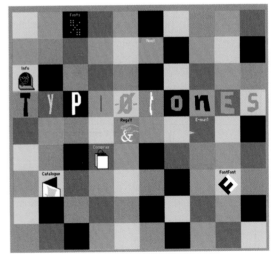

11.

9.
An example of a tatami mat layout illustrates the flexibility and proportional beauty of this modular system.

10.
A book cover divided into a grid of eighty squares is used as an organizational system. Five squares forming the Swiss cross provides a window into Swiss architecture.
(Designer: Paul Rand)

11.
Located within assigned squares, spinning letterforms and animated images entice users to navigate the website.
(Designer: type-ø-tone)

Grids may consist of primary and secondary divisions of space. For example, the grid used in this book consists of two columns as the dominant structure, with an optional structure of five columns (note the visible grid lines on this page). Concurrent grids not only provide added flexibility, they also enable the designer to layer typographic elements, achieving the illusion of three-dimensional space (Fig. **22** and **23**).

22.

Concurrent grids and multi-column grids with irregular column intervals can be used to accommodate information desiring special treatment. Specific parts of information can inhabit assigned columnar zones to preserve their autonomy. In the example shown, the far right column is reserved for the display of alphabetic characters.

23.

Multi-column grids can be applied to many different situations, as in this format consisting of three panels, each divided into three columns.

Typographic Design:
Form and Communication

A grid is a skeletal framework used by designers to organize, relate, and control content within a spatial field. It is a system characterized by the dualities of freedom and constraint, simplicity and complexity.

The whole duty of typography, as with calligraphy, is to communicate to the imagination, without loss by the way, the thought or image intended to be communicated by the author. And the whole duty of beautiful typography is not to substitute for the beauty or interest of the thing thought and intended to be conveyed by the symbol, a beauty or interest of its own, but, on the one hand, to win access for that communication by the clearness and beauty of the vehicle, and on the other hand, to take advantage of every pause or stage in that communication to interpose some characteristic & restful beauty in its own art. We thus have a reason for the clearness and beauty of the first and introductory page and of the title, and for the especial beauty of the headings of chapters, capital or initial letters, and so on, and an opening for the illustrator as we shall see by and by. The whole duty of typography, as with calligraphy, is to communicate to the imagination, without loss by the way, the thought or image

22.

Typographic Design:
Form and Communication

A grid is a skeletal framework used by designers to organize, relate, and control content within a spatial field. It is a system characterized by the dualities of freedom and constraint, simplicity and complexity.

The whole duty of typography, as with calligraphy, is to communicate to the imagination, without loss by the way, the thought or image intended to be communicated by the author. And the whole duty of beautiful typography is not to substitute for the beauty or interest of the thing thought and intended to be conveyed by the symbol, a beauty or interest of its own, but, on the one hand, to win access for that communication by the clearness and beauty of the

vehicle, and on the other hand, to take advantage of every pause or stage in that communication to interpose some characteristic & restful beauty in its own art. We thus have a reason for the clearness and beauty of the first and introductory page and of the title, and for the especial beauty of the headings of chapters, capital or initial letters, and so on, and an opening for the illustrator as we shall see by and by. The whole duty of typography, as with calligraphy, is to communicate to the imagination, without loss by the way, the thought or image intended to be communicated by the author. And the whole duty of beautiful typography is not to substitute for the beauty or interest of the thing thought and intended to be conveyed by the symbol, a beauty or interest of its own, but, on the one hand, to win access for that communication by the clearness and beauty of the vehicle, and on the other hand, to take advantage of every pause or

A grid is a skeletal framework used by designers to organize, relate, and control content within a spatial field. It is a system characterized by the dualities of freedom and constraint, simplicity and complexity.

Typographic Design:
Form and Communication

23.

Experimentation with multi-column grids can yield visually surprising and functional results. Columns can be shifted horizontally and vertically, placed at opposing angles, or behave in ways extending typographic tradition. However, such effects should only be used when they contribute to the interpretation of the text (Figs. **24–27**).

24.

Strict adherence to a two-column grid proves an orderly environment for the presentation of text and paintings by artist and designer Bart van der Leck. (Designer: Wigger Bierma)

25.

The purity and serenity of climbing is reflected in this elegant and restrained design. The magazine layout consists of three columns that facilitate a balanced integration of text and spectacular photographs. (Editor/Creative Director: Christian Beckwith; Designer: Sam Serebin)

24.

25.

33.

The MeBox is a customizable cardboard box storage system. The ends of each box have a grid of perforated disks that can be punched out as needed to make initials, numbers, symbols, and text. The boxes can be arranged in rows to create longer messages. (Designer: Graphic Thought Facility, London)

34.

Visual unity among the many components of the Grasslands outdoor exhibition is established through a modular system of squares. By combining the smallest square unit into larger groups of rectilinear units, images and type are presented in many different sizes for visually dynamic displays. (Exhibition designers: Michael Mercadante and David Whitemyer; graphic designer: Polly Johnson)

35.

The Web site for Demographik – a design agency based in Florida that develops media solutions – is based on an animated system of square modules. While navigating the site, "tiles" appear to lift from the surface of the screen, casting shadows, and dynamically spinning into new locations where transformed spaces reveal information about the company. (Designer: Juan Benedit)

33.

34.

35.

37.

36.

36.
Vitra, in collaboration with internationally renowned designers, is a manufacturer and developer of high-quality furniture. Visitors to the Vitra Web site are stimulated by an expansive and layered modular environment. Typography is integrated into modular units with refined simplicity, while vivid color, contrasting shapes, and visual repetition yield drama and sophistication. (Designer: Uli Weidner, Virtual Identity AG)

37.
IF/THEN is a book utilizing concurrent grid structures that provide visual variety while also preserving unity among pages. (Designer: Mevis & Van Deursen)

Improvisational structures

Improvisational structures evolve in response to the specific elements of information as opposed to modular grids, which are predetermined organizational devices. A complete grasp of the visual material in question enables designers to understand the relationships between parts and to create visual hierarchies among them. In the metaphorical sense, typographic designers are information architects – they "build" typographic environments for clear and accessible information.

Typographical materials are the building blocks of improvisational structures. Once it is known which elements are dominant, subdominant, and subordinate, they are translated into typographic forms reflecting their hierarchical status. These forms, consisting of different sizes and shapes, are then introduced into the spatial field and intuitively arranged until a rational and aesthetic solution is found. For a poster announcing a lecture series, designer David Colley has organized the information into five distinct zones: title, speakers, venues, sponsor, and tertiary information. The improvised structure not only communicates clearly through legible typography and the effective organization of contrasting parts, it also provides a dynamic viewing experience based on the language of asymmetrical composition (Fig. **38**).

This flexible construction process involves inserting typographic forms in space to establish form and content relationships, substituting these forms with revised forms as necessary, and omitting forms that are inconsequential.

Working with improvisational structures calls for a firm understanding of asymmetrical composition, the dynamics of positive and negative space, and the essential role of visual contrast among typographic elements.

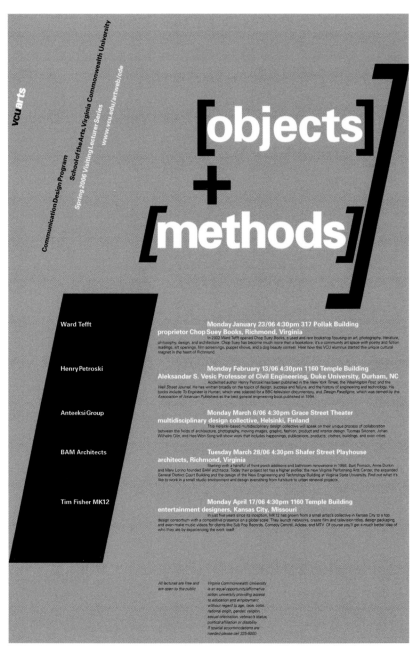

38.

38.
The improvisational structure inherent in this poster is built upon dynamic relationships between horizontal, vertical, and diagonal axes. (Designer: David Colley)

Typographic messages pervade our culture to the degree that they are often taken for granted or not noticed at all. Typographic messages are most effective when they are distinguished from the competition. Messages that clearly communicate and are etched into the mind and memory are those characterized by absolute clarity in form and content. This chapter introduces typography as a language of potent visible signs, a language capable of educating, persuading, informing, and entertaining. When typographic signs are created with an informed eye and mind, they achieve both lucidity and aesthetic beauty.

ping pong
ping pong ping
pong ping pong
ping pong

1.

1.
"ping pong" (Poet: Eugen
Gomringer)
4.
Title lettering for De Stijl.
(Designer: Theo van
Doesburg)

A multidimensional language

The typographic message is verbal, visual, and vocal. While typography is read and interpreted verbally, it may also be viewed and interpreted visually, heard and interpreted audibly. It is a dynamic communication medium. In this sense, early twentieth-century typography became a revolutionary form of communication, bringing new expressive power to the written word. Consider the concrete poem "ping pong" (Fig. **1**). The geometric structure of this poem is composed of a repetition of the words *ping* and *pong*. As these words are repeated, they signify the sound of a bouncing ping-pong ball, and the circular letters *p, o,* and *g* reflect the shape of the ball. The full impact of this poem is achieved when it is read aloud. By hearing the sounds and viewing the typographic forms, the typographic message is strengthened.

Significant departures from the use of conventional typographic forms occurred in Europe at the beginning of the twentieth century. During this activist period, experimentation in all the visual and performing arts was affected by potent social and philosophical changes, industrial and technological developments, and new attitudes about aesthetics and modern civilization. Typographic design was pulled into this artistic revolution as poets and visual artists realized that both meaning and form could be intensified in typographic communications.

The Futurist manifesto, written by the Italian poet Filippo Marinetti in 1909, profoundly influenced thinking in Europe and Russia. Futurism praised technology, violence, danger, movement, and speed. Futurist typography, known as "free typography," demonstrated these ideas in a highly expressive manner (Fig. **2**; and see Chapter 1, Fig. **125**). The chill of a scream was expressed in bold type, and quick impressions were intensified through italics. Letters and words raced across the page in dynamic motion.

Among the movements affected by Futurism were Dadaism in France, Switzerland, and Germany; de Stijl in Holland; and Constructivism in Russia. Each of these historical movements has had a penetrating effect upon typography. Artists and designers associated with these movements saw typography as a powerful means of conveying information relating to the realities of industrialized society (Figs. **3-5**; also see Chapter 1, Figs. **129–35**). They disdained what typography had become: a decorative art form far removed from the realities of the time. The architect Otto Wagner further emphasized that "all modern forms must be in harmony with the new requirements of our time. Nothing that is not practical can be beautiful." Written in 1920, the second de Stijl manifesto clearly demonstrated the concern for a new, expressive typography (Fig. **6**). With dramatic changes taking place in the form and content of typography, the typographic message became a multifaceted and expressive form of communication. Typography needs to be read, seen, heard, felt, and experienced.

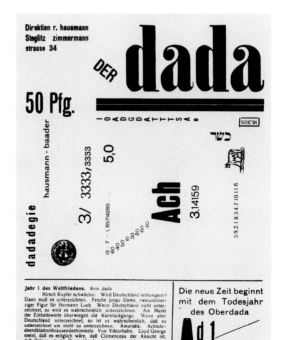

3.
Cover of the first issue of
Der Dada. (Editor: Raoul
Hausmann)

2.
Les mots en liberté futuristes.
(Designer: Filippo Marinetti)

5.
Constructivist cover design
for *Veshch, Gegenstand,
Objet.* (Designer: El Lissitzky)

BERLIN 1922

OBJET

ВЕЩЬ

A=3

GEGENSTAND

REVUE ● INTERNATIONALE ● DE L'ART ● MODERNE ●
МЕЖДУНАРОДНОЕ ● ОБОЗРЕНИЕ ● СОВРЕМЕННОГО ● ИСКУССТВА ●
INTERNATIONALE ● RUNDSCHAU ● DER KUNST ● DER GEGENWART

In language, signs are joined together to create messages. Words as verbal signs, grouped together in a linear fashion, attain their value vis-à-vis other words through opposition and contrast. Words can also evoke meaning through mental association. These associative relations are semantically derived. Since typography is both visual and verbal, it operates in a linear fashion, with words following each other in a specific sequence, or in a nonlinear manner, with elements existing in many syntactic combinations. For example, in the visual poem "O Christmas Tree," the choice of the typeface, Futura Light, is very important. The capital letter *O* is a perfect circle, signifying ornaments; the linear strokes of other letterforms suggest the texture of evergreen needles (Fig. **11**). This typographic message is derived from the mental associations formed by contrasting typographic signs.

Two terms important to the understanding of signs are denotation and connotation. When considering the meaning of typographic signs, denotation refers to objective meaning, the factual world of collective awareness and experience. For example, a denotative interpretation of a yellow *O* would be: "This is a yellow letter *O*" or "This is a yellow circle." Connotative interpretations of the yellow *O* might be: "This is the sun, a slice of lemon, or a golden ring." Connotative observations are often conditioned, for they relate to overtones and are drawn from prior personal experience.

Typographic signs are both verbal and visual. The associations formed between the verbal and visual attributes are verbal/visual equivalencies, which are found in a variety of configurations. These reveal the associative nature of signs composing the typographic message and help us further understand its multifaceted attributes. Figures **12-24** illustrate the nature of some of these verbal/visual equations.

12.
Visual substitution: The visual
sign of an ear is substituted
for the letters *E, A,* and *R.*
(Designer: Lou Dorfsman)

14.

Simultaneity: The numeral *8* functions as the letter *g* in this logotype used for a group exhibition of paintings by the early-twentieth-century American art group The Eight.

15.

Visual transformation: A mother, father, and child are suggested through the visual transformation of the letters *l* and *i*. (Designer: Herb Lubalin)

Taking Things Apart and Putting Things Together

what chemistry is what chemists do and what the results have been

sponsored by the American Chemical Society on the occasion of its 100th anniversary

Union Carbide 270 Park Ave. New York, N.Y. 10017

April 5-May 28, 1976 9:30-4:30 weekdays Closed April 16, 17 and Sundays Admission: free

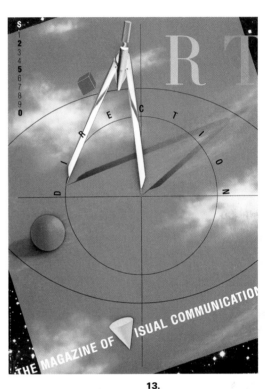

13.

Visual substitution: The visual sign of a compass is substituted for the letter *A* and an inverted cone is substituted for the letter *V*. (Designer: Harold Burch)

16.

Visual exaggeration: The irregular syntactic treatment of typographic signs exaggerates the process of taking things apart and putting things together. (Designer: Steff Geissbuhler)

the American premiere at the Depot in Urbana
of the play by Marcel Achard

translated by Sue Huseman Moretto
directed by Jose Moretto

October 31, November 1, 2, 3 1974
November 7, 8, 9, 10
at 8:00 pm, Friday and Saturday also at 10:30 pm

tickets at Record Service
704 South Sixth Champaign
and at the Depot 223 North Broadway
on nights of performance

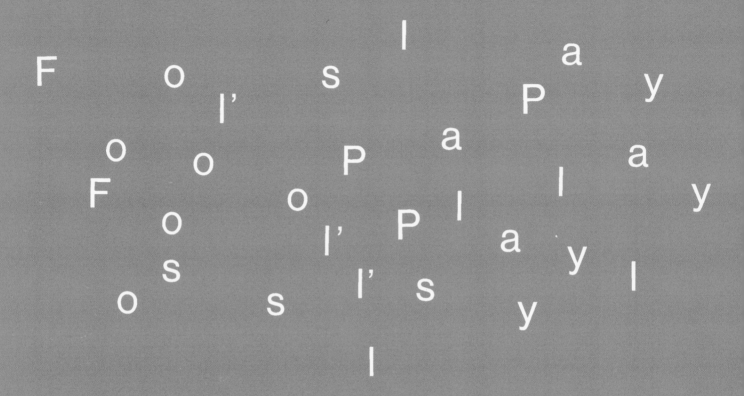

18.
Form combination: Visual and verbal signs are combined into a single typographic statement, creating trademarks that suggest the nature of various industries: an electrical contractor, a maker of plastic fibers for carpets and draperies, and a lithographic printer. (Designer: Don Weller)

18.

19.
Form combination: Verbal signs are combined with visual signs (cables). The resulting forms suggest the qualities of cable transmission. (Designers: Jerry L. Kuyper and Sheila de Bretteville)

20.
Parallel form: The Olivetti logotype and electronic calculator have similar visual characteristics that parallel each other. (Logotype design: Walter Ballmer)

21.
Verbal/visual correspondence: The syntactic qualities of this typographic sign correspond to the graffiti found in an urban environment. (Designer: Jeff Barnes)

22.
Verbal/visual correspondence: The visual characteristics of this typographic sign correspond to the form of a zipper. This is achieved by a repetition of letters and a horizontal shift within the word. (Designer: Richard Rumble)

19.

C A B L E

20.

city

21.

17.
Visual exaggeration: The repetition and playful treatment of typographic forms effectively reinforces the content of the drama *Fool's Play,* for which this poster was designed. (Designer: David Colley)

ZIIIIIIIIIIIIIPPPER

22.

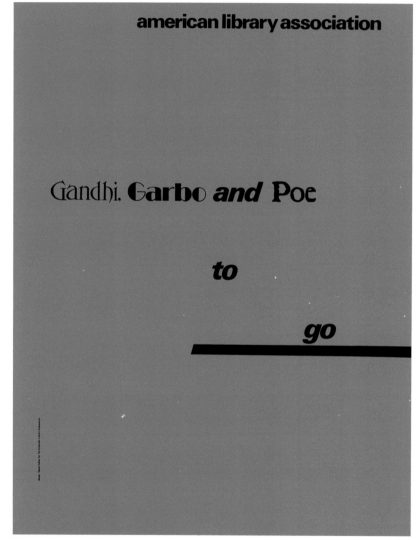

american library association

Gandhi, Garbo *and* Poe

to

go

23.

Unity 1924

Xiiunity

Anspach
Grossman
Portugal
Inc

24.

23.
Verbal/visual correspondence:
The visual qualities of the
typefaces chosen for the signs
Gandhi, Garbo, and Poe make
direct reference to time and
culture. The message is
further strengthened by the
sounds associated with the
words. (Designer: David
Colley)

24.
Verbal/visual correspondence:
The visual repetition of this
word – unified by the shared
letters *u* and *n* – express the
concept of unity. (Designer:
Steff Geissbuhler)

Function and expression

Functionalism is a term used to describe the utilitarian and pragmatic qualities of designed objects. During the early twentieth century, functionalism was generally equated with designed objects of clarity, purpose, and unornamented simplicity. However, it has since evolved as a subjective notion that varies widely according to the needs of the audience and the objectives of the designer.

For example, if comfort in the design of a chair is defined as plushness and cushiness, an upholstered automatic recliner complete with footrest and vibrator might satisfy the criteria of a functional chair.

In contrast to the automatic recliner is the red/blue chair, a central artifact of the de Stijl movement, designed in 1918 by Gerrit Rietveld (Fig. **25**). Members of de Stijl sought a restrained expression and a new philosophy for living. With its hard, flat surfaces, the red/blue chair appears very uncomfortable; however, Rietveld's desire was for the chair to promote alert mental activity through rigid support. The seat and backrest planes are attached at only one edge, enabling the pliable wood to adjust to the user's weight. In this regard, the chair functions according to Rietveld's intentions. In an interior environment, Rietveld's red/blue chair has the presence and visual harmony of a piece of sculpture. The needs for a functional object (seating) and for aesthetic experience are fulfilled in this one object.

In typography, function is the purposeful communication of information to a specific audience. Although the range of possible typographic design solutions is infinite, the appropriateness of a solution always depends upon the purpose for which it was intended. Varying degrees of formal reduction or elaboration can be effective when solving specific typographic problems.

25.
Red/blue chair, 1918.
(Designer: Gerrit Rietveld)

26.

The elemental shape and sequence of letters in the word *eye* visually suggest two eyes and a nose. Set in News Gothic, this typographic configuration serves as the masthead for *eye, The International Review of Graphic Design*. (Designer: Stephen Coates)

27.

Required to appear on all food packaging in the United States, the standardized *Nutrition Facts* label clearly provides consumers with important information about the nutritional value of foods. Typography responsibly assumes an objective, informational role. (Designer: Berkey Belser)

28.

The "A" stamp is the official priority stamp of the Swiss Post Office. A simple configuration of three interlocking shapes suggests an uppercase *A*. The trilogy of shapes represents the co-dependent parts of the mailing process: message, sender, and receiver. (Designer: Jean-Benoît Lévy)

29.

The vitality of *Rolling Stone* magazine is revealed in this monumental, three-dimensional letterform, a deconstructed element used in the traveling exhibition *The 30th Anniversary Covers Tour*. (Designer: J. Abbott Miller, James Hicks, Paul Carlos, and Scott Davendorf)

30.

This sequence of frames represents the animated "splash page" of a Web site designed to teach children how to read. The letter *O*, containing the remaining vowels, rolls onto the screen. As the letterforms transform in color, they roll off of the screen and disintegrate. (Designer: John Stratiou)

Formal reduction can be used to create optimum clarity and legibility, presenting complex information, such as news or scientific data, in a clear and straightforward manner. Orderly presentation guides the eye from one element to another, preserving reader interest and attention (Figs. **26** and **27**).

Another approach, expressionism, accomplishes its purpose through formal elaboration and ornamentation, creating visual impact. When appropriate, attention can be given to experimental, expressive, and ornamental possibilities. Ornament serves a variety of practical needs. Because it is semiotic, iconographic, and historical, it identifies the object with which it is associated. Expressive and ornamental typographic forms place objects in time, reveal their purpose, and clarify their structures (Figs. **28-30**). The formal elaboration of objects in architecture, industrial design, and the fine arts can significantly influence typographic possibilities. Figures **71** and **119** (Chapter 1) and **31-33** possess strong ornamental qualities. Innovative typography can emerge when a designer fully understands communication needs and is able to assimilate a diversity of visual ideas.

On this subject, Ladislav Sutnar commented that "an eccentric visual scandal or visual shock of the outrageous and of the unexpected can catch the attention of the astonished eye . . . it may also delight the eye to see a fresh design concept or a message so orderly presented as to make comprehension fast and easy." A designer can avoid conventional solutions to typographic problems when innovation is appropriate. A single approach to typographical design, induced by stylistic convention and predetermined formulas, is a routine activity lacking the vitality of meaningful typographic invention. Sound principles and a trained vision should supersede dependency upon preconceived formulas. For typography to be truly functional, satisfying the needs of an audience, a designer must understand both the verbal and visual attributes of a typographic message.

30.

26.

27.

28.

31.

A field of typographic forms, illustrations, and the colors orange and black charge this poster with expression. (Designer: Todd Timney)

32.

This view book acquires its robust and expressive quality through vivid color, varying typographic textures, and structural complexity. (Design: Rob Carter)

33.

Expressive text type is achieved on a spread of the book *Elvis+Marilyn* by its configuration into the letter *R*. (Designer: Mirko Ilić)

The invention of typography has been called the beginning of the Industrial Revolution. It is the earliest mechanization of a handicraft: the handlettering of books. Typographic design has been closely bound to the evolution of technology, for the capabilities and limitations of typesetting systems have posed constraints upon the design process. At the same time, typesetting has offered creative challenges as designers have sought to explore the limitations of the available systems and to define their aesthetic and communicative potential.

From hand composition to today's electronically generated typography, it is important for designers to comprehend the nature and capabilities of typographic technologies, for this understanding provides a basis for a thoughtful blending of design and production.

Hand composition

The traditional method of setting foundry type by hand is similar to the method used by Gutenberg when he invented movable type in 1450. For centuries, hand composition was accomplished by assembling individual pieces of type into lines. A typographer would hold a composing stick (Fig. **1**) in one hand while the other hand placed type selected from a type case (Fig. **2**) into the stick. Type was set letter by letter, line by line, until the desired setting was achieved. When it was necessary to justify a line, additional spaces were created in the line by inserting metal spacing material between words. Letterspacing was achieved by inserting very thin pieces of copper or brass between letters until words appeared to be evenly spaced. When additional space between lines was desired, strips of lead were inserted between the lines until the type column was the proper depth. By adding lead, the exact proportion and size of the column could be formed, assuring readability through consistent spacing.

Once type was set, it was "locked up" in a heavy rectangular steel frame called a *chase* (Fig. **3**). This was done on a table called a *stone.* The type was surrounded by wood or metal spacing material, called *furniture,* and the contents of the chase were made secure by tightening steel, wedgelike devices called *quoins.* After the type was secured in the chase, it was ready to be transferred to a

2.
Type case.

Chase

Wood furniture

Type

Quoins

3.
A chase containing type "locked up" and ready for printing.

126

press for printing, and after printing, the individual pieces of type were distributed back into the type case by hand.

Hand composition was tedious and time consuming. When typesetting became automated as a result of the invention of Linotype and Monotype machines, hand composition was used only for setting small amounts of type or for display type. Currently, hand composition is obsolete as a practical means of setting type, but as an art form there has been a revival. Private presses produce limited-edition books and a variety of experimental materials by hand. Many of our typographic conventions and traditions have their origins in the rich heritage of handset metal type.

Linotype

One of the most profound developments in typesetting technology was the invention of the Linotype machine (Fig. **4**) by Ottmar Mergenthaler in 1886. This machine represented the first great step toward typographic automation. Its name was coined because it produced a single line of type to a predetermined length specified by the keyboard operator.

The operation of the Linotype was based on the principle of a circulating matrix. Each time a key was pressed, a single brass matrix (Fig. **5**) was released from an overhead magazine, divided into ninety vertical channels, each containing matrices for one character. The magazine was the character storage case for the machine. Once an entire line had been typed, the matrices moved into an automatic casting mechanism where the line of type was cast from molten lead. As each line was being cast, the operator typed the next line. After the casting process was complete, cast lines of type called slugs (Fig. **6**) were ejected from the mold, and the matrices were automatically returned to their appropriate slot in the magazine for reuse.

The advantages of machine composition as compared to hand composition were obvious. It was faster and more accurate; the problem of type distribution (returning characters to the type case) was eliminated, for the cast lines of type were

7.
Monotype keyboard.

simply melted, and the lead was reused. Justification of type was automatic, eliminating the tedious process of inserting spaces between letters and words. A standard Linotype could cast lines up to thirty picas in length.

An important development for linecasting type was the Teletypesetter. This perforated tape-driven machine – an attachment to Linotype and Intertype – was introduced in 1928. Tape, which was punched by a machine similar to a standard typewriter, could be generated from a distant office and transmitted to the linecaster by wire, which made the machine invaluable to news services.

Monotype

Another significant achievement leading to fully automated typesetting was the Monotype machine, invented by Tolbert Lanston in 1887. This machine cast one character at a time rather than an entire line. it was composed of two parts: a keyboard and a typecaster (Fig. **7**). When an operator typed at a keyboard, a perforated paper tape was generated. This coded tape was used to drive the second part of the system – the typecaster. Compressed air, blown through the punched holes of this revolving spool of coded paper, determined which characters would be cast by the typecaster. Actual casting of type occurred when hot metal was forced into matrices from the matrix case (Fig. **8**). Once the cast characters had cooled, they were placed into a metal tray called a galley, where the lines were assembled. Monotype lines could reach a maximum length of about sixty picas.

Monotype became an efficient way to set type for several reasons. Corrections could be made by changing individual letters instead of complete lines. Therefore, complex typesetting, such as scientific data and tabular information, was easier. The Monotype matrix case held many more characters than a Linotype magazine, and the casting machine was relatively fast, casting one hundred fifty characters per minute. Since the system consisted of two separate machines, an operator could generate type away from the clatter of the casting machine. In fact, several operators could keyboard information for later setting.

8.
Monotype matrix case.

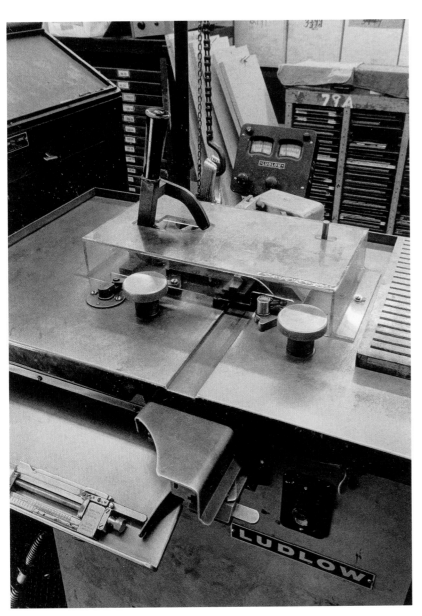

Ludlow

Ludlow, a semiautomatic linecaster, is another machine that found a place in the development of automated typesetting (Fig. **9**). Unlike the Linotype and Monotype, the Ludlow did not have a keyboard but combined both hand and machine production. An operator took matrices from a matrix case similar to a handset type case and placed them into a special composing stick, one by one. The stick would automatically justify or center lines by inserting blank matrices where necessary. Once a line of matrices was assembled, it was placed into a casting device where it was automatically cast into slugs. If a correction was necessary, matrices were inserted into the stick, cast, locked up, and printed. Although partially automated, this process was time consuming. Distributing the matrices back into the type case by hand added to the production time.

Type produced by the Ludlow machine ranged from 6 to 144 points. Its major use was to produce display type for headlines and other purposes requiring larger typefaces. As was true in the case of handset composition, the Ludlow was neither practical nor efficient for setting large volumes of type.

9.
Ludlow linecaster.

Phototypesetting

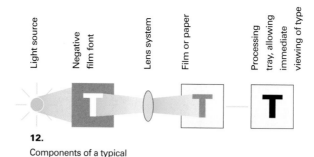

12.
Components of a typical
display phototypesetter.

Phototypesetting is a cold-type process, for type is set not from molten cast metal, but by exposing film negatives of characters onto photographic paper. Although photographic typesetting was explored as early as the 1880s, its potential was not fully recognized until after World War II. As printing advanced from letterpress to offset lithography, typography underwent a similar evolution. Hand composition of metal display type, and cast metal machine-set text type, yielded to photographic typesetting. Two kinds of phototypesetting systems were developed: display phototypesetters, for larger headlines and titles; and keyboard phototypesetters, used to set text type through keyboard input. Phototypesetting gradually replaced metal type during the 1960s, as the technology improved rapidly.

Display phototypesetting
In display phototypesetting machines (Fig. **10**), light is projected through film negatives and a lens to expose letters, numbers, and other symbols onto a strip of photographic paper. While a font of type in hand composition consisted of a drawer full of raised metal letters, a font for display photo composition consists of clear images on a long strip of film (Fig. **11**) wound on two reels. This film font slides between an amber safe light and a lens. Characters are projected onto a strip of photo paper resting in a shallow tray of developer. An operator uses hand cranks to roll the strip from one drum to another, putting the next letter in position to be exposed. By pressing a button, the operator causes a bright white light to flash thorough the lens, exposing the character to the photo paper (Fig. **12**). The character immediately begins to develop, so the operator sees it while using a lever to advance the photo paper. The projected image for the next character is positioned by winding the film strip on the reels with hand cranks. Character by character, a line of display type is exposed on the photo paper, then developed and fixed. Because the operator can view recently set characters as they develop, letterspacing is precisely controlled (Fig. **13**). This spacing flexibility was a major innovation. Many design advantages of display phototypesetting made it the dominant method for setting headlines by the late 1960s. No longer constrained by the

fixed sizes of metal type, the designer could now specify display type set from the film font (whose capitals were about an inch tall) in a wide range of sizes. Type could be enlarged up to two times the master font size, for two-inch capitals, or reduced to a one-fourth size, with capitals as small as a quarter inch high. Enlarged and reduced type retained perfect sharpness, unlike metal type, which became very ragged when enlarged. Metal fonts had a limited number of characters, while photo type had an unlimited number of characters, because the same negative could be exposed over and over again.

The constraints of metal blocks yielded to the elasticity of photographic processes, and innovative designers rapidly explored new possibilities. The lens system permitted photographic distortion. Characters could be expanded, condensed, italicized, and even backslanted (Fig. **14**). The tremendous expense of introducing new metal typefaces, requiring punches, cast letters, and matrices, was replaced by the cost of one economical film font. As a result, many new display typefaces – as well as revivals of earlier styles that were no longer available – were introduced at a rapid pace.

11.
Film font for a display
phototypesetter.

10.
A display phototypesetter.

Typography
Typography
Typography
Typography

13.
Unlike hand composition, where every letter is cast on a block of metal and cannot be easily kerned, display phototype interletter spacing is visually controlled by the operator and can be set wide, normal, tight, or even touching.

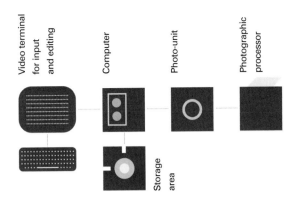

Video terminal for input and editing — Computer — Photo-unit — Photographic processor — Storage area

16.

Components of a typical keyboard phototypesetter.

14.

Normal, expanded, condensed, backslant, and italic (top to bottom).

aaaaaaaa

aaaaaaa
aaaaaaa
aaaaaa

aaaaaaaaa
aaaaaaaaaa
aaaaaaaaaa

aaaaaaaa
aaaaaaaa
aaaaaaaa

aaaaaaaa
aaaaaaaa
aaaaaaaa

Keyboard phototypesetters

Keyboard phototypesetters were introduced in 1950. Two major types of phototypesetting systems (Fig. **15**) were developed: photo-optical and photo-scanning systems. They have the same basic components (Fig. **16**); the primary difference is how the photo paper or film is exposed.

Photo-optical systems store characters as a master font on film discs, drums, grids, or strips. The letters, numbers, and other symbols in the text are input on a keyboard. A typical film disc or drum spins at several thousand revolutions a minute, and a computer controls the exposure of light through the negative characters and a lens, onto light-sensitive paper or film. At the same time, the computer advances the paper or film in a transport device, moving it forward by the set width of the previously exposed character and into position for the next character to be exposed. Different lenses are used for different magnifications, so the typesetter can set different sizes of type. The computer makes very precise adjustments in spacing for the specific type size, and increases interletter and interword spacing when setting justified text columns. These systems are capable of setting hundreds of characters per minute. Early phototypesetting systems used a special keyboard to code punched paper tape that was fed into the phototypesetter to control the typesetting process. Paper-tape systems were replaced by magnetic tape systems, then by magnetic disks and diskettes.

A newer generation of photo-scanning typesetters replaced the photo-optical systems with an electronic system. Fonts are stored as electronic data. These digitized characters are projected as typeset text on a cathode ray tube (CRT) screen. A lens focuses the type on the CRT screen onto light-sensitive film or paper. A full page of type, including many different sizes and typefaces, can be divided into a grid of several blocks, each the size of the CRT screen, and stored in the computer's memory. Photo-scanning typesetters are much faster than photo-optical systems. They reproduce sections of the page rapidly, one block at a time, setting up to ten thousand characters per second.

Phototypesetters are flexible and fast, compared to hot-metal typesetting machines, which could set only about five characters per second. Hot-metal machines had many mechanical parts, while phototypesetters were operated electronically. Photo type needs little storage space because it is stored on flat photographic paper or film, while metal slugs are very heavy and require enormous amounts of storage space. Phototypesetting permits electronic editing, with corrections and changes made at the keyboard.

Phototypesetting freed designers from the physical restrictions of metal type. Increased flexibility in spacing typographic elements included greater control over kerning, interletter and interline spacing, overlapping, and special effects such as runarounds (type running around elements such as images). Designers who understood the potential of this technology used it to great advantage.

15.

A keyboard phototypesetter.

Digital typesetting

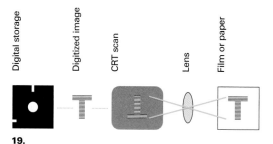

Digital storage · Digitized image · CRT scan · Lens · Film or paper

19.
Digital-scanning typesetter.

The digital computer in combination with the high-resolution cathode ray tube (CRT) and laser revolutionized the communications industry. Because digital computers have no mechanical parts and are entirely composed of electronic components, they set and process type at speeds never thought possible. In addition, the text type from digital typesetters has now been developed to rival the quality of phototype.

Knowledge of digital-computer functions is critical to an understanding of digital typesetting. A digital computer is an electronic device that uses electricity to process information. It can perform repetitive logical and arithmetic operations and store the results in memory. A computer system is composed of hardware and software. Hardware consists of the physical components of a computer; software is the program data that controls the operation of the hardware.

The computer component that controls all other parts, performs logical operations, and stores information is the central processing unit (CPU). All components that do not belong to the CPU are called peripherals. A typical digital-typesetting system is composed of a CPU and various peripherals that perform the functions necessary to the setting of type – for example, editing and storing text, displaying text on a screen, and printing typeset copy. In the main memory of a computer, called random access memory (RAM), data is stored and retrieved.

In digital typesetting, when an operator punches a key to enter a letter or issue a command (such as line length or paragraph indent), the computer receives it as binary code. Once information has been entered, it can be stored, edited, and sent to a peripheral device for typesetting.

Digital typesetting systems encode typographic characters digitally on a grid, defining the shape of each letter as a certain number of distinct points. Every detail of a letter is defined, including horizontal strokes, vertical strokes, and curves. The coded characters are stored electronically as digital instructions designating the x and y coordinates of the character on the grid. In the earliest digital typesetters, these instructions were sent to a CRT, where the character is generated onto the computer screen.

A CRT has a vacuum tube with a cathode at one end and a plate of phosphorous and aluminum at the other. When the CRT receives the digital instructions from the computer, defining the shape of the characters, the cathode emits a beam, which scans the tube in a series of parallel back-and-forth sweeps. The light emitted by the plate defines each character being typeset. The type is then digitally exposed to photographic paper.

The degree of resolution in digital letterforms is an important consideration. Basically, the more dots or lines used to describe a letterform, the higher the resolution. Because letters are constructed on a grid, the curved lines consist of a series of stair-stepped contours (Fig. **17**). When more dots are used to represent a curve, the curve appears smoother to the eye. The quality of letterforms is determined not only by their design but also by their digital resolution (Fig. **18**).

Resolution is improved through a process called *hinting* (see Chapter 4), which mathematically encodes letterforms in a manner true to their original design. Each size of a well-designed typeface possesses characters with unique proportional characteristics, and hinting preserves these characteristics, a concern particularly relevant for typefaces of smaller size. Details of curves, strokes, and serifs maintain optical integrity.

Scanning and laser systems
There are two classes of digital typesetters: digital-scanning systems, first introduced in 1972, and digital-laser systems. In digital-scanning systems (Fig. **19**), photographic characters were digitally

18.
Examples of digital letter-forms, demonstrating decreasing resolution, from top to bottom, as the number of elements is reduced.

17.

132

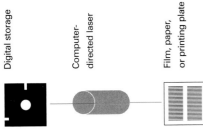

20.
Digital-laser typesetter.

21.
A morphology of multiple-master fonts, originating with four master fonts interpolated along the axes of weight, width, and optical size. Weight and optical size occur along the vertical axis; width occurs along the horizontal axis. Though the variations seem very subtle, each represents an individual font.

22.
Walker, a typeface designed by Matthew Carter, enables designers to "snap-on" five variations of serifs at will.

scanned and recorded electronically on a magnetic disk or tape. The characters were translated into a grid of extremely high resolution and then transmitted as a set of instructions to a CRT. Next, the characters were generated onto the CRT by a series of scan lines. The letterform images were then projected from the CRT onto paper, film, or an electrostatic drum. Because the output type is digital, it could be modified automatically to reflect a number of typographic variations. For example, it could be made heavier, lighter, slanted, condensed, or expanded at the command of the operator.

Rather than employing a CRT to generate characters, digital-laser systems (Fig. **20**) used a laser beam that scanned photographic paper as it read digital information stored in the typesetter. As the paper was scanned, a series of dots forming the characters were exposed to the paper. The information controlling the laser included the font, as well as spacing, paragraph configuration, hyphenation, and kerning.

Digital typesetting technology continues to improve and evolve, and with the introduction of electronic page design, and the responsibility for typesetting having shifted from a compositor to the designer, the nature of typographic communication has changed drastically. The ability of a designer to dynamically edit and alter individual letterforms and entire fonts with the aid of new software has in many ways redefined the way type is used. For example, multiple-master typefaces, developed by the Adobe Corporation in 1991, readily enable designers to interpolate and therefore change fonts along several design axes (Fig. **21**). These axes include weight, width, optical size, stroke shape, and serif configuration.

Other developments depart entirely from traditional typesetting methods. The typeface Walker, for example, designed in 1995 by Matthew Carter for the Walker Art Center, provides "snap-ons," that is, variant serifs treated as separate characters that can be added to or removed from letters as desired (Fig. **22**). Future innovations in digital typesetting will continue to shape and define typographic culture.

21.

22.

Each major typographic process has its own place in the evolution of technology. Increased efficiency, control, flexibility, and the design of letterforms have been affected by continuous research and innovation. The nature of the typographic image has been changed as well (Fig. **34**). The microphotographs by Mike Cody demonstrate the differences. Letterpress printing of metal type impressed the letterform into the fibers of the paper. Phototype, usually printed by offset lithography, provides a precise image with a comparatively smooth contour. As the microphotographic enlargement shows, digital type evidences the stepped contour caused by the digitization of the image into discrete elements.

In the most advanced digital-typesetting systems, the discrete elements are so small that they become indiscernible to the naked eye.

Technology develops rapidly, and designers must work to keep abreast of innovations that influence the design process and the typographic image. Designers should view typographers as partners in the design process, for their specialized knowledge of the typesetting system and its capabilities, along with an understanding of typographic refinements, can help the designer achieve the desired quality of typographic communication.

34.
Microphotographic enlargement of letterforms.

Metal type on newsprint

Metal type on coated paper

Phototype

Digital-photo type

Many of the educational projects in the following
chapter represent theoretical and exploratory
investigations. They are structured to teach
typographic history, theory, spatial concepts, form,
and meaning. The goal of typographic education is
to prepare young designers for the complexity of
applied problem solving. The case studies
presented in this chapter describe specific
typographic design problems encountered in
professional practice. The nature of each problem
is analyzed, and the rationale for the solution
is discussed.

These ten studies cover a wide range of typographic design: integrating type and image on
posters, publication designs, environmental
typography, CD-ROM and Web-site design,
typographic motion-picture titles, and permutations of a title page.

**Integrating type and
image in poster design**

1.
Alignment of the letterspaced
type along the angled edges
of the stars unifies word and
image. (Designer: Jean-Benoît
Lévy; photographer: Tom
Wedell, Boston)

A remarkable integration of type with image is
found in posters designed by Jean-Benoît Lévy,
who has studios in Basel, Switzerland, and San
Francisco, California. Lévy collaborates with pho-
tographers; he approaches their images as three-
dimensional fields whose space is activated and
extended by type. On the last day of class when
Lévy was a student, teacher Armin Hofmann told
him to place type *in* the photograph rather than *on*
the photograph. Lévy says, "From that moment
on, I knew what to do." In his inventive designs,
words and images become a unified composition.

The large star in a "Happy New Year" poster (Fig.
1) for the Basel studio AND (Trafic Grafic) conveys
a sense of energy and motion through repetition
on a diagonal axis. The background transition
from orange to blue signifies earth to sky. *Happy*
aligns with the two white stars, unifying the type
and background. The sky is signified in three
ways: symbolic stars; a photograph of clouds; and
the lines and dots of a star chart. Subtle symbols
of the world's major religions, and small type
identifying each religion's deity or founder, date,
and number of adherents, add another level of
meaning in the bold celebratory message.

Grid structures for graphic designs are often
implied, but in a poster (Fig. **2**) for the fashion
store Inflagranti, the horizontal and vertical pattern
of window blinds superimposed with a double
portrait of a fashion model provides a visible
structure of the placement of type. The translu-
cency and graded tones of the vertical store name
echo the translucent portrait and blended tones
of the blinds, further uniting word and image.

The curved forms of watch parts, their shadows,
and watch-face numerals were photographed in
atmospheric space for a Montres et Bijouterie
Bosch watch and jewelry store poster (Fig. **3**).
Widely letterspaced type set in arcs reflects the
curves in the photograph. Color is used to create
harmony, for the yellow, white, and orange letters
repeat the photograph's warm tones in contrast to
the predominantly gray background. Lévy says the
orange dots from the text signify seven planets,
with the Sun in the exact center.

1.

2.

Three different sizes and amounts of tracking create variety, while using the same typeface brings unity to the design. (Designer: Jean-Benoît Lévy; photographer: Jean-Pascal Imsand)

3.

The simple geometry and spatial dispersion of the type echos these qualities in the photograph. (Designer: Jean-Benoît Lévy; photographer: Franz Werner)

2.

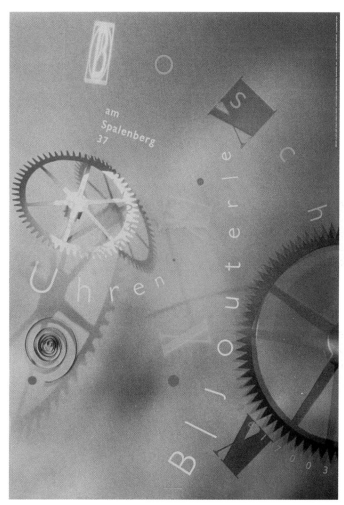

3.

4.

By making the x-height of the larger words the same height as the smaller words, a strong visual relationship is maintained. (Designer: Jean-Benoît Lévy; photographer: Jean-Pascal Imsand)

5.

Lévy carefully retained enough of the overlapped letters to ensure their legibility. (Designer: Jean-Benoît Lévy; photographer: Alexandre Genoud)

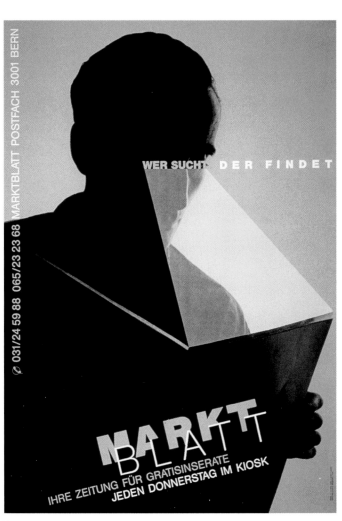

4.

5.

For the Savoy Intercoiffure hair salon poster (Fig. **4**), Lévy used a photograph shot from a low viewpoint of a woman moving her head, causing her hair to fling about in a blurred shape. The photograph was carefully cropped to bleed on the right side and bottom, making a dynamic dark shape against the soft flat background. Two diagonal lines of condensed sans serif type are a sharp contrast to the blurred shape. One line links the top and bottom of the head, while the other links the top of the hair to the edge of the poster. The first word in each line is larger, and the tracking is increased for emphasis.

The *Markt Blatt* is a free newspaper of advertisements in Bern, Switzerland. A sidelit man (Fig. **5**) reads the paper against a warm yellow background. A trapezoid of light becomes a symbol for the process of reading, connecting the reader's eyes with the printed page. Alignment of the typography with the angles of the horizontal and vertical edges of the poster, and the diagonal of the newspaper page creates a structured relationship. By making the type on the photograph yellow and the type on the background white, further integration is achieved. The bold and light type, and overlapping of the two words of the title, produce an arresting visual element.

6.

Across the top, eight rows of modules are filled in with a darker pencil tone to spell the bookstore name in geometric letterforms. The condensed all-capital sans serif type at the bottom of the poster is two modules tall; this unifies with the labyrinth. (Designer and photographer: Jean-Benoît Lévy)

7.

The letters of the bookstore name were executed in outline slab-serif letterforms that are drawn to conform to the horizontal, vertical, and diagonal movements of the labyrinth image. (Designer and photographer: Jean-Benoît Lévy)

6.

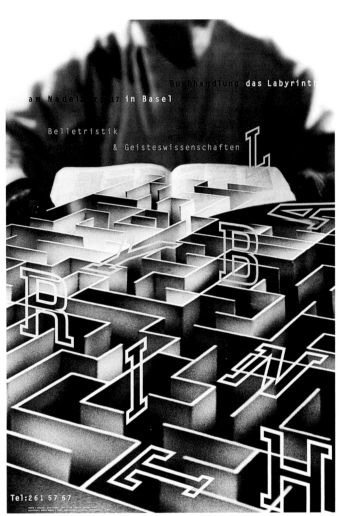

7.

In this poster (Fig. **6**) for the Labyrinth bookstore in Basel, the maze or labyrinth appearing on the poster reinforces the store's name. Lévy carefully drew his complex labyrinth in pencil on a modular grid. The soft pencil tones bring warmth to the rigid geometry. This labyrinth can actually be solved by a viewer standing at the poster kiosk. A photograph of a young man reading a book is superimposed over the labyrinth. "Reading," Lévy says, "is like entering a labyrinth." The organic properties of the human image provide contrast to the stark geometry of the labyrinth, softening and enriching the poster.

In a subsequent poster (Fig. **7**) for the Labyrinth bookstore, Lévy created an image of a three-dimensional labyrinth moving back into space. This compelling image fades back into an out-of-focus, tightly cropped photograph of a reader. These hover in space over the labyrinth; their openness and transparency echo its edges and open channels. A three-dimensional graphics program and Photoshop™ were used to execute this poster. As in Lévy's other posters, a dynamic integration of word and image is achieved through unexpected and original compositional relationships between pictorial and typographic forms.

12.

to the title bar and may be complementary colors, contrasting colors, or black. These bars are 25 points wide, and one is always placed across the bottom of the folder. Display type is sometimes reversed from the bars.

The Unigrid System emphasizes clarity by clearly separating the elements. Type seldom overlaps images, and maps are not obscured by picture inserts or overlaps. Neutral grays and beiges, used to create backgrounds behind text areas or unify groups of images, are part of a standard palette of twenty-four colors, created from four-color process inks and a limited selection of secondary colors. This color palette creates continuity between various park publications.

Planning layouts are created using computer-generated typography, images, map windows, and the master grid sheets. A typesetter with a contract to set National Park Service typography uses electronic page makeup to format and position type, rules, and bars, providing repro-quality output for mechanicals.

Standardized formats and typographic specifications enable National Park Service designers to focus on content and design, rather than developing formats and specifications for each project. The Unigrid System is flexible, permitting unique solutions appropriate to specific messages, while leading to consistent graphic excellence and a unified visual identification.

Massimo Vignelli was the inventor and remains consulting designer for the Unigrid System. The program gained its vitality because the original design team remained intact over the first dozen years, and included Vincent Gleason (chief), Melissa Cronyn, Nicholas Kirilloff, Linda Meyers, Dennis McLaughlin, Phillip Musselwhite, and Mitchell Zetlin.

11.

**Design and typography
for *Interiors* magazine**

14.

15.

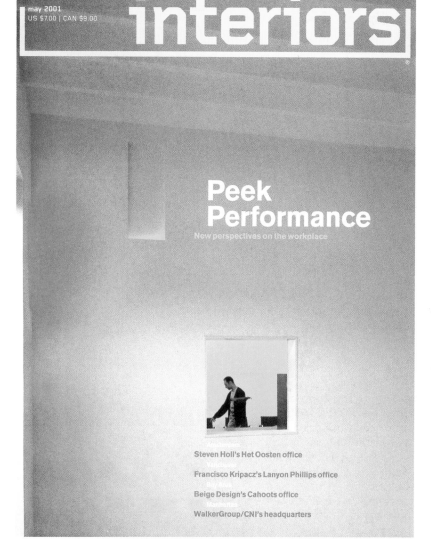

While the National Park Service design program used standardized formats and typographic specifications to maintain consistency in hundreds of printed designs, the needs of *Interiors* magazine are very different. Art director Paul Carlos and editor Julie Lasky required a design system consistent enough to create an identity for the magazine, but with sufficient design flexibility to enable them to express a wide variety of interior design, architecture, and product design subjects.

The masthead (Fig. **13**) consists of the word *interiors* set in lowercase Gridnik, a bold geometric sans-serif font whose curved strokes are replaced by forty-five-degree diagonals. The junctions where diagonals join horizontals and verticals are softened by subtle curves. The name *interiors* is within an open-top, three-sided box. This becomes a subtle metaphor, as the word *interiors* sits in the interior of the box. This ruled-line device and typeface are used for the headers of regular departments to tie the editorial content together and reinforce the visual identity.

The masthead appears prominently on each cover in the same size and position, but its color changes for contrast or harmony with the photograph. Only one major article or theme is presented on each cover. Cover typeface style, size, and placement are selected to express content and/or become part of the photographic composition (Figs. **14–16**). Type colors are carefully chosen to complement the photograph's colors while having sufficient contrast for good legibility.

interiors

13.

13.
Interiors magazine masthead. The *r* and *t* were shortened to improve the spatial intervals inside the word. (Designer: Paul Carlos; typeface: Gridnik by Wim Crouwel)

14.
For a special issue on designing for the entertainment industry, a typeface evoking stage lights appears over a backstage photograph. (Art director: Paul Carlos; photographer: KAN Photo Studio)

15.
A lengthy quotation from a panel discussion about the decline of hardwood forests in America engages the reader. (Art director: Paul Carlos; photographer: Graham McIndoe)

16.
To complement the understated elegance of a minimalist interior, small type in analogous colors is placed on the open space and aligned with the windows. (Art director: Paul Carlos; photographer: Paul Warchol)

17.

Page numbers on the contents page are in the margin, and a line-space interval separates type units. Titles are in large bold type, with italic authors' names and roman subheads. (Art director: Paul Carlos; photographer: KAN Photo Studio)

18.

A three-column grid, fine vertical rules separating items sharing a page, and silhouette photographs bring order and vitality to carefully balanced layouts. (Art director: Paul Carlos; photographer: supplied by manufacturers)

The double-page contents section (Fig. **17**) always uses the same format. The spread is divided horizontally, with photographs below and type above. Fine ruled lines separate elements, with departments on the left and features on the right. A clear and precise typographic plan enables readers to easily navigate the contents.

Design flexibility is achieved by using two-, three-, and four-column grids for various text settings in the magazine, reflecting a variety of content. The distinctive texture of the Quadraat Sans type family, used for all text settings, brings continuity to the pages. Other unifying factors are consistent use of type sizes, leading, and flush-left, ragged-right column alignment.

The "matter monthly" department (Fig. **18**) presents new furniture, wall coverings, and fabrics. The top two-thirds of each spread contains images of the products, handsomely composed with generous white space. Text type columns under each product are unified by a flow line. Captions are within fine ruled boxes placed close to the identified product, making figure numbers or directional words unnecessary.

The layout and typeface selection for editorial spreads opening each article reflect the subject matter and photography. A full-page photograph presents perforated metal panels, a vertical structure, and a luminous recessed window in a Dutch housing corporation pavilion (Fig. **19**) designed by Steven Holl. Carlos responded with a spatial echo effect. A black page (Fig. **20**) intensifies the glowing luminosity of the restored Hotel Burnham's terra-cotta facade.

The design of *Interiors* magazine represents a balance between a systematic approach using consistent text type, folios, margins, and flow lines for continuity, while other elements – notably feature article opening-spread display type and design elements – have great variety to express the visual and conceptual nature of the subject matter. There is sufficient consistency for easy navigation, and enough variety to delight and surprise readers.

17.

18.

19.

A graphic structure with large title type and a repetitive texture of dots mimics the photograph. The green subtitle repeats the bright green color of the trees outside the window. (Art director: Paul Carlos; photographer: Paul Warchol)

20.

Text type set in the shape of the building, display type reflecting the palette of the hotel exterior, and use of color terra cotta to set the words *terra-cotta* complete the resonance between photography and typography. (Art director: Paul Carlos; photographer: Hedrich Blessing)

19.

20.

Referring to a movie advertisement that used letterforms "painted by light," typographic historian Beatrice Warde wrote, "After forty centuries of the necessarily static Alphabet, I saw what its members could do in the fourth dimension of Time, 'flux,' movement. You may well say that I was electrified." Through advanced animation and computer graphics techniques, graphic designers are transforming typographic communication into kinetic sequences that might almost be called "visual music."

Richard Greenberg has distinguished himself as a leading innovator in graphic design for film titles, movie previews, special effects, and television commercials. He considers film titles to be a "visual metaphor" for the movie that follows, setting "the *tone* of the movie. You have to take the people who have just arrived at the theater and separate them from their ordinary reality – walking onto the street, waiting in line; you bring them *into* the movie. You want to tell them how to react: that it's all right to laugh, that they are going to be scared, or that something serious is going on."

In the titles for the Warner Brothers film *Superman – The Movie,* bright blue names and the Superman emblem streak through space like comets, stop for a moment, then evaporate into deep space (Fig. **21**). The speed and power of this film's fantasy superhero are evoked. This effect is accomplished by tracking rear-illuminated typography in front of an open camera lens. Each frame captures a streak of light that starts and stops slightly before the light streak recorded on the next frame. When shown at twenty-four frames per second, this series of still images is transformed into a dynamic expression of zooming energy.

21.

22.

23.

For the Warner Brothers movie *Altered States,* the title sequence opens with a wide-angle image of a researcher in an isolation tank (Fig. **22**). Superimposed over this image, the two words of the title – transparent, as if they are windows cut from a black background – overlap each other as they move slowly across the screen. The film credits are superimposed in white typography in front of this lively pattern of typographic forms and counterforms. Behind the title the background slowly darkens while the camera pulls away from it, causing the letterforms to become smaller and smaller. Finally, the complete title, *Altered States,* appears in its entirety before the totally black screen. In the title, set in Avant Garde Demi, the repetition of this unusual configuration unifies the two words and serves to make the title a unique and memorable signification.

An ominous mood is created in the title sequence for the Twentieth Century-Fox production *Alien* (Fig. **23**). Deep in outer space, the dark side of an immense planet (suggested by a sweeping curved edge) moves slowly onto the screen. Gradually, it passes from right to left, engulfs the screen in blackness, and then continues until it disappears from sight. As the planet passes, small white rectangles appear one by one, then undergo a metamorphosis to form a five-letter title letterspaced across the screen. An elevated sense of mystery is achieved by the harmonious juxtaposition of the passing planet and the typographical transformation. The impending arrival of aliens is evoked.

A striking three-dimensional effect is achieved in the seamless title sequences for *True Lies,* a film about a secret agent who learns about his wife's extramarital affair and pursues her using intelligence resources available in his profession, which is a job he kept secret from her. The title begins with four faint blue streaks that start to rotate in space (Fig. **24**). As the lines rotate, the flat, planar letters of the word *true* are revealed. These letterforms continue to rotate, appearing as independent cubelike structures, with the final sequence revealing the letters of the word *lies,* reversed and appearing in black on the adjacent surfaces of the structures. This simple and elegant visual transformation provides a surprising tension between the two opposing words of the film's title.

Martin Riggs, the lead character in the film *Lethal Weapon 3,* finally meets his match in Lorna Cole, a beautiful but tough policewoman. Together with his partner, Roger Murtaugh, the three attempt to expose the illegal arms racket of a fellow police officer. The heightened suspense of the film is established with the visceral image of fire licking the surface of a calm body of water. As the flames erupt from left to right along the screen, typography presenting the names of the film's stars follows their movement (Fig. **25**). In this film title, the synergistic relationship between type and image is fully developed as they move in time and space. This film title provides an excellent example of the integration of type into image, unlike many designs where type is merely added to, or placed upon, an image.

The time-space orientation of digital media enables the typographic designer to add motion, scale change, sequence, and metamorphosis to alphabet communication. As demonstrated by the work of Richard Greenberg, this opens new vistas of expressive communication.

24.

25.

**Hancock Park: interpretive exhibit
for the La Brea Tar Pits**

Hancock Park is a unique urban setting situated along Wilshire Boulevard in the Miracle Mile section of Los Angeles. Home to both the Los Angeles County Museum of Art and the Page Museum of La Brea Discoveries, Hancock Park is a natural historic site where both science and art are combined in a public setting. The park, which contains natural tar pits and fossils, dates back to the Miocene and Pliocene eras when the Los Angeles basin was covered by sea. In 1913, G. Alan Hancock gave the 23-acre tract of land to the County of Los Angeles for the purposes of preserving and exhibiting its scientific features.

Project director Paul Prejza, project manager Holly Hampton, and designer Niv Kasher teamed together on this project with the objective to enhance the social as well as the aesthetic value of Hancock Park as both a natural and cultural attraction.

From the offset, the didactic nature of the exhibits implied the importance of the role that typography would play. Consideration in the selection of type styles was given to legibility, color, and form as well as compatibility with existing typographic systems for museums located at this site. The final result was a system that combined the sans serif font Frutiger Roman with the serif font Fenice.

26.

27.

28.

Frutiger was the natural choice for the sans serif face. It not only provided exceptional legibility but also helped to establish a visual link to the Los Angeles County Museum of Art, which was also identified under the umbrella of Hancock Park. With this in mind the park itself needed an identity that would work well when combined with the sans serif font. To complement the clean strokes of Frutiger, the modern, somewhat condensed straight serif form Fenice was chosen and developed in combination with the Gingko leaf symbol as a vertical reading logotype for the park. Fenice was used for the body copy of the

29.

30.

31.

33.

34.

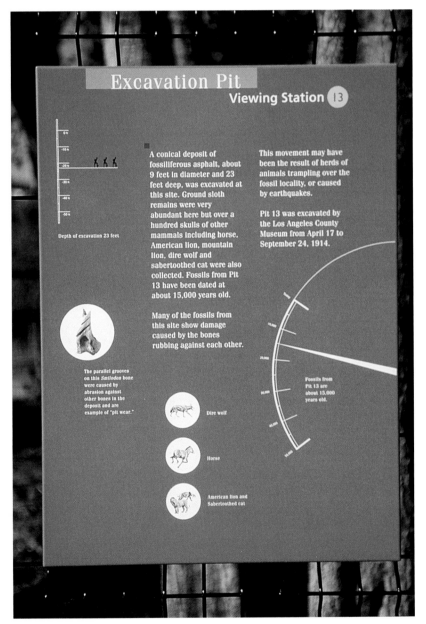

32.

exhibition portion of the project as well. A quarter-inch cap height with proper leading allowed for ease of legibility at a comfortable viewing distance.

Because of the expansive size of this outdoor exhibit environment, directional signage for optimal wayfinding was an important component of the system. To enable visitors to read signs from a distance, carefully letterspaced Frutiger was chosen for this task. Legibility was also strengthened by presenting black letters on yellow backgrounds (Figs. **26** and **27**). Note the unusual directional arrow. This form is visually consistent with the Gingko leaf symbol used as the park's logo (Fig. **28**).

This primary locator sign (Fig. **29**) introduces passersby to the park and identifies the Los Angeles County Museum of Art, Page Museum, and La Brea Tar Pits. The logotype and typographic units are sized and grouped for maximum clarity. Secondary locator signs within the park feature a logical hierarchy of type, images, diagrams, and maps to provide navigational clarity and give visitors the confidence to freely explore the area. The large numerals enclosed within circles on the locator signs clearly identify the park's various attractions (Figs. **30** and **31**).

The scientific interest in the tar pits is reflected in the written and visual history of the site. Porcelain enamel interpretive panels are located at the six major excavation sites within the park and identify the best view for each station. The content of the didactic panels combines typography, photography, and illustration. These elements are designed to visually display quantitative information including geologic time, animal life, and the preservation of the fossils excavated at Hancock Park. The interpretive panels reveal the compositional flexibility of the typographic system. While the treatment of the heads, text, captions, color, and asymmetrical organizational strategy remain constant, the panels exhibit a wide variety. For primary text, Fenice is set flush left, ragged right with generous interline spacing for ease of reading (Figs. **32–34**).

35.

36.

Nothing in the Hancock Park exhibit system is left to chance: differences in signage for womens' and mens' restrooms are established through variations in color, sign shape, figure, and plant icons (Fig. **35** and **36**); parking signs are identified with a large capital letter *P* to distinguish them from other park signs (Fig. **37**); the heights of graphic panels and rails are carefully determined to satisfy the needs of a wide-ranging audience (Fig. **38**), and exhibit components and signage are assigned different colors based on their given function: orange is for supplementary information, yellow for directional information, and red for interpretive information.

In designing environmental graphics at this major attraction for young and old alike, the researchers and designers gave every consideration to ensuring clear, concise communication. All elements, from the final installed height of the panels to the dynamics of color, typography, and composition, work together to signal the viewer from afar and draw them in for a closer look.

38.

37.

CD-ROM design for *Crank Call:*
a holiday typeface by MetaDesign

Multimedia is likely the most profound educational and entertainment tool to have been developed. It is powerful because, as its name suggests, it is capable of employing several media – video, animation, sound, text, and pictures – into a single highly engaging sensory experience. Because multimedia is also interactive, users travel from place to place, forward and backward at will. In such environments, typographical concerns have also changed. Unlike a book, where typography sits still on the page, typography on a screen is active; it is a kinetic element in a highly flexible environment, aiding in the navigational process of the user. While typography has traditionally been rooted in space only, in interactive environments it is also rooted in time: pacing, transition, and motion are important new facets that affect both legibility and aesthetics. Careful attention must be paid to how type appears on a screen (see Chapter 4), and how readers interact with it.

39.

The title page of the CD-ROM – saturated in holiday red – contains the title set in the *Crank Call* typeface. Secondary information is clearly presented in Meta. Anticipating what is to come, the architecture and primary graphic elements of the interactive experience are suggested in subtle, muted tones. A pulsating directional button in the form of an arrow cues the visitor to click it for entry into the presentation.

40.

In contrast to the expressive nature of the subject typeface, the introduction page, typeset in Meta, describes the project with clarity, restraint, and refinement. The text adheres also to legibility concerns specific to the world of the screen: type size, interletter and interline spacing, line length, and color contrast are carefully balanced.

41.

With another click of the mouse, visitors are taken to a page that provides entrance into the type-design process. A single click forward advances the user to the next letter of the alphabet; a single click backward retreats the user to the previous letterform.

39.

40.

41.

Sonoma County Woodworkers Association Web site

51.
The title's dominant position in the visual hierarchy is established by its central high position and wide linespacing, rather than its size, weight, or color.

52.
When the cursor moves over the contents list, a subtitle appears at the lower center of the screen.

53.
The brown line becomes an important compositional device, linking elements into an open rectangle above the organic fish image.

In designing the Web site for the Sonoma County Woodworkers Association, designer Maureen Kringen of Kringen, Inc., in Sebastopol, California, sought to evoke an aesthetic response to the art and craft of woodworking. A clean, contemporary site was desired; but at the same time Kringen wanted to convey a feeling for the rich warmth of fine woods and the traditional heritage of excellent craftsmanship. Her final solution was based on a dark background, punctuated by understated, elegant typography and warm photographs of handmade objects designed and created by members of the association.

During the design process, important decisions about the site characteristics were made. The dark background was selected because Kringen felt it brought out the warmth of the wood in the photographs. She decided to make the type small and understated to focus the viewer's attention on the visual images rather than the typography. The opening page, often called the splash screen (Fig. **51**), establishes the design theme for the site. The organization's name is set in Classical Garamond BT, an elegant all-capital Old Style font that is highly readable on-screen. The five sections of the site are listed to the left in green letterspaced, all-capital Arial Black; a statement of the organization's purpose appears on the right in a Garamond Bold Italic. The color, texture, and spacing separate these three type elements into discrete units. They appear structured because they form a dynamic asymmetrical triangle. The green line between the contents list and title strengthens the vertical structure created by the flush edges.

Navigation is an important consideration in Web design. Kringen carefully developed visual cues to give the viewer easy access to information on the site. These include a warm brown bracket embracing a section title when the cursor moves over it (Fig. **52**), and the addition of "Home" to the contents list (Fig. **53**) so visitors can return to the opening page from any section of the Web site.

51.

52.

53.

54.

The title page for the "Gallery" section of the site contains a second contents list of artists whose works are on display. Web-site content is set in Arial; initial caps are Arial Bold.

55.

Clicking on an artist's name takes one to a scrolling portfolio, shown here in its entirety, of images by that artist.

56.

Clicking on any image on the scrolling portfolio opens a window with a larger photograph of the art object.

57.

Clicking on "Contact the artist" brings up a screen with contact information; the navigational device "Back to Portfolio" is important in preventing viewers from becoming trapped in a dead end.

54.

56.

55.

Section title pages have subtle background images depicting details of woodwork. Some of these fade softly into the background. Smaller images also showing woodwork details animate the screen by appearing and changing while each page is viewed. The screens are carefully composed to achieve a lively asymmetrical balance (Figs. **54-60**).

This site evidences how careful planning, consistent visual characteristics, and superb images can be used with understated type to create an effective and engaging Web site.

57.

58.

The "Resources" page uses fine brown lines as visual punctuation to separate and structure a long scrolling list of available videotapes.

59 and 60.

The "Newsletter" and "Membership" title pages use a subtle color change and underlining to emphasize type with links to other information.

By changing the placement and horizontal or vertical orientation of the background images, and the location of the small photographs, variety is achieved within the unified site.

58.

SCWA • RESOURCES

ABOUT SCWA
GALLERY
NEWSLETTER
RESOURCES
MEMBERSHIP
HOME

The Sonoma County Woodworkers Association maintains a selection of video and publication resources dedicated to the art and craft of fine woodworking. The following videos are available for viewing to all association members. Contact resources@sonomawoodworkers.com for more information.

#	TITLE	PRESENTER
1	Bowl Turning	Del Stubbs
2	Carving Techniques & Projects	Sam Bush & Mack Headley, Jr.
3	Finish Carpentry	
4	The Hole Story	
5	How to Hang a Door	
6	Installing Trim	Craig Savage
7	SCW Seminar - July '91	James Krenov
8	Not Available	
9	The Woodwright's Shop: Planes	
10	Refinishing Furniture	Bob Flexner
11	Repairing Furniture	Bob Flexner
12	Router Jigs	
13	Not Available	
14	Small Shop Tips & Techniques	Jim Cummins
15	Turning Wood	Richard Raffan
16	Wood Finishing 2 copies	Frank Klausz
17	Wooden Planes & Cabinet Scrapers	
18	Lacquers, Stains & Colors (water based)	Hydrocote Supply Co.
19	4-Shaper System, 6-Shaper System, Dado Saw & Wide Belt Sander	L.A. Weaver Co.
20	Lumber Company	
21	Maximum Woodworking: How to Buy the Right Machine for the Job	Mini Max
22	Multi-router	JDS Company
23	Build a Shaker Table	Kelly Mehler
24	Small Shop Projects: Boxes	Jim Cummins
25	Making Mortise & Tenon Joints	Frank Klausz
26	Dovetail a Drawer	Frank Klausz
27	Wood Turning	Stewart Tools
28	Turned Forms	Irving Lipton Collection

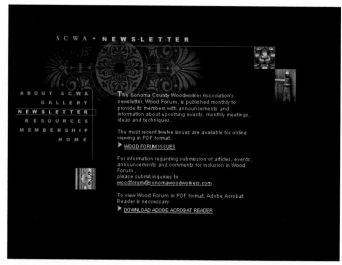

SCWA • NEWSLETTER

ABOUT SCWA
GALLERY
NEWSLETTER
RESOURCES
MEMBERSHIP
HOME

The Sonoma County Woodworker Association's newsletter, Wood Forum, is published monthly to provide its members with announcements and information about upcoming events, monthly meetings, ideas and techniques.

The most recent twelve issues are available for online viewing in PDF format.

▶ WOOD FORUM ISSUES

For information regarding submission of articles, events, announcements and comments for inclusion in Wood Forum, please submit inquiries to woodforum@sonomawoodworkers.com.

To view Wood Forum in PDF format, Adobe Acrobat Reader is necessary.

▶ DOWNLOAD ADOBE ACROBAT READER

59.

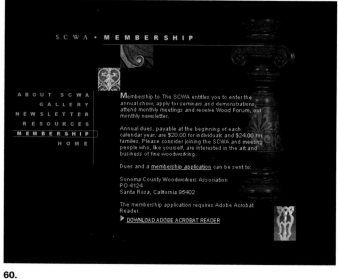

SCWA • MEMBERSHIP

ABOUT SCWA
GALLERY
NEWSLETTER
RESOURCES
MEMBERSHIP
HOME

Membership to The SCWA entitles you to enter the annual show, apply for seminars and demonstrations, attend monthly meetings and receive Wood Forum, our monthly newsletter.

Annual dues, payable at the beginning of each calendar year, are $20.00 for individuals and $24.00 for families. Please consider joining the SCWA and meeting people who, like yourself, are interested in the art and business of fine woodworking.

Dues and a membership application can be sent to:

Sonoma County Woodworkers Association
PO 4124
Santa Rosa, California 95402

The membership application requires Adobe Acrobat Reader.

▶ DOWNLOAD ADOBE ACROBAT READER

60.

Book design for
Listen Up: The Lives of Quincy Jones

61.
Type was expanded and condensed by computer to form a column, but the designers were very careful to minimize awkward optical distortions.

62.
Quincy Jones's friends call him "Q"; this inspired the large red *Q* on the cover, which is repeated on the title page.

The release of a major motion picture about musician and composer Quincy Jones was accompanied by an oversize book. Design director Kent Hunter and designers Thomas Bricker, Riki Sethiadi, and Johan Vipper of the Frankfurt Gips Balkind design office responded to the structure and content of the movie, which had a syncopated rhythm of rapid cuts, musical performances, and interviews. This inspired a lively design approach using typography for expression and interpretation. The background material for this 192-page montage included hundreds of photographs, long and short quotations gleaned from the film soundtrack, and 800 pages of transcripts, and a lengthy essay by jazz journalist George Nelson.

Jazz albums from the 1950s and 1960s influenced the use of the sans serif Franklin Gothic type family, especially its condensed versions, for display type. This was combined with Sabon old style for the running text. A lively dissonance resulted from the contrast between Franklin Gothic's bold verticality and Sabon's lighter, more organic forms. On the book jacket (Fig. 61), a vertical column of type was printed in red over a photograph of Jones. This typographic configuration was also used on the soundtrack packaging and movie publicity to unify graphics for the book, film, and recording.

Upon opening the book (Fig. **62**), the reader experiences dynamic typographic scale, including informational copy on the brown-and-black jacket flap; the blue-and-black shapes of the words *Quincy Jones* printed on the inside of the jacket; and a large red *Q* that wraps around the front and back book cover.

61.

62.

64.
Large outline letters were freely arranged on the computer screen to create an electronic collage using a drawing program. The areas were then filled with colors.

63.
Layering, overlapping, and extreme scale changes were qualities generated using the capabilities of electronic page design.

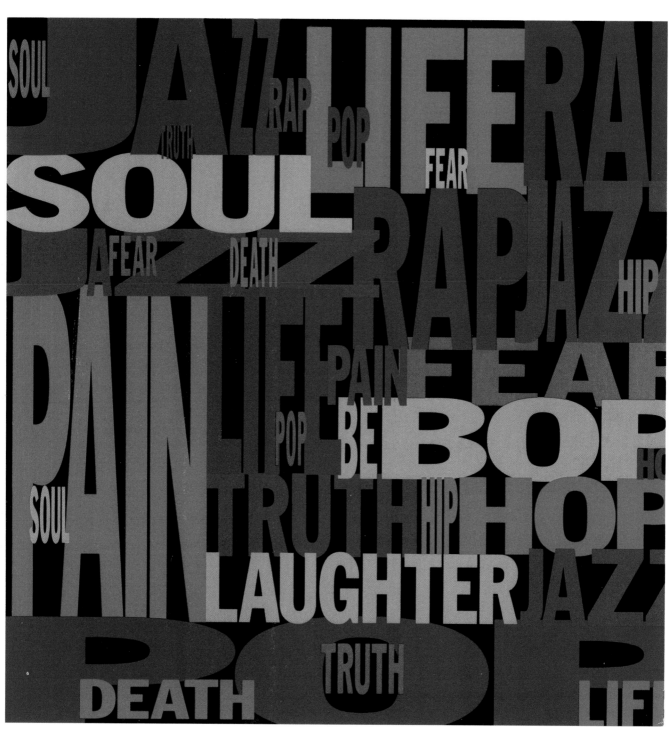

65.

The light texture of widely
leaded gray Sabon is
punctuated by red Franklin
Gothic Condensed; two bleed
photographs give the layout
a lateral expansiveness.

66.

A dozen full-page bleed
photographs of musicians
each have a large color initial
letter, the musician's name,
and a narrow column of
Franklin Gothic Condensed
text superimposed over the
image.

The back cover (Fig. **63**) is a typographic montage of words expressing music and life. This typographic montage reappeared in animated form for the film titles, further tying the two works together. Typographic experimentation to express content and a thorough understanding of electronic page design enabled the design team to make *Listen Up: The Lives of Quincy Jones* an outstanding example of innovative typography.

The book is divided into seven chapters representing periods of Quincy Jones's life and work, entitled "Early years," "Player," "Film scorer," and so on. Each section opens with a large typographic design (Fig. **64**) of overlapping letters in black, gray and a bright color, such as red in the first title page shown here, opposite a full-page photograph. Quiet pages (Fig. **65**) are introduced periodically as calm areas after more complex, energetic pages to bring variety to the visual flow; that is, sequential movement, repetition, and rhythm from spread to spread. Unity within tremendous diversity is achieved through the repetition of several themes throughout the book. These include a series of full-page bleed photographs of musicians accompanied by Quincy Jones's remembrances (Fig. **66**), and pages combining one or more small photographs with quotations from the movie as well as other sources (Fig. **67**).

The essay takes about one-fourth of the book's pages. The running text was placed on gray rectangles (Fig. **68**). These rectangles containing text type help the reader find the essay after it skips several pages. The essay becomes a thread running throughout the book, contributing to the visual flow. The content suggested typographic themes to the designers. A double-page spread (Fig. **69**) uses type to express the cadence and dissonance of rap music.

If Ray had followed the strict commercial line, he may have had more hits, but he would have had less meaning. People buy an armful of Ray Charles cassettes or discs, and what they're buying is an armful of **integrity.** – Jesse Jackson

"*Every music has its soul. And if you really are sincere and surrender to it and explore it, it's all soulful.*" – *Ray Charles*

When he became the vice president in charge of **A**rtists & **R**epertoire of Mercury Records, the first black person to reach that level, I absolutely was so proud, it was just unbelievable. And then he says, "I'm going out to Hollywood!!" – Lloyd Jones

I just dropped everything and just took that chance. I said, "Maybe I won't make it out there, but **I'm going!**" – Quincy

65.

66.

67.
Quotations from the movie expressing contradictory opinions about Jones's trumpet-playing skills are asymmetrically composed around a centrally placed photograph.

Scale, weight, and color are used to emphasize key words in the comments.

68.
Negative leading was specified on the computer, squeezing interline space from between the lines to create a rhythmical cadence.

69.
Typography becomes a visual metaphor for the auditory intensity of rap music. The text type's alignment and structure are influenced by the large letters and words.

"Quincy was a **tremendous** jazz trumpet player." – Lionel Hampton

"He **wasn't that good** a trumpet player." –Bobby Tucker

"Turned out to be a **marvelous** trumpet player." – Clark Terry

"He was a **horrible** trumpet player." – Billy Eckstine

YOU GOTTA WRITE YOUR OWN TICKET IN THIS LIFE BECAUSE IF YOU DON'T THEN SOMEBODY IS DEFINITELY GONNA WRITE A TICKET FOR YOU, AND YOU AIN'T GONNA RIDE FIRST CLASS. YOU'LL JUST FALL VICTIM TO WHATEVER THE STREET DICTATES TO YOU INSTEAD OF TRYING TO DICTATE SOMETHING TO THE STREET. – MELLE MEL

67.

68.

69.

A typographic program
for the 17th Street Farmers' Market

70.
The bold, vector-based tractor silhouette, straightforward spatial composition, and vivid color are characteristics that would define the essence of the Market's graphic program.
71.
The sun sets on a horizon of aligned text type in this implied farm landscape.

71.

The 17th Street Farmers' Market in the Shockoe Bottom district of Richmond, Virginia, is one of America's first public markets. It originated as an outdoor market around 1737 and was officially established in 1779. The first structure on the site was an open wooden shed, replaced two years later with a brick building and colonnade. The Market expanded in the years to follow, and by 1854 a larger brick building – The First Market House – was built on the corner of 17th Street and Main. During the Civil War, this building served as a strategic gathering place for Confederate soldiers. Later in the war, Union troops occupied it as barracks. After the war and into the 1900s, the market prospered; but by mid-century the Shockoe Bottom district declined and the Market could no longer be sustained; the First Market House was demolished in the 1960s. The Market was again revived in the 1980's, and the current open-air pavillion was built during this time.

In recent years, the Market has thrived as a vital center for various community events, and as a venue for farmers, artists, flea and antique dealers, and bakers to sell their products.

The current success of the 17th Street Farmers' Market is largely attributable to a visionary period of time when the Market's manager departed from the conservative thinking of the city officials and the advisory board to embrace the power of forward-thinking graphic design and typography.

Initially, John Malinoski was asked to design a poster for one of the Market's events. The poster proved so successful that it soon became the pilot project for the Market's identity and the inspiration for developing the graphic program (Fig. **70**). The visual language of the program is based on compelling ideas and bold, iconographic forms rather than what might be considered the obvious market vernacular – nostalgic photographs and engravings laden with obvious period typography. The silhouetted icon of the farm tractor serves as the Market's identity mark and as a central unifying element in posters, postcards, bumper stickers, and various other printed materials (Fig. **71**).

70.

167

74.

75.

72.

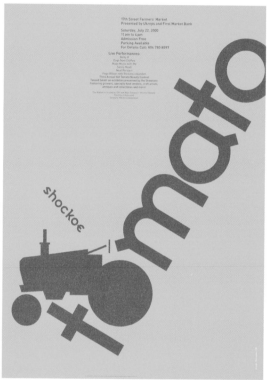

73.

72 and **73.**

The tractor icon is inventively introduced into different environments and contexts to surprise and delight viewers. Considerable effort was made to identify a typeface that visually accommodates the tractor wheel.

74.

Reminiscent of travel baggage stickers and tickets, the postcard communicates the international scope of the event. The warm colors suggest autumn.

75.

The contrast between the sturdy wheelbarrow and the delicate type creates a convincing image. The wheelbarrow is filled with items found at the Market.

Malinoski can be considered a second generation modernist who pays allegiance to the universal principles of rationality, simplicity, and visual economy. He nurtures these ideals like a dedicated parent, but does so with wit, humor, and intelligence. It is possible that several visits to Holland contributed to shaping his design vision, for Dutch design has street presence and is a reflection of the processes and pragmatics of everyday living. Malinoski adheres to the idea that understatement is the most potent statement.

Malinoski's work for the Market is also street savvy. The striking simplicity and boldness of the posters and other materials command the attention of people both walking and driving. Often the tractor combines with other images or typography to excite the curiosity of viewers. In one poster, a tractor hauls a giant tomato to create

a highly exaggerated and memorable image (Fig. **72**). In another example, the wheel of a farm tractor is substituted for the letter *o* in the word *tomato*. The large scale and oblique angle of the type, and the hot color set the stage for a hot summer event (Fig. **73**).

Other farm implements are sometimes used in combination with type to create thought-provoking messages. Examples include a postcard for the *International Brunswick Stew Festival,* where the tractor, a passenger jet, and a bowl are objectively displayed as a series of international symbols (Fig. **74**); and a brochure featuring a wheelbarrow loaded with type (Fig. **75**).

168

Sometimes type and image combine in surprising ways to tell a story or to convey an abbreviated narrative. For a Market event focused on pets, a tractor is placed in a doghouse (Fig. **76**), and in an announcement for *Saturday Arts on the Market,* a living room setting with a framed image of the tractor suggests that art was purchased at the Market (Fig. **77**).

When departing from farm-related images, as in a poster announcing the Market's opening season, the consistent use of robust icons preserves visual unity (Fig. **79**).

The universal feel of the graphic system is supported by the use of DIN as the text typeface. Designed by H. Berthold AG in 1936, *DIN* stands for *German Industrial Standard,* and is the face used for road signage throughout many parts of Europe. When larger amounts of text occur in materials, it is set into basic flush-left, ragged-right blocks, as seen in a flyer for a film festival. (Fig. **78**). But the inherent simplicity of the graphic program belies the careful attention paid to every conceivable typographic detail.

76.

77.

78.

79.

76 and **77.**
Incongruent combinations of type and image challenge the expectations of viewers.

78.
Multiple readings of typographic images can add mystery, intrigue, and humor to messages. The highlighted *esp* reveals "extra sensory perception."

79.
Here, the word *opening* refers to the opening of the Market's season and the emergence of a spring flower. The typeface selected for the word is both organic and geometric, effectively corresponding to the flower image.

Exhibition design for the Jewish Historical Museum Amsterdam, Netherlands

80.

A quiet space that can be seen from outside the building in which the synagogue complex and its relationship to the Jewish Quarter is explained through text and historic photographs.

All photographs in this case study are by Liselore Kamping.

80.

The Jewish Historical Museum possesses the largest and best preserved collection of Dutch Jewish sacred and ceremonial objects known, dating from the late sixteenth century to the late twentieth century. The collection of objects, made by and for Jews, covers the entire religious, cultural, social, and economic history of Jews in the Netherlands and its colonies.

The museum was founded in 1930, opening officially in 1932. At the time of World War II, the collection consisted of about 940 objects. In 1943, approximately 610 objects were confiscated by the German occupiers, but efforts to restore the collection resumed after the war, resulting in the current collection of around 30,000 objects, documents, and photographs.

The war had left the synagogues in derelict condition, and out of respect for the victims they were never again used as houses of worship. Restoration of the buildings began in the mid-1960s, and in 1987, the museum moved to this complex on the Jonas Daniel Meijerplein. The museum building actually consists of a complex of four synagogues; the Great Synagogue is the oldest and was built in 1671. The most recent is the New Synagogue, built in 1752. Maintaining historical and architectural integrity, the buildings are connected as a continuous space with the use of modern forms and materials. Located in the Jewish Quarter of Amsterdam, the museum strives to communicate its role as part of a neighborhood, as part of a city, as part of a country (Fig. **80**).

Presenting and describing the objects in the collection is the museum's principal task, mandating the importance of scripts in Jewish life. For this reason, typography plays a pivotal role in the exhibits.

In addition to a regular program of thematic exhibitions related to Jewish art, life, and culture, four permanent exhibits are housed within the synagogue complex. Beginning in 2001, a new design program was initiated to update these exhibitions in terms of visitor navigation,

81.

82.

presentation of interpretive texts, and emotional resonance. Designers Victor Levie and Marit van der Meer of atelier MV levievandermeer are responsible for the concept development of the new exhibitions and for overseeing graphic design and typography.

81 and **82.**

In the upstairs historical exhibition, layers of typographic information applied to exhibition surfaces provide textural beauty, an intensified sense of three-dimensionality, and a clear visual hierarchy. Light filters through the space where banners, display cases, and artifacts contribute to an ethereal and rhythmic environment.

83.

The focus of this display case, located in the historical exhibition, is three sacred objects: a book, a silver platter, and a painting. It is clear that the primary duty of the typography is to support, illuminate, and interpret these objects.

84.

A display case in the downstairs religious exhibition reveals a rail of intepretive text that can be easily replaced with updated information.

85.

A very large display case features "the beauty of holiness," a collection of ritual silver. Careful lighting illuminates the objects to create an opulent setting. Text set on transparent material intensifies this effect.

86.

Downstairs in the New Synagogue, a symmetrical space – articulated through colored banners and *Fresco* type – divides the space into blue (private) and red (collective) sides. Objects displayed in these areas relate either to life at home, or life in the Jewish community.

87.

A bold and colorful poster featuring the typeface *Fresco* reflects the visual style of the new Jewish Historical Museum.

The new installations present a layered typographic environment where visitors can decide how much time they wish to spend and how much information they wish to glean. A visitor may spend a day or only an hour contemplating the collections. This is achieved by applying typography in a graded arrangement of sizes to walls, banners, and display cases. Type set in the largest sizes and placed on banners identifies general themes (Figs. **81** and **82**). Display cases consist of three levels of information: display titles, display text, and small texts describing the objects in detail. These are printed on clear stickers that can easily be changed as objects are rotated in and out of the exhibits. For improved legibility and ease of reading, the detailed text referring to the objects is placed on transparent pedestals at an angle (Figs. **83-85**).

When the designers were considering a new logotype and visual identity for the new exhibitions they chose the typeface *Fresco,* designed by Fred Smeijers at about the same time (Fig. **8**). Consisting of serif and sans-serif variations, this design capably reflects the 300-year timespan reflected in the collections. Sans serif is used exclusively in the exhibitions, while museum publications also employ the serif version. Looking from the entrance of the New Synagogue, one sees the use of *Fresco* on banners identifies the "red side" (collective side) and the "blue side" (private side) of the synagogue (Fig. **86**).

The sensitive, unobtrusive, and respectful integration of typography into the exhibitions contributes to the primary mission of the museum, which is to provide information about religious life and the history and culture of the Jews in the Netherlands, communicating knowledge about the past to future generations.

83.

84.

85.

86.

nieuw

jh

joods historisch
museum

jm

www.jhm.nl

The rapid advance of technology and the expanding role of visual and audio-visual communication
in contemporary society have created new
challenges for typographic education. Faced with a
complex communications environment, and the
changes that are occurring and are anticipated,
how can a designer nurture sensitivity to
typographic form and communication? An
appreciation of our typographic heritage, an ability
to meet the standards of contemporary design
practice, and an innovative spirit in facing
tomorrow's challenges are required.

The following assignments, ranging from basic
theoretical exercises to complex applied projects,
were selected to provide an overview of contemporary typographic design education. An effective
curriculum is composed of perceptual and
conceptual development, technical training, and
processes for solving multifaceted design problems. These projects were selected with emphasis
upon building the perceptual and conceptual
abilities that provide a foundation for effective and
innovative typographic design practice.

Cece Cutsforth

Portland Community
College

Gordon Salchow

University of Cincinnati

A series of designs each used
one or more copies of a single
letter to demonstrate a series
of design concepts:
scale, communicating large
and small by comparison;
positive and negative space,
with the spaces surrounding
the letter becoming equal to
the letter itself; *pattern,* using
repetition to create a distinctly
articulated pattern;
congestion, where letters
encroach upon one another's
space; *tension,* with placement and angle conveying
instability; and *playfulness,*
with letters conveying a
carefree sensation.

The examples shown here are
from the pattern segment of
the project. The choice of
letterform, size, angle, and
figure/ground relationships
determines the tonal density
and degree of consonance
or dissonance.

33–35
Designers: Portland
Community College students

33.

34.

35.

36.

37.

A letter has been altered in
a series of steps until it is
transformed into a simple
object, an abstract shape, or
another letterform (Figs.
36–38). An understanding of
typographic sequencing,
permutation, and kinetic
properties is developed.
Students can gain an awareness of form and counterform
relationships, and the unity
that can be created in complex
configurations.

38.

36–38
Designers: University of
Cincinnati sophomores

Experimental compositions
with found typography

Katherine McCoy

Cranbrook Academy of Art

Using all of the typography found on a product label, a grid-based composition was produced exploring size relationships, spatial interval, and weight (Fig. **39**). A second composition was generated with more dynamic movement and scale change (Fig. **40**). Visual notations were made of each, analyzing eye movement, massing, and structure (Figs. **41** and **42**). Tone, texture, and shape are substituted for the typographic elements.

This project is designed to encourage an understanding of the abstract properties inherent in existing typo-graphic forms. An exploratory attitude toward space and visual organization is developed.

39.

40.

41.

42.

39–42
Designer: Ryoji Ohashi

Syntactic explorations using onomatopoeic terms

Frank D'Astolfo

Rutgers University–Newark

An onomatopoeic term (a word that sounds like the thing or action denoted) was selected and used in syntactic explorations. The first level involved drawings exploring syntactic variations using a grid to create visual relationships. These studies evolved into complex type compositions expressing the term.

Level two saw an additional word added as a simple linear element. Unexpected yet meaningful relationships were sought. Visual relationships were created through alignment, balance, juxtaposition, and direction.

In level three, a photograph was added, completing the composition and forming a meaningful message. Unexpected, ironic, or complex associations were encouraged. A spectator or fan at a sporting event (Fig. **43**) adds a new dimension to the *ver* sound of a fan. Rabbit ears cause *schhh* (Fig. **44**) to denote the static of poor television reception. The meaning of the word *croak* (Fig. **45**) is changed by the gun. The *ding-dong* (Fig. **46**) comes from the bell in a boxing match after a prize fighter is added to the design.

This project addresses a complex set of issues. Type style, size, and placement can express the meaning of words. Effective visual organization is achieved with the help of a grid. Words and pictures strengthen and even alter each other's meaning.

FAN

43.

static

44.

ready *di*

croak

45.

46.

43.
Designer: Elisa Robels;
Ver, fan, and spectator.

44.
Designer: Kelly Olsen;
Schhh, static, and rabbit ears.

45.
Designer: Cheri Olsen;
Ribbitt, croak, and gun.

46.
Designer: Paris Jones;
Ding Dong, ready, and boxer.

Type chronology booklet

R. Roger Remington

Rochester Institute
of Technology

A comparative study of ten typefaces was made by each student. The information was organized chronologically in a booklet with four pages devoted to each typeface. In Figure **47**, the opening spread juxtaposes descriptive text and a complete font opposite a large letterform. The following spread contains a historical application of the type opposite a contemporary application created by the student.

This problem develops research skills, an understanding of typographic history, and an ability to work with different typefaces. Large amounts of complex data are organized; a consistent format is developed; diversity is created within this format.

47.

47.
Designer: Heinz Klinkon

Expressive typography: form amplifies message

Computer improvisation and manipulation

Douglas Higgins

University of Cincinnati

Design students were introduced to computer typography in a project that explored the potential of computer techniques to intensify typographic messages. Content derived from scientific newsletters was used to create typographic identifiers that clearly summarize factual information contained in the article. By employing a source of subject matter that is usually designed routinely, the temptation to appropriate a solution was minimized.

Special attention was given to the role of visual hierarchy and typographic contrast while developing computer drafting skills useful in professional practice. The ease with which the computer generated variations facilitated visual refinements.

Douglas Higgins

Ringling School of Art and Design

Two letterforms in structural opposition were combined to create a "seed" configuration (Figs. **51** and **52**). Successive improvisations depart from the original while preserving the basic structural form, as basic computer operations are learned (Fig. **53**). Parallels are established between typographic concepts and computer techniques needed to explore them. Electronic page layout software was used to document the entire design process in book form.

Using a computer to deconstruct and manipulate digital type images allows students to hasten their understanding of letterform analysis and elemental structures governing each letter's legibility. Assignment goals include an understanding of letterform complexities and using forms inherent in a letter's design as points of departure for applied problem-solving.

51.
Designer: Michelle Carrier
52.
Designer: Teresa Leard

48.

51.

52.

48–50.
Designers: University of Cincinnati juniors

49.

50.

Warren Lehrer

SUNY Purchase

About this project, Lehrer states, "Students investigate a subject. Working with one to three primary texts, they develop four panels that approach typography as metaphor. The first panel is composed of paragraphs, sentences, phrases. The second panel, individual words. The third panel, syllables. The last panel, individual letters. Through research, critical thinking, mind-mapping, and experimentation, students give form to metaphoric implications through compositional arrangement, juxtaposition, and typographic manipulation. This project can really help design students go beyond utilitarian, over-literal, or pre-ordained approaches to typography. The examples shown here are from my Advanced Typography class at the School of Art+Design, SUNY Purchase, and from an Experimental Typography class I taught at The Cooper Union. I was first introduced to a variation of the Type as Metaphor project by Mike Schmidt (University of Memphis) who picked it up from Andrew Blauvelt."

53.
Designer: Kerry De Bruce
54.
Designer: Nakyoung Sung
55.
Designer: Rob Dieso
56.
Designer: Jason Marconi

53.

54.

55.

56.

Jan Conradi

Ball State University

David Colley

University of Illinois at Champaign-Urbana

Students design multiple solutions with the same content as a way to explore the relationship between legibility. Innovation is pursued while working within strict parameters and investigating the impact of typeface selection, size, leading, position, line length, tonal contrast, and tactile qualities. In the first of an eight-composition series, each student tries to maximize legibility while using a uniform type font, size, and weight, with no tonal variations. Subsequent compositions introduce geometric grids, then organic forms and multiple type weights and sizes (Figs. **57** and **58**). Images are added but remain subordinate to type. The final compositions emphasize texture and emotional impact rather than legibility (Figs. **59** and **60**).

Students are encouraged to reflect on the visual hierarchy of information and logical reading flow. The consequences of illegibility and people's emotional response to design are considered. Students learn that type can be as potent as images in achieving unique and identifiable communicative designs, and black and white can equal the visual impact of full color.

57.

58.

59.

60.

61.

A series of posters was designed to encourage local high school students to attend symphony concerts (Fig. **61**). Emphasis was placed on writing interpretive copy and selecting typefaces appropriate to that message. Diversity of expression to parallel the concert season was an important consideration. (These posters were printed by offset and donated to the symphony.)

This project introduces the student to the importance of the message in typographic communication. Language devices including metaphor, sound repetition, and rhyme were used to make the content memorable. The relationship of form and meaning was addressed; the nature of each composer's music was considered in the selection of typeface, size, placement, and color. In the examples shown, typographic dissonance in the Stockhausen poster parallels the composer's musical dissonance; word substitution occurs in the Brahms poster; and an auditory double meaning is found in the Bach poster.

61.
Designers: University of Illinois undergraduate students

57.
Designer: Dennis Good
58.
Designer: Dennis Good

59.
Designer: Autumn Musick
60.
Designer: Pam Lemming

Information design:
changing typographic parameters

Marcia Lausen

University of Illinois at Chicago

Selecting their own subject matter, students explore changing typographic parameters and the resulting effect of these changes upon communication in four exercises. Typographic variables change for each exercise: one size and one weight; two sizes or two weights; any number of sizes and weights; and incorporation of an image with any number of type sizes and weights.

Projects presented here are based upon a Chicago Transit Authority timetable (Figs. **62–65**), and statistical data for a student's vintage muscle car (Figs. **66–69**).

Related goals of the project include instructing students in the use of numeric figures in typography, the relationship of subject and data to visual presentation, the different forms of emphasis and hierarchy in typography, the interaction of type and image, and the basic systems of structure and alignment in typography.

Information design is a growing specialty of graphic design. The ability of designers to interpret, envision, and communicate information in typographical and graphical terms has become increasingly important. The Internet and other information media requiring nonlinear forms of communication are becoming increasingly important in the study and practice of visual communication.

62–65.
Designer: Eric Roth
66–69.
Designer: Tim Russow

62–65.

66–69.

Typographic cubes

R. Roger Remington

Rochester Institute
of Technology

A visual presentation combining typography, images, and symbols was created as an extension of a self-assessment study by advanced design students (Figs. **70–72**). The students made a formal analysis of their past experiences and future goals. This part of the project stressed research and information gathering. The collected materials were evaluated for their communicative effectiveness in a complex design.

Transforming diverse information into a three-dimensional cube poses a complex design problem. Each side of the cube functions as part of a totality; the four contiguous sides are graphically and communicatively integrated.

70.

71.

72.

70.
Designer: Beth April Smolev
71.
Designer: Katherine St. James
72.
Designer: Bruce Morgan

Calendar typography

Josef Godlewski

Indiana University

Calendar pages were designed using typographic elements to organize the space and direct eye movement on the page (Fig. **73**). Emphasis was placed upon experimentation, creating unity and movement on each page, and developing a visual elaboration over twelve pages. A grid structure was established and used to achieve diversity and order within a sequence of twelve designs. Graphic elements were limited to typography and rules.

This assignment enables students to explore interrelationships between graphic elements and the surrounding space.

73.

73.
Designer: Jean
Brueggenjohann

**Unity of form
and communication**

Christopher Ozubko

University of
Washington at Seattle

After selecting a historical
event as subject, students
were asked to develop a
typographic message using
the visual properties of type
and space to amplify content
(Figs. **74–77**). This project
develops an understanding of
the inventive potential of
typographic form. As a
message carrier, typography
can intensify and expand
content and meaning.

74.
Designer: Steve Cox
75.
Designer: Kyle Wiley
76.
Designer: Bill Jolley
77.
Designer: Susan Dewey

74.

the worlds deepest submarine

nov

17

1973

dive

32.820ft

75.

Amelia Earhart   July 2 1937   Disappeared in flight over the Atlantic Ocean

76.

ChristianBarnardFirstSuccessful   Transplant12/3/67

Heart

77.

San Francisco

great earthquake and fire

april 18, 1906   5:12 am

Typeface history posters

Performance typography

Jan Baker

Rhode Island
School of Design

Paul Bruner

Rutgers University

Each student in the class was assigned a typeface to study and use in a poster design, communicating its essential characteristics (Figs. **78** and **79**). Letterforms that reveal the unique properties of the typeface were emphasized. The typeface name and entire alphabet were required components of the design.

This project enables students to establish a visual hierarchy in a poster format, while introducing them to the visual characteristics of typefaces.

78.
Designer: Holly Hurwitz
79.
Designer: Luci Goodman

In this project, typography is defined as performance art – a personal form and expression actualized through the typographic medium. Each student wrote a personal poem, not by plan but by feeling. Through the process of typographic design, each student gave visual form to the felt content of the personal poem. This process was conceived as the essence of performance. The poems and their typographic realization are conceived as art, so the project was conducted in an atmosphere of unconditional positive regard, with no attempt to make value judgments about student's typographic usage or feelings expressed in the poems.

The poems were assembled in handmade-boxed folios. Paul Bruner believes that, "this approach to feeling and reading stands in radical contrast to the information processing and sight-reading of so much attention-getting novelty-type-image displays in mass communications publications."

78.

79.

80.

81.

THE SATANISTIC THOUGHTS OF DOCTOR MCCALLISTER

82.

80.
"Untitled." Author/designer:
Jason Bass
81.
"PX." Author/designer:
Kara Lukasik

82.
"The Satanic Thoughts of Dr. McCallister." Author/designer:
John Jankowski

190

Type in motion

83.

86.

Claudia Dallendörfer
Jean-Benoît Lévy

Academy of Art University
Department of Computer Arts
and New Media, San Francisco

This project, taught by two designers from different areas of expertise – one new media and the other print – focuses on the development and production of two-dimensional, black-and-white animations. Students first select a small toy that is accompanied by a set of non-verbal instructions revealing how the toy is assembled. (Figs. **83, 86**). Using words and sentences, these instructions are interpreted verbally and translated into typographic compositions (Figs. **84, 87**). These compositions serve as "scores" for typographic animations that communicate the process of assembling each toy. A primary objective of the project is to explore the communicative potential of moving typography and sound (Figs. **85, 88**).

84.

87.

85.

88.

83-85.
Designer: Hung Che Lin
86-88.
Designer: Chih Fan Ting

Type and image in the third dimension

Marcia Lausen

University of Illinois
at Chicago

In 1952, Charles and Ray Eames created the House of Cards, a set of interlocking playing cards for children and adults. This project is an adaptation of this now-famous design system.

The two-sided cards enable students to study on opposite sides of the twenty individual cards the structural and conceptual dualities (as related to semiotics, color theory, symbolism, etc.) of their chosen subject matter. The interlocking feature of the cards allows for an exploration of type and image in dimensional form and space.

Three excellent examples of this project include *Fourteen Generations,* the Holing family lineage traced to the voyage of the Mayflower (Fig. **89**); *Catalog of Building Materials* (Fig. **90**); and *Cards of Mystery,* where type and image are manipulated to express different emotions and sensations (Fig. **91**).

89.
Designer: Allison Holing
90.
Designer: Chul Kam
91.
Designer: Kyra Jacobs

89.

90.

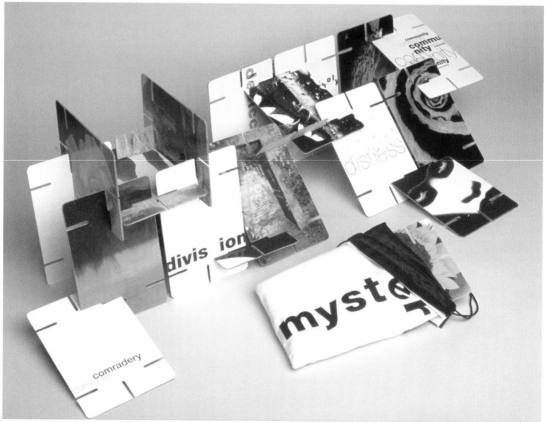

91.

Comparative relationships: type and image

Jan Conradi

Ball State University

In this two-part project, students considered visual relationships between type and image. After selecting photographs, students chose typefaces and letterforms that related to the image through visual characteristics such as shape, weight, decorative embellishments, and other design attributes. Part one involved hand drawing the letterform in a side-by-side comparison of form (Figs. **92** and **93**).

In part two, the relationship was explored further by integrating the letterform into the image (Figs. **94** and **95**). Attention to typeface selection, scale, repetition, color, and balance allowed the merger of type and image into a single entity.

This project helps students who are innately image-oriented to understand how design characteristics of typefaces are individualized and distinctive. Selection of an appropriate font can enhance the communicative message, and type and image can be composed into a unified composition.

92.

93.

94.

95.

92.
Designer: Brandon Luhring
93.
Designer: Brandon Luhring
94.
Designer: Trina Denison
95.
Designer: Kara Holtzman

Directional poster:
from your house to the university

98.

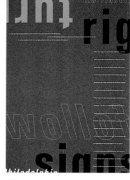

99.

Malka E. Michelson

Philadelphia University

Typographic posters reveal the directional path between students' homes and the university. Message content, hierarchy, sequencing of letters, words, and lines of type were explored to enhance the development of a typographic landscape. Bumpy, smooth, straight, jagged, curvy, up, down, slow, traffic jams, smooth sailing, bumper to bumper, confusing, farmland, city, over water, and through tunnels are examples of concepts explored through typographic space to amplify and expand content, context, and meaning (Figs. **96–99**).

96.
Designer: Todd Duchynski
97.
Designer: Monique Maiorana
98.
Designer: Erin Roach
99.
Designer: Susan Ulsh

96.

97.

103.

Paul Nini

Ohio State University

Students create a series of three typographic history posters, each based upon one of the following structural themes: 1) orthogonal/grid, 2) diagonal/integral, and 3) combination of orthogonal and diagonal. An orthogonal/grid structure enables a composition consisting of flush-left typographic elements arranged within a grid structure (Fig. **100**). Compositions based on a diagonal/integral structure consist of flush-left typographic elements arranged upon a diagonal axis (Fig. **101**), and a combination structure provides students with an opportunity to explore in a fluid manner the interpretation of information (Fig. **102**).

Phase two of the project is the design of an accordion-fold booklet that profiles any three of the modern typographers appearing on the posters. Students conduct research about the typographers, gathering information and images for inclusion in the booklet. Shown here is a sample cover (Fig. **103**).

100–103.
Designer: Matthew Franco

100.

101.

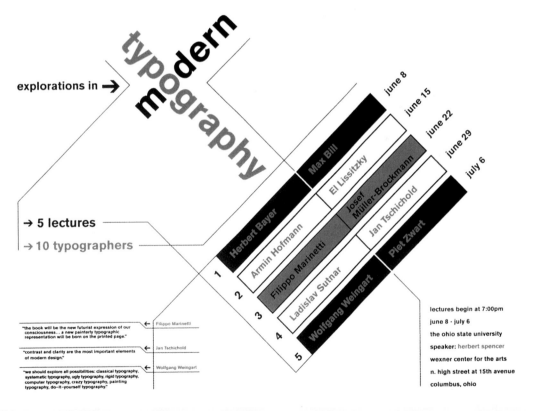

102.

Sandra Wheeler

Virginia Commonwealth
University

Using only the letters of the alphabet and punctuation, students created a ten-second (120 frame) typographic narrative with an expressive aspect. After concepts were developed through preliminary sketches, storyboards were produced to explore the conversion of still images to sequential frames representing motion over time. The storyboards reveal and emphasize that type as a formal element is rooted not only in space but also in time. As such it offers endless possibilities for exploring rhythmic and sequential structures.

The storyboards provided the plan for the animated sequence using a 550 pixel x 400 pixel stage size and frame rate of twelve frames per second. Designing ten-second typographic animations develops an ability to create kinetic typographic splash pages for Web sites.

The animation of two "Gs and a Dot" brings energy to the screen (Fig. **104**). A large Ultra Bodoni capital *G* appears on the screen, then a Futura sans serif capital *G* enters from the left and moves in front of the bolder letter. A turquoise dot resting on the Ultra Bodoni *G* begins to roll through the circle of the Futura letter, while the two letters rotate in space, creating a series of dynamic shape configurations. At the end of the animated sequence, the turquoise dot

falls from the screen and the *G*s return to their normal position.

In "Little ä in Traffic" (Fig. **105**), an *ä* with an umlaut (German accent consisting of two dots over a vowel) looks to the left and right, then its "eyes" widen as a stampede of letters rushes past it. Finally, after the letters go by, the little *a*'s mother, a capital *A*, arrives to comfort and protect its child. Letters, motion, and color are used to tell a complex metaphorical story in a few seconds.

"Truth/Fiction" (Fig. **106**) explores the metamorphosis of the word *Truth* into the word *Fiction*. Starting as a horizontal word, the letters swing into a vertical position as they transform, ending with a stacked configuration of letters. Going from a five- to a seven-letter word is nicely resolved by treating the two *l*s as offshoots from the capital *T*.

104.
Designer: Bryan Keplesky
105.
Designer: Nancy Digman
106.
Designer: April Meyer

104.   **105.**   **106.**

196

Typezine: my favorite typeface

Rob Carter
Henk Groenendijk

Virginia Commonwealth
University

After considering many possibilities, students were asked to select their favorite typeface – one with which they would choose to have a "love affair." On the basis of the selected typefaces, six pages were designed by each student to be combined into a single collection (Figs. **107** and **108**). The content for each page consists of the following: title, type specimens, image having a metaphorical relationship to the typeface, love letter to the typeface, experimental interpretation of the typeface, and a page revealing the research process.

This project exposes students to the enormous range of available typefaces, creating an awareness of the history, form, and function of different typefaces.

107.
Designer: C.J. Hawn
108.
Designer: Jung Kwon

107.

108.

Type history posters

Larry Clarkson

Weber State University

After a thorough investigation into all aspects of a particular period in graphic design history, student teams designed a large poster. Preliminary research included an examination of issues having an impact on the period, including economic conditions of the time, prevailing and developing technologies, popular culture, key design figures, design theory and style, and examples of significant work. This research culminated into a poster composed of the most pertinent content gleaned: a period identity mark, text and captions, examples of work, design theory score, and historic timeline. Each poster was designed in the vernacular of the period communicated (Figs. **109-111**).

109.

110.

111.

109.
Designers: Miki Eto,
Shinsuke Ito

110.
Designers: Anthony Alestra,
Romelle Domingo
111.
Designers: Hana Sullivan, Lisa
Olson, Christine Burton

Typeface design: mind/machine

Max Kisman
Rob Carter
Henk Groenendijk

Virginia Commonwealth
University

This project was launched by Max Kisman as part of a visiting lecture series. Due to the short length of his visit, the project was completed under the tutelage of Rob Carter and Henk Groenendijk. Students were asked to design a typeface based on the concept mind/machine. Kisman's premise that "an alphabet can be anything and anything can be an alphabet," encouraged students to pursue open-ended and unique designs. Typefaces derived from a variety of methods and tools were realized using font design software (Figs. **112, 115**). Other components of the project include a short movie about each typeface (Figs. **113, 116**), a folder containing specimens and a poster (Figs. **114, 117**). The two examples shown are the typefaces *Alphemotibots* and *Franklin Zombie*.

112.

113.

112-114.
Designer: Erin Hall
115-117.
Designer: Ginnie Winston

114.

198

116.

117.

ABCDEFGHI
JKLMNOPQ
RSTUVWXYZ
abcdefghij
klmnopqrst
uvwxyz

115.

Ned Drew

Rutgers University–Newark

Cultural diversity serves as the underlying context for this project. Students are asked to design a series of banknotes in three sequential denominations, both front and back sides (Figs. **118** and **119**). They begin by researching the country of their origin, engaging in word lists, mindmaps, visual notations, and image gathering. The goal of the project is to design a currency system revealing pertinent historical, social, and environmental aspects of the home country, providing the system with functionality and aesthetic beauty. Ultimately, the new banknote designs should attempt to surpass the quality and communicative effectiveness of those currently in use.

118.
Designer: Alan Bayot
119.
Designer: Christian Pearson

118.

119.

The creative process is a struggle with the unknown. Whether composing music, making a painting, or designing a chair, one is faced with the challenge of how to begin and how to end. Every project offers unique challenges, and no fail-safe formula exists for solving problems.

The design process can range from the use of highly structured methods to the serendipity of chance operations. Often, designers work in a realm somewhere between these two extremes – somewhere between intuition and logic. The solution to a problem emerges on rare occasion as a brilliant scrawl on a dinner napkin; but most often the problem-solving process is a journey that requires courage and patience, and confidence in finding one's way through uncertain terrain.

The design process is a sequence of events that begin as soon as the designer takes on a problem. It continues until either a deadline is reached or problem criteria have been met. Rarely is the process predictible, a progression in a straight line from point A to point B. The design process is more like reading a road map; there are many ways of reaching the final destination. If side roads are taken, it will probably take longer to get to the destination. But side roads are almost always more interesting than well-travelled highways.

A traditional model

1.
This typographic diagram reveals the design process as a flexible, dynamic, and unpredictable mental journey. Diverse lines of thought and activity lead eventually to closure. (Designer: Chris Malven)

This chapter will explore the design process and its role in typographic problem solving. Many models exist that schematically represent the design process. But in fact, there is no single process or method for working through problems. Most designers approach their work in a highly individual manner, some using a combination of traditional and digital tools and methods. Digital technology has played an enormous role in the evolution and individualization of design processes.

A well-known model of the design process consists of five steps, which are explained below. Traditionally, these steps have been thought to occur in a linear manner, beginning with *defining* the problem and progressing toward *realizing* the solution. But rarely, if ever, is the process so smooth and predictible. Design formulas certainly can be devised and followed letter by letter, ending in solutions lacking imagination and mental rigor. But perhaps it is more helpful to think of the process as five fields of activity that overlap each other in a multidimensional environment of intellectual discourse. The process is not linear; rather, it is one of interaction and ambiguity where paths appear to meander aimlessly toward durable and innovative solutions (Fig. **1**).

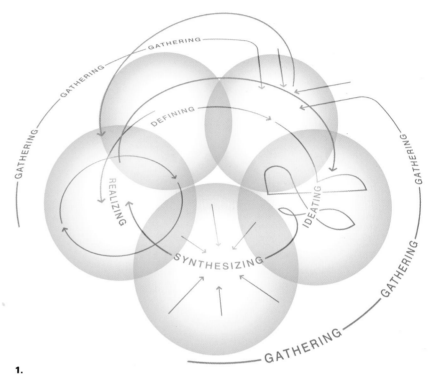

1.

Defining. Immersion into the design process begins by defining the problem and its parameters. What are the client's needs, and what is the sphere of the client's activity? What are the goals and objectives of a potential solution? Who is the audience? What are the budget and production limitations? To answer these and other pertinent questions is to set the problem's parameters. These parameters may change at any time during the process and should not be too tightly defined.

Gathering. This phase provides the essential information needed by the designer regarding all aspects of the problem. This includes gathering information about the client, problem content, and production requirements. While gathering information, designers should make use of all available resources. Experts, libraries, museums, antique shops, and movie theatres are all excellent information-gathering venues. The Internet is also an invaluable information-gathering resource. As new developments arise later in the process, designers may find it necessary to gather additional information. A designer's curiosity is the key to informed practice, and the ability to openly and clearly communicate with colleagues and clients.

Ideating. The worst enemy of the design process is thinking inside the proverbial "box." The mind should be open to lateral, sideways, and

202

3.

unconventional thinking. Often, experienced designers rely upon formula or knowledge-based intuition to solve problems. But these approaches often limit the vast potential for new possibilities.

Synthesizing. Whereas the ideation phase is concerned with expanding possibilities, the synthesis phase concentrates on narrowing options and coming to closure. Often, the most effective solutions are readily apparent; they meet initial problem criteria and are formally and aesthetically superior to weaker solutions. Short of using sophisticated marketing techniques, the best way to evaluate the effectiveness of a solution is to weigh it point by point against the criteria established at the outset of the problem. However, if necessary and appropriate, the original criteria can change at this stage and the solution can be adjusted.

Realizing. Implementation cannot go forward without client approval. Usually, designers and clients communicate on a regular basis throughout the process, which prevents confusion and misunderstanding at the end. More often than not, clients are not visually oriented people, thus making it the designer's responsibility to educate them and communicate with them clearly and without the use of jargon or highly technical language. Such communication breeds mutual trust and respect. Upon final approval, the design moves into final production. Successful implementation requires the designer to manage production processes such as printing and manufacturing with an eye on intermediate and final deadlines.

Processing typographic form and ideas

The typographic design process involves a search for typographic form and its meaning. Any change in form (syntactics) results in a shift in meaning (semantics). The goal, therefore, in typographic problem solving is to identify or discover the appropriate form, content, and structure for the defined problem. Ideas evolve and are realized as typographic form moves through different transformational processes. The following methods and techniques can aid the designer in this search.

2.

2.

Sample spreads from a sketchbook reveal drawings, collected artifacts, and notes. (Designer: Laura Kang)

3.

A process book unfolding in time, documents the "typographic" language of the Anasazi and Fremont cultures. (Designer: Rob Carter)

Sketchbooks

Most designers are highly curious people who crave visual stimuli and make it a habit to record their daily experiences. Always with a camera and a sketchbook on hand, they record thoughts and impressions through drawing, writing, photographing, and collecting. An effective sketchbook is not an ordinary scrapbook; rather, it is a reflective archive of experiences that can jog the memory and stimulate thinking while working on projects (Fig. **2**).

Process books

While a sketchbook is an ongoing exercise of recording visual and verbal ideas, a process book is a visual and verbal record of the process of a specific project as it unfolds (Fig. **3**). Figure **3** is an example of a process book generated during a research excursion into the desert of southern

4.

Any subject can serve as the nucleus for a mind map. Mindmapping is an invaluable exercise where the designer's thought processes are revealed as an ever-expanding universe of possibility and potential. (Designer: Matt Klimas)

5.

Polar opposition occurs in both the syntactic and semantic realms. In this example, the letters *S* and *T* stand syntactically in opposition in terms of shape and weight. The lightness and solitude of peace stand in opposition to the heaviness and aggressiveness of war.

7.

Gathering images and organizing them thematically aids in generating ideas. (Designer: Jessica Salas)

7.

8.

Utah. This handmade book measures only 4 x 4 inches, making it easy to pack and carry. But its accordian-folded pages stretch thirty-five feet when opened, reflecting the horizontal expanses of petroglyph panels. The drawings record thousands of years of the pictographic language of the Anazasi and Fremont cultures. Notations within the book reveal their location and dimensions. Making a process book keeps the designer consciously aware of what activities and thinking lead to a problem solution.

Brainstorming. Brainstorming is perhaps the most familiar ideation strategy for design teams. Though it has its detractors, it remains an effective approach if conducted according to basic ground rules. These include deferring judgement of all ideas during a session, generating as many ideas as possible, and being open to both good and bad ideas. The basic theory is that the group is a deep reservoir of experience, and that one idea leads to new and unique possibilities.

Mindmapping. Related to free association, mindmapping is a nonlinear brainstorming process with a word or concept at its nucleus. By making lighting-quick associations of the concept, a web of related themes reflecting mental patterns emerges (Fig. **4**). The satellite concepts generated from mindmapping help designers identify areas of possible content, both visual and verbal.

Word lists and interaction matrix structures
Making lists of analogous words and descriptive phrases related to specific umbrella topics, or spontaneously generating random words derived from brainstorming or mindmapping can stimulate thinking and open the mind to broader visual possibilities. When lists of words are integrated into the structure of a matrix, new and improbable relationships can be forged between unlikely and contrasting word pairs. Often the most intriguing concepts emerge from the interaction of polar or nearly polar opposites. A sign is understood more clearly and achieves greater impact when juxtaposed with an opposite sign (Fig. **5**). Interaction matrix structures can also accommodate the interaction of words with

4.

	fear	courage	hate	lust	resentment	anger	trust	seduction	happiness	frustration
elephant										
giraffe						●				
possum		●								
chipmunk										
whale					●					
eagle						●			●	
ant										
rattlesnake	●									
iguana				●						
porcupine										

6.

S T

peace

WAR

5.

9.

10.

11.

images, or images with other images. Collecting an abundance of material related to given content and applying it to an interaction matrix can aid the designer in identifying and defining a problem, or in developing fresh ideas outside of conventional thinking. When engaging in these processes, it is helpful to unleash the "play instinct," release the child within, and hush any tendency toward self-criticism. In the sample matrix structure, the red dots are placed at points of potential interaction (Fig. **6**).

Visual notations and comprehensives

Ideas that remain only in the mind and not articulated visually do little to move the process ahead. Design students often convey their ideas to teachers and classmates verbally. This is where ideas begin, but until they are expressed visually in the form of sketches or notations, their effectiveness cannot be evaluated. Thumbnail notations can be created with a variey of tools and materials – from pencil and paper to computer.

The design process can be thought of as beginning at the broad base of an inverted pyramid. Options are expansive at first, but as one moves through the pyramid toward its apex, the vision of a viable outcome – the solution to a problem – becomes more specific. The process may begin as a mindmapping session, progress into a series of general notations, then advance to comprehensive sketches. A project conducted at Rutgers University by Professor Ned Drew is used to illustrate this progression. Visual notations and sketches leading to the design of banknotes are shown (Figs. **7-15**); and see Chapter 9, Figs. **118** and **119**. Another example shows notations exploring preliminary concepts for the Web site about this book (Fig. **16**).

12.

13.

14.

15.

8-10.
Preliminary visual notations exploring a wide range of concepts and typographic concerns. (Designer: Alan Bayot)

11 and **12.**
Sketches with accompanying notes explore thematic possibilities.
(Designer: Chinedue Chukwu)

13.
Small but highly articulated thumbnail notations search for a typographic system that will unify the series of banknotes.
(Designer: Roland Ilog)

14 and **15.**
A distinct progression in visual refinement can be seen in this comparison of a preliminary and a final comprehensive.
(Designer: Roland Ilog)

16.
Sketches and notes investigate the navigational architecture and visual approach to the *Typographic Design: Form and Communication* Web site.
(Designer: Chris Malven)

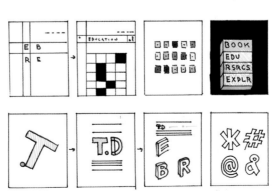

16.

17.

‘ DOES
THE
IMAGE
D U P L I C A T E
CERTAIN
ITEMS
OF
I N F O R M A T I O N
IN
THE
TEXT,
BY
A
P H E N O M E N O N   ROLAND BARTHES
OF

REDUN
DANCY

OR
DOES
THE
TEXT
ADD
A
BRAND
NEW
ITEM
OF
INFORMATION
TO
THE
IMAGE? ’

Metaphorical thinking

In language, a metaphor is a subset of analogy, a figure of speech suggesting that something appears, sounds, or behaves like something else. Letterforms can suggest objects and ideas beyond their function as symbols for spoken language. They possess visual qualities and can be manipulated to suggest other objects, sounds, and images. Typographic metaphors are derived through any number of syntactic manipulations, including those of spacing, position, rhythmic sequencing, and color. Metaphorical thinking is a conceptual process focused on finding relationships between dissimilar ideas and objects; some are highly abstract, others more concrete. Metaphors are successful when the mind makes a conceptual leap and perceives shifts in context. New contexts are established when visual signs are combined to make new signs or when the mind makes an association based on past experience. Fragmented and exploding letterforms suggest fireworks; forms organized into a syncopated rhythm imply a jazz orchestra. Every typeface is also a potential metaphor capable of suggesting meaning beyond the mere content of the words and text. Some typefaces march, others dance (Figs. **17** and **18**).

17.
Reorganizing letters in the word *redundancy* translates into a typographic metaphor of the word. (Designer: Todd Timney)

18.
Selected letters from the alphabet, *Dutch Doubles,* with designs by thirty-seven Dutch type designers. Designers of the letters shown:
A: Jacques Le Bailly
I: Assi Kootstra
K: Sander Kessels
M: Marc Lubbers
O: Harmen Liemburg
P: Peter Bilak
S: Swip Stolk
T: Richard Niessen
Y: Mark van Wageningen
?: Rutger Middendorp
*: Martin Majoor
.,_.: Max Kisman

18.

19.
A page in a computer application measuring approximately 100 x 50 inches serves as a huge digital sketch pad for the development and processing of form and ideas. (Designer: Brad Rhodes, eudesCo)

Typographic processes and the computer

The introduction of the computer as a major design tool has dramatically changed the typographic design process, and many designers have adopted hybrid problem-solving methods. Some begin with hand-drawn sketches and proceed to the computer to refine and produce the final designs. Others scan rough sketches and import them as templates into chosen applications, which are then rendered digitally. In a reciprocal process, Swiss designer Jean-Benoît Lévy often begins with hand sketches, redraws them on a computer, prints them out, applies changes and color by hand, and returns to the computer once again. Designer Brad Rhodes creates digital palettes often containing hundreds of elements that are combined and manipulated in search of problem solutions (Fig. **19**). It is not unusual for designers to begin the problem-solving process by going directly to the computer and developing ideas by means of digital sketches and permutations. All approaches are valid as long as the process delivers an effective and creative solution. Each designer is faced with embracing a unique relationship with the computer and all other methods, tools, and techniques that may be on the horizon.

Whenever working at the computer, it is advisable to save documents using the "save as" command rather than simply using the "save" command. Each new design permutation can be given a new name, which preserves the last permutation for possible future reference. Otherwise the process is lost in cyberspace. File management is now an essential part of the design process, and is a design problem in and of itself. A major challenge facing designers is how to adequately archive digital files for future reference and, as appropriate, for posterity.

Morphologies

A morphology is a menu of visual possibilities. It consists of a list of syntactic and/or semantic variables that can be systematically or randomly explored in a search for typographic solutions (Fig. **20**). Morphologies can be tailored in size and scope to accommodate a wide range of problems and applications. Just as the twenty-six letters of the alphabet can be combined to form an infinite number of words, so too, can morphological factors be employed to achieve a vast number of typographic effects. When used freely and creatively, morphologies liberate rather than constrain the creative mind. Several precedents exist for the development and use of morphologies in typographic design practice, including the pioneering work of Karl Gerstner who developed logical morphologies based on the formal language of type. Gerstner believes that working with "morphological boxes" enables randomness, serendipity, and a kind of invention. He writes, "Working by the morphological method is value-free and unprejudiced – and at least makes it easier to find pioneer solutions where they are possible."

20.

The morphology to the left features a collection of typographic factors that can be freely appropriated in the course of solving typographic problems. The challenge and joy of using a morphology is to combine the components of the various categories in a search for visual alternatives. Figures **125-128** present typographic posters designed with the aid of this morphology. (Morphology designer: Todd Timney)

1.1 SIZE	**1.11** SMALL	**1.12** MEDIUM	**1.13** LARGE	**1.14** COMBINE					
1.2 WEIGHT	**1.21** LIGHT	**1.22** NORMAL	**1.23** BOLD	**1.24** COMBINE					
1.3 CASE	**1.31** LOWERCASE	**1.32** UPPERCASE	**1.33** COMBINE						
1.4 SLANT	**1.41** SLIGHT	**1.42** EXTREME	**1.43** REVERSE SLIGHT	**1.44** REVERSE EXTREME	**1.45** COMBINE				
1.5 CATEGORY	**1.51** SERIF	**1.52** SANS SERIF	**1.53** SCRIPT	**1.54** PIXEL	**1.55** PICTURE	**1.56** WOODTYPE	**1.57** HANDWRITE	**1.58** COMBINE	**1.59** OTHER
1.6 ALIGNMENT	**1.61** LEFT	**1.62** RIGHT	**1.63** CENTERED	**1.64** COMBINE					
2.1 LETTER SPACE	**2.11** OVERLAP	**2.12** TIGHT	**2.13** NORMAL	**2.14** LOOSE	**2.15** EXTREME	**2.16** COMBINE			
2.2 WORD SPACE	**2.21** NONE	**2.22** NORMAL	**2.23** LOOSE						
2.3 LEADING	**2.31** OVERLAP	**2.32** WITHOUT	**2.33** NORMAL	**2.34** EXTRA	**2.35** COMBINE				
2.4 COMPOSITIONAL	**2.41** SYMMETRIC	**2.42** ASYMMETRIC	**2.43** BALANCED ASSYMETRY	**2.44** COMBINE					
2.5 LINEAR DIRECTION	**2.51** VERTICAL	**2.52** HORIZONTAL	**2.53** DIAGONAL	**2.54** CIRCULAR	**2.55** COMBINE				
2.6 REPETITION	**2.61** FEW	**2.62** MANY	**2.63** TEXTURAL	**2.64** PATTERN	**2.65** COMBINE				
2.7 DEPTH	**2.71** SKEWING	**2.72** OVERLAP	**2.73** ATMOSPHERIC	**2.74** COMBINE	**2.75** COMBINE				
3.1 DISTORTION	**3.11** PIXELATE	**3.12** MUTILATE	**3.13** SKEWING	**3.14** FRAGMENT	**3.15** COMBINE	**3.16** OTHER			
3.1 DIMENSION	**3.11** VOLUMETRIC	**3.12** SHADOWING	**3.13** COMBO						
4.1 RULED LINE	**4.11** HORIZONTAL	**4.12** VERTICAL	**4.13** DIAGONAL	**4.14** CURVED	**4.15** COMBO				
4.2 SHAPE	**4.21** ORGANIC	**4.22** GEOMETRIC							
4.3 IMAGE	**4.31** PHOTO	**4.32** ILLUSTRATION							

Exploring typographic permutations

The range of potential solutions to a typographic problem is seemingly infinite. Variations, permutations, and transformations can be developed, exploring changes in both fundamental aspects and subtle details. Processing typographic form in search of solutions involves a process of insertion, substitution, and omission. After freely exploring ideas and selecting those for further development, the designer explores many permutations by inserting elements into the typographic space. The space may be organized by a predetermined grid structure, or the visual dynamics of the elements may define their own structures. This initial process enables the designer to consider the placement of parts, and most importantly, the relationship of the parts to the whole. Limiting initial elements to the same size and weight provides a solid base for the expansion of syntactic possiblities.

The substitution process replaces initial elements with alternative elements in an effort to test and improve the hierarchy and legibility of the text, as well as to heighten visual resonance. This is achieved by assigning different sizes, weights, spacings, positions, as well as other syntactic variations.

The omission phase eliminates superfluous or meaningless elements, reduces elements to their essential form, and simplifies the typographic field

as a whole. The process then repeats itself until all possibilities are exhausted and a viable solution to the problem is revealed.

For the design of a title-page, designer Thomas Detrie developed a sequence of possible solutions. Detrie's approach to the design process is based on his beliefs that "solutions come from within the problem" and "ideas come from working with the material and are not supplied or preconceived."

Detrie's personal problem-solving method is a three-stage design process: preliminary exploration, message investigation, and visualization of solutions. In his preliminary exploration, Detrie considered the nature and content of the problem and made sketches to explore possible directions. Typographic information (title, subtitle, authors, and publisher) was assigned priority. Detrie raised the question, "For the book *Basic Typography,* what is basic to typography that can be signified in a visual solution?" His answer established parameters appropriate to the given problem: a right-angled system, black on white, printed and unprinted areas, and a clear message. These considerations became the criteria for the investigation.

This project commenced in the postgraduate program in graphic design at the Basel School of Design, Switzerland. The encouragement and criticism of Wolfgang Weingart are gratefully acknowledged.

Ruedi Rüegg/Godi Fröhlich

ABC Verlag Zürich   Handbuch für Technik und Gestaltung
**Typografische
Grundlagen**

Editions ABC Zurich   Manual pour technique et conception
**Bases
Typographiques**

ABC Edition Zurich   Handbook for technique and design
**Basic
Typography**

21.

22.

23.

24a.

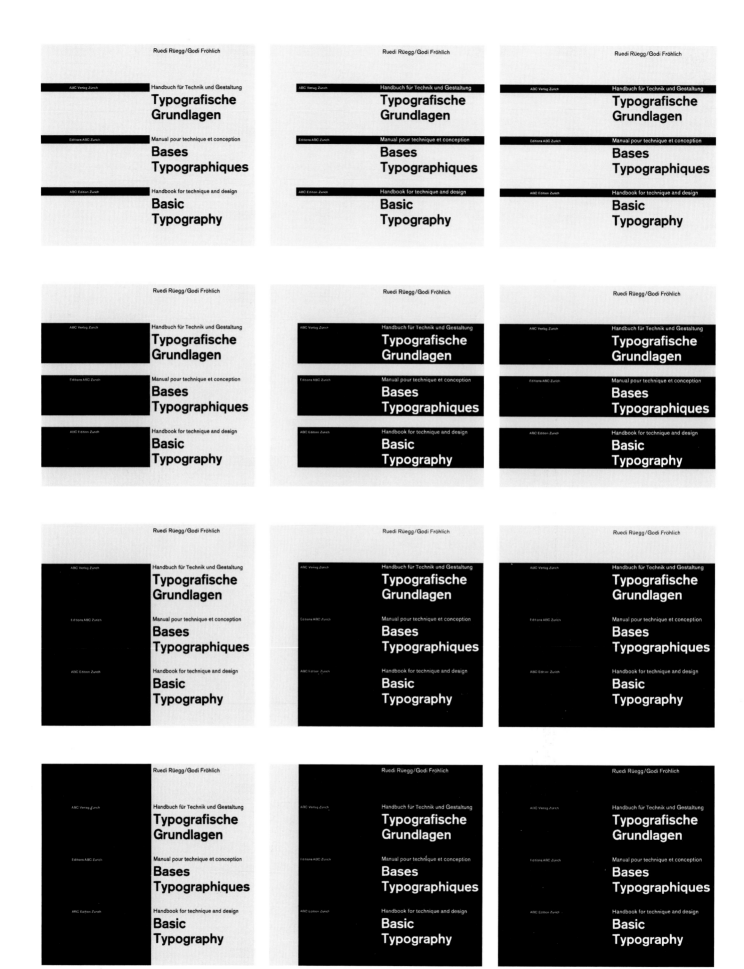

24b.

To investigate the range of typographic possibilities for the clear presentation of the manuscript, actual type was set and used in the initial visualizations for accuracy. A sans-serif face was chosen, and the message was printed in three sizes and two weights for use as raw material in these typographic studies. While maintaining the message priorities determined in the first stage, a variety of visual solutions were executed.

Decisions were made through subtle comparisons of type sizes and weights to select those that provided the best visual balance and message conveyance. Detrie did not place the type upon a predetermined grid; rather, he allowed the organizational structure to evolve from the process of working with the type proofs. Selecting the basic typographic arrangement was an intermediate step in the design process (Fig. **21**).

Next, Detrie developed a series of variations of this arrangement by investigating the application of horizontal and vertical lines, positive and negative shapes with positive type, and positive and negative shapes with positive and reversed type. Figure **22** demonstrates nine permutations with the application of vertical lines to the basic typographic schema. Permutations range from type alone to the addition of linear and rectilinear elements to a solid black page with reversed type (Fig. **23**). A graded arrangement of twenty-four of the many solutions is shown in Figure **24**. Observe the horizontal and vertical sequencing.

Unlimited solutions are possible in typographic design, and selection becomes an integral part of the design process. Not every possible solution is appropriate; the designer must continually evaluate each one against the problem criteria.

Because the practice of typography intersects both the visual and verbal worlds, it is an activity that draws inspiration and support from a wide variety of sources, including direct observation of nature, the fine arts, literature, photography, music, architecture, and popular culture.

An experimental project conducted by Sandra Wheeler in the graduate graphic design program at Virginia Commonwealth University traces the design processes of ten designers. In conjunction with a larger project, the international group of designers was asked to typographically explore the concept *green*. Though this general departure point was the same for each designer, the paths taken to examine and explore visual possibilities and message-making were worlds apart and inspired by a wide range of influences and interests. Each designer was responsible for identifying how their investigative processes would finally be realized. The pages that follow provide a comparative glimpse into each designer's typographic journey. As a collection, the diverse experiences of the designers reveal the vast exploratory potential inherent in the design process, and investigate many of the potent ideas that *green* can signify.

Typographic designers solve communication problems. Typically, these problems are pre-supplied by clients. But increasingly designers are asking important questions and seeking problems impacting culture and the environment. The open-ended nature of the *Green* project encouraged stepping into the roles of both of problem-seeker and problem-solver. Though many of the processes and experiments represented in the following pages appear not to have an obvious or direct relationship to the end product, each nonetheless contributed conceptually to the process.

Book design:
The Feminine Other

Designer:
Heather Boone

25.
Possible concepts were first collected in a process book.
26–31.
Using Adobe Illustrator and various weights of Univers, a study of "green"-related concepts were arranged, laser printed, crumpled and photographed digitally in low light without flash, and processed further in Photoshop. These investigations were a significant part of the process, for they led to provocative imagery and a unique typographic approach for a book design. Many visual effects – torn and crumpled paper, printouts with smeared edges, and overlapping images created with transparent material – served as indexical signs referring abstractly to original sin and the subsequent stress and guilt felt by some women. Words were also exploited for multiple meanings. In one example, one can read both *lie* and *life*.
32.
The process is applied to a book design entitled *The Feminine Other*. Shown here is the cover and details of sample spreads.

Green is original sin.

This typographic investigation, which led to the concept and design of an artist's book, did not develop in a precisely linear manner. Rather, it bubbled and simmered, one idea spilling into the next for a layered and enriched portrayal of feminism. "Green" is the woman in the photograph. She is living, breathing, complex, and flawed. A fascination with the egg as a symbol of birth, beginnings, and potential, led to musings about the Garden of Eden, original sin, and a woman's inherited guilt. Typographic permutations were developed with these themes in mind.

25.

26.

27.

28.

29.

30.

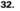
31.

32.

Film: *Planet Sartre*

Designer:
Matt Gardner

33.

34.

35.

36.

33-36.
Initially, words were altered in form to suggest reinvented language.
37-40.
Highly skilled drawings of Planetoids (referred to by the designer as amateur planets) symbolically represent the entirety of human experience in a single point.

41 and **42.**
The primary planetoid embodies an existential proclamation by Jean-Paul Sartre.
43.
This planetoid, along with *City Planet, Moon Serif Planet, Peeled Planet, Comma Planet,* and *Volcano Planet* are the subjects of a mysterious and evocative science fiction film.

Green is the planet Sartre.

"On the surface typographic design appears a process fraught with limitations. Clients, commissions and convention can dictate form and content. Unacknowledged delimitations such as language, standards of taste and technology abound, forcing a designer into seemingly narrow avenues of communication. Add to this the ambiguous gray area of readability and the fragile anatomy of the symbols used; it is little wonder that typographic expression is most often a collection of ready-made elements. However, a skillful designer can, like Zeno's rabbit, find infinite distance between two points. The multifarious manifestations of typographic experimentation can have the dynamic range of figural painting. While design has more traditionally allied with abstraction, this connection is merely formal. Design is not the invention of a new language; it is the extrusion and embellishment of an existing one. The addition of a new word does not mean that one is no longer speaking English. Again, the illusion of restraints presents itself, the conceit that some avenues are closed to the designer's practice. Still, just because we cannot reinvent the wheel doesn't mean we cannot create a better vehicle."

MPG

37.

38.

39.

40.

41.

42.

43.

Interactive user interface:
Dynamic Typography

Designer:
Benjamin Gaydos

44.

45. **46.** **47.**

Green is not found in a jail cell.

Joshua Berger states in *Restart: New Systems in Graphic Design,* that type is "the building blocks of meaning in whatever form that meaning arises. . . . Type can now be image. Type can be a sound. Type can be color."

This investigative process began with the concept of green as liberation. The goal was to "liberate" type from conventional forms and structures, and to explore typography as a dynamic, kinetic, and evolving meta-language. The primary communicative responsibility shifts from the text to a new dynamic visual syntax. Explorations in deconstruction, extrusion, and mutation informed the process, and digital tools enabled the realization of a real-time, interactive user interface.

44.
The process began by freely manipulating the forms of classic typefaces. It was found, however, that the choices were purely aesthetic. If the goal was to "liberate" the form from the original meaning, a different approach was needed.

45-47.
The word green was then extruded to imply the third dimension. This manipulation challenged the functionality of traditional letterforms and led to the development of dynamic and expansive alphabetic forms.

48. and **49.**
Using video and computer software, the letterforms were animated to achieve a constant state of movement and mutation. In *Dynamic Typography,* viewers are transported into fascinating typographic landscapes wherein classic typefaces dramatically morph into abstracted kinetic forms.

48.

49.

68.

69.

70.

71.

Typographic film

Designer:
Karen Stein

108.

108.
Visual transparency and ambiguity are explored through hand-constructed exercises in reference to the wabi-sabi idea that all things are impermanent, imperfect, and incomplete.

109.
Clothing patterns appropriated as the substrate for several typographic experiments metaphorically suggest aspects of wabi-sabi. These patterns are like the processes and patterns of aging; they are fragile and wrinkled, yet they are resilient and strong.

110 and **111.**
Projected typography, photographic imagery, and words reflecting the contradictory nature of wabi-sabi are explored for formal and communicative potential.

Green is wabi-sabi

If a concept, object, or expression can raise within human emotion a sense of longing, melancholy, or spirituality, it can be said to be wabi-sabi, the ancient Japanese practice that teaches three fundamental realities: nothing lasts, nothing is finished, and nothing is perfect. Wabi-sabi is a way of life that appreciates and accepts the contradictions of nature and of everyday living. As a concept, *green* is steeped in contradiction: while it is a symbol of life itself, a reference for green space, nature, and recycling, it is also the color of less desirable human traits: greed, jealousy, and envy. The design process featured here began with a visual study of green in this context. These investigations contributed to a typographic film on the subject of wabi-sabi.

109.

110.

111.

DISCORD GREED DESTRUCTION

Fire and Ice
Some say the world will end in fire,
Some say in ice.
From what I've tasted of desire
I hold with those who favour fire.
But if it had to perish twice,
I think I know enough of hate
To say that for destruction ice
Is also great
And would suffice.

Robert Frost

g

u

112.

112.

The design process is seldom predictible; it is often informed by digressions in thought and by activities seemingly unrelated to the problem itself. A Robert Frost poem, for example, encountered by the designer echoes the inherent themes of wabi-sabi.

113-117.

Further investigations with clothing patterns, stock-market newspaper pages, and typographic configurations seek to visually express contradictory themes.

118.

Sample frames from a poetic film about wabi-sabi reveal floating spheres and transitory typography in an expression of this ancient philosophy.

118.

113.

114.

115.

116.

117.

Poster series

Designer:
Todd Timney

119.

120.

121.

Green is many voices.

A mindmapping exercise yielded relationships between the root concept *green* and aspects of human nature and culture. Should a visual message be made as simple as possible, or should it be as layered and exciting as the culture it reflects? This question – asked at the beginning of this theory-oriented process – led to experiments in multiplicity and repetition, and the affect of visual and verbal redundancy on messages. At the conclusion of several typographic experiments, and with the aid of a morpho-logical typecase, a series of interpretive posters were designed. The morphological approach to problem solving offers a multiplicity of syntactic options that when intuitively employed can lead to effective visual messages.

122.

123.

124.

119.
A mindmap reflecting the rigorous process of associative thinking.

120.
Letterforms are constructed with a cross-stitch pattern of diagonal lines, and structured with the aid of a grid. The redundancy and repetition of parts echo the diversity found in culture.

121.
Words derived from the mindmap are examined for their similarities and differences. The resulting concrete poem evokes an emotional response.

122.
Computer printouts of the words *change* and *engage* are cut into strips and woven together. The resulting image intensifies the meaning of the word and further explores the notion of multiplicity.

123 and **124.**
The foregoing exercise is extended through the integration of photographic imagery and combining the words *life* and *death* into a single typographic image.

125-128.
A series of experimental posters were generated with the aid of a morphology from which variables were intuitively selected (see Fig. **20**, page 108). The content of the posters is based on a loose interpretation of *One,* a song composed by Adam Clayton, David Evans, Paul David Hewson and Laurence Mullen, and performed by Johnny Cash and U2. The singularity of the number one is juxtaposed by the manifold visual possibilities offered by the morphological choices.

125.

126.

127.

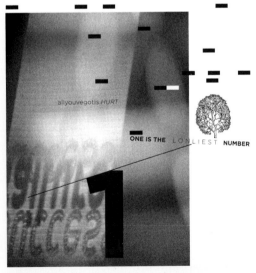

128.

Poster design

Designer:
Shuangshuang Wu

129.
Recalling childhood memories of smell and taste, these pencil drawings are of the aromas and vapors of green tea.

130.
A quick and intuitive interpretation of memory: fuzzy, fleeting, changing.

131 and **132.**
Experiments with light and gauze. These are interpretations of memory as dimmed, blurred, and mysterious.

133.
Memory is faded. The word green is written with Chinese ink in a sink. Water washes it away, and as this is occurring, rice paper is pressed into the fading letterforms.

134.
Memories overlap and they are complicated, uncertain, and indistinguishable. A sponge carved with letterforms is pressed into ink. The vague impression is then photographed using back lighting.

Green is memory.

Prior to immersing herself in process, Shuangshuang Wu gained inspiration from several readings. The most significant of these are *The Lover,* by Marguerite Duras and *Remembrance of Things Past,* by Marcel Proust. Perhaps her own childhood experiences while growing up in China proved the most poignant inspiration. Of the concept green, she says, "Green reminds me of jade, which has a special meaning in my country. Handed down from one generation to the next, we believe it brings good luck and protects whoever wears it." Shuangshuang's processes are highly experimental and she is not afraid to get her hands dirty or to challenge herself with unconventional ideas and methods.

129.

130.

133.

131.

132.

134.

135.
Photographic studies lead to experimentation with the language of shadows.

136 and **137.**
Memory is a reflection of real life, but is uncertain, impalpable and distorted. Memory and reality are reciprocal, interactive, and simultaneous. Type casting shadows is photographed to suggest these impressions.

138.
Memories of different people emerge. They are often contradictory. Strips cut from photographs and type express this idea.

139.
Memories build on each other and transform into new memories. A computer-generated system of linear elements is photographed in various stages of change.

140.
An earlier drawing was combined with a poem and integrated into an interpretive poster about memory, longing, and remembrance (overleaf).

135.

136.

137.

138.

139.

Throughout the long winter

mysterious tears r... ...r glass eyes

and lie on her ch... ...not falling.

It's just the damp, say skeptics.

A miracle, say I, respectfully...

But why does she weep?

REMEMBRANCE OF GREEN

The uses of typographic specimens by graphic designers have changed dramatically in the age of digital technology. Earlier generations of designers used specimens to determine which fonts and sizes to specify and order from typesetting companies, and for reference or tracing purposes when drawing layouts. A limited range of sizes were manufactured, and specimen sheets or books showed all available sizes.

Digital computers make an infinite range of sizes and style variations available, and designers can study and purchase fonts from digital type foundry Web sites. Today printed specimens are used for study and comparison purposes. The typeface specimens in this chapter were selected from outstanding type families to provide examples of the major historical classifications: Old Style, Transitional, Modern, Egyptian, and Sans Serif. More extensive specimens of Old Style and Sans Serif fonts are included, for these are the most widely used categories.

A bewildering number of typeface variations are available today, including versions originally designed for hand-, machine-, or phototype composition. Excellent newer varieties have been designed specifically for digital media. Designers need to study the subtlety of form and spacing in fonts, because their quality can vary widely.

ORONTII FINEI

DELPHINATIS, REGII MATHEMA-TICARVM PROFESSORIS, DE ARITHMETICA PRACTICA LIBRI QVATVOR.

LIBER PRIMVS, DE INTEGRIS: HOC EST, eiuſdem ſpeciei, ſiue denominationis tractat numeris.

De fruĉtu, atqᵉ dignitate ipſius Arithmeticæ: Proœmium.

NTER LIBERALES MA- thematicas, quæ ſolæ diſciplinæ vocâtur, Arithmeticam primum locum ſibi vendi- caſſe: nemo ſanæ mentis ignorat. Eſt enim Arithmetica omnium aliarum diſciplina- rum mater, & nutrix antiquiſſima: nume- rorũ qualitates, vim, & naturam, ac id ge- nus alia demonſtrans, quæ abſolutum vi- dentur reſpicere numerum. Cuius prin- cipia tanta excellunt ſimplicitate, vt nul- lius artis videatur indigere ſuffragio: ſed cunĉtis opituletur artibus. Ad cuius puritatem illud etiam plurimum facit: quoniam nulla diuinitati adeò cõnexa eſt diſciplina, quantùm Arithmetica. Nam vnitas omniũ numerorũ radix & origo, in ſe, à ſe, ac circum ſeipſam vnica vel impar- tibilis permanet: ex cuius tamen coaceruatione, omnis cõſurgit & ge- neratur, omniſque tandem in eam reſoluitur numerus. Quemadmo- dum cunĉta quæ ſeu diſcreta, ſiue compoſita inſpeĉtentur Vniuerſo, à ſummo rerum conditore in definitum digeſta, redaĉtáve ſunt, & demũ reſoluenda numerum. Quot autem vtilitates cognita, quótve laby- rinthos ignota præbeat Arithmetica: conſpicere facile eſt. Numerorũ etenim ratione ſublata, tollitur & muſicarum modulationũ intelligen- tia: geometricorum, cæleſtiúmve arcanorum ſubtilis aufertur ingreſ- ſio: tollitur & vniuerſa Philoſophia, ſiue quæ diuina, ſeu quæ contem- platur humana: imperfeĉta relinquitur legũ adminiſtratio, vtpote, quæ

Dignitas arithmeticę.

Fructus arithmeticę.

A.iij.

Old Style

Garamond
Minion

Additional
Old Style fonts

1.

Page 3 of the French Renaissance book *Arithmetica* by Oronce Fine, printed by Simon de Colines in Paris, 1535.

Although Old Style typefaces trace their heritage to the printers of the Italian Renaissance, their heritage extends to an earlier time, for Roman inscriptional letterforms (see Chapter 1, Fig. **18**) inspired their capital-letter design. The Caroline Minuscules (see Chapter 1, Fig. **27**) from medieval manuscripts inspired writing styles during the fifteenth century, and these became the model for Old Style lowercase letters.

Many Old Style typefaces bear the name of Claude Garamond, a leading typeface designer and punchcutter working in Paris when the book *Arithmetica* (Fig. **1**) was published. In the heading material, the designer has used bold capitals for

the author's name, two sizes of capitals for the title, and italics for the subhead. The spatial intervals between these units have been established with great care. Fleurons (printer's flowers), paragraph marks, a woodcut headpiece, and a large initial letter *I* intricately carved on a woodblock bring vibrancy to this elegant example of French Renaissance book design and letterpress printing.

For more than five hundred years, designers have created lively typeface variations inspired by Italian and French Old Style fonts of the fifteenth and sixteenth centuries. The specimens in this section display digitized versions of traditional typefaces with distinctive design attributes.

Adobe Garamond

A digital version designed by
Robert Slimbach for Adobe
Systems and released in 1992.

abcdefghij

klmnopq

rstuvwxyz

$1234567

890(.,'"-;:)!?

ABCDEF
GHIJKL
MNOPQ
RSTUV
WXYZ&

140 point

abcdefghijklmnopqrstuvwxyz
ABCDEFGHIJKLMNOPQR
STUVWXYZ$1234567890
(.,'"-;:)!?&

abcdefghijklmn

opqrstuvwxyz

ABCDEFGHIJK

LMNOPQRSTU

VWXYZ$12345

67890(.,'"-;:)!?&

abcdefghijklmnopqrstuvwxyz
ABCDEFGHIJKLMNOPQRS
TUVWXYZ1234567890
(.,'"-;:)!?&

26 point

abcdefghijklmno

pqrstuvwxyz

ABCDEFGHIJK

LMNOPQRSTU

VWXYZ$12345

67890(.,'"-;:)!?&

81 point

abcdefghijklmnopqrstuvwxyz
ABCDEFGHIJKLMNOPQR
STUVWXYZ$1234567890
(.,'"-;:)!?&

26 point

abcdefghijklmno

pqrstuvwxyz

ABCDEFGHIJK

LMNOPQRST

UVWXYZ$1234

567890(.,'"-;:)!?&

81 point

Adobe Garamond

The whole duty of typography, *as with calligraphy,* is to communicate to the imagination, without loss by the way, the thought or image intended to be communicated by the author. And the whole duty of beautiful typography is not to substitute for the beauty or interest of the thing thought and intended to be conveyed by the symbol, a beauty or interest of its own, but, on the one hand, to win access for that communication by the clearness and beauty of the vehicle, and on the other hand, to take advantage of every pause or stage in that communication to interpose some characteristic & restful beauty in its own art. We thus have a reason for the clearness and beauty of the first and introductory page and of the title, and for the especial beauty of the headings of chapters, capital or initial letters, and so on, and an opening for the illustrator as we shall see by and by. Further, in the case of poetry, verse, in my opinion, appeals by its form to the eye, as well as to the

8/10

The whole duty of typography, *as with calligraphy,* is to communicate to the imagination, without loss by the way, the thought or image intended to be communicated by the author. And the whole duty of beautiful typography is not to substitute for the beauty or interest of the thing thought and intended to be conveyed by the symbol, a beauty or interest of its own, but, on the one hand, to win access for that communication by the clearness and beauty of the vehicle, and on the other hand, to take advantage of every pause or stage in that communication to interpose some characteristic & restful beauty in its own art. We thus have a reason for the clearness and beauty of the first and introductory page and of the title, and for the especial beauty of the headings of chapters, capital or initial letters,

9/11

The whole duty of typography, *as with calligraphy,* is to communicate to the imagination, without loss by the way, the thought or image intended to be communicated by the author. And the whole duty of beautiful typography is not to substitute for the beauty or interest of the thing thought and intended to be conveyed by the symbol, a beauty or interest of its own, but, on the one hand, to win access for that communication by the clearness and beauty of the vehicle, and on the other hand, to take advantage of every pause or stage in that communication to interpose some characteristic & restful beauty in its own art. We thus have a reason for the clearness and beauty of the first and introductory page and of the title, and for the especial beauty of the headings of chapters, capital or initial letters,

10/12

The whole duty of typography, *as with calligraphy,* is to communicate to the imagination, without loss by the way, the thought or image intended to be communicated by the author. And the whole duty of beautiful typography is not to substitute for the beauty or interest of the thing thought and intended to be conveyed by the symbol, a beauty or interest of its own, but, on the one hand, to win access for that communication by the

12/14

The whole duty of typography, *as with calligraphy,* is to communicate to the imagination, without loss by the way, the thought or image intended to be communicated by the author. And the whole duty of beautiful typography is not to substitute for the beauty or interest of the thing thought and intended to be conveyed by the symbol, a beauty or interest of its own, but, on the one hand, to win access for that communication by the clearness and beauty of the vehicle, and on the other hand, to take advantage of every pause or stage in that communication to interpose some characteristic & restful beauty in its own art. We thus have a reason for the clearness and beauty of the first and introductory page and of the title, and for the especial beauty of the headings of chapters, capital or initial letters, and

8/12

The whole duty of typography, *as with calligraphy,* is to communicate to the imagination, without loss by the way, the thought or image intended to be communicated by the author. And the whole duty of beautiful typography is not to substitute for the beauty or interest of the thing thought and intended to be conveyed by the symbol, a beauty or interest of its own, but, on the one hand, to win access for that communication by the clearness and beauty of the vehicle, and on the other hand, to take advantage of every pause or stage in that communication to interpose some characteristic & restful beauty in its own art. We thus have a reason for the

9/13

The whole duty of typography, *as with calligraphy,* is to communicate to the imagination, without loss by the way, the thought or image intended to be communicated by the author. And the whole duty of beautiful typography is not to substitute for the beauty or interest of the thing thought and intended to be conveyed by the symbol, a beauty or interest of its own, but, on the one hand, to win access for that communication by the clearness and beauty of the vehicle, and on the other hand, to take advantage of every pause or stage in that communication to interpose some

10/14

The whole duty of typography, *as with calligraphy,* is to communicate to the imagination, without loss by the way, the thought or image intended to be communicated by the author. And the whole duty of beautiful typography is not to substitute for the beauty or interest of the thing thought and intended to be conveyed by the symbol, a beauty or interest of its own,

12/16

**Adobe Minion
Display Regular**

The Minion type family was
designed by Robert Slimbach
for Adobe Systems in 1990.

abcdefghij

klmnopqr

stuvwxyz

$12345678

90(.,'''-;:)!?

ABCDEF

GHIJKL

MNOPQ

RSTUV

WXYZ&

abcdefghijklmnopqrstuvwxyz
ABCDFGHIJKLMNOPQRSTU
VWXYZ$1234567890
(.,'"-;:)!?&

25 point

abcdefghijklmn

opqrstuvwxyz

ABCDEFGHIJKL

MNOPQRSTU

VWXYZ$12345

67890(.,'"-;:)!?&

75 point

244

abcdefghijklmnopqrstuvwxyz
ABCDFGHIJKLMNOPQRSTU
VWXYZ$1234567890
(.,'"-;:)!?&

abcdefghijklmno

pqrstuvwxyz

ABCDEFGHIJKL

MNOPQRSTU

VWXYZ$1234567

890(.,'"-;:)!?&

abcdefghijklmnopqrstuvwxyz
ABCDFGHIJKLMNOPQ
RSTUVWXYZ$1234567890
(.,'"-;:)!?&

abcdefghijklmn

opqrstuvwxyz

ABCDEFGHIJKL

MNOPQRSTU

VWXYZ$12345

67890(.,'"-;:)!?&

**Adobe Minion
Regular**

abcdefghijklmnopqrstuvwxyz
ABCDEFGHIJKLMNOPQRSTUVWXYZ
$1234567890(.,'"-;:!)!?&
abcdefghijklmnopqrstuvwxyz
ABCDEFGHIJKLMNOPQRSTUVWXYZ
8 point *$1234567890(.,'"-;:)!?&*

abcdefghijklmnopqrstuvwxyz
ABCDEFGHIJKLMNOPQRSTUVWXYZ
$1234567890(.,'"-;:)!?&
abcdefghijklmnopqrstuvwxyz
ABCDEFGHIJKLMNOPQRSTUVWXYZ
9 point *$1234567890(.,'"-;:)!?&*

abcdefghijklmnopqrstuvwxyz
ABCDEFGHIJKLMNOPQRSTUVWXYZ
$1234567890(.,'"-;:)!?&
abcdefghijklmnopqrstuvwxyz
ABCDEFGHIJKLMNOPQRSTUVWXYZ
10 point *$1234567890(.,'"-;:)!?&*

abcdefghijklmnopqrstuvwxyz
ABCDEFGHIJKLMNOPQRSTUVWXYZ
$1234567890(.,'"-;:)!?&
abcdefghijklmnopqrstuvwxyz
ABCDEFGHIJKLMNOPQRSTUVWXYZ
12 point *$1234567890(.,'"-;:)!?&ß*

The whole duty of typography, *as with calligraphy,* is to communicate to the imagination, without loss by the way, the thought or image intended to be com municated by the author. And the whole duty of beautiful typography is not to substitute for the beauty or interest of the thing thought and intended to be conveyed by the symbol, a beauty or interest of its own, but, on the one hand, to win access for that communication by the clearness and beauty of the vehicle, and on the other hand, to take advantage of every pause or stage in that communication to interpose some characteristic & restful beauty in its own art. We thus have a reason for the clearness and beauty of the first and introductory page and of the title, and for the especial beauty of the headings of chapters, capital or initial letters, and so on, and an opening for the illustrator as we shall see by and by. Further, in the case of poetry, verse, in my opinion, appeals by its
8/10

The whole duty of typography, *as with calligraphy,* is to communicate to the imagination, without loss by the way, the thought or image intended to be communicated by the author. And the whole duty of beautiful typography is not to substitute for the beauty or interest of the thing thought and intended to be conveyed by the symbol, a beauty or interest of its own, but, on the one hand, to win access for that communication by the clearness and beauty of the vehicle, and on the other hand, to take advantage of every pause or stage in that communication to interpose some characteristic & restful beauty in its own art. We thus have a reason for the clearness and beauty of the first and introductory page and of the title, and for the especial beauty of the
9/11

The whole duty of typography, *as with calligraphy,* is to commu nicate to the imagination, without loss by the way, the thought or image intended to be communicated by the author. And the whole duty of beautiful typography is not to substitute for the beauty or interest of the thing thought and intended to be con veyed by the symbol, a beauty or interest of its own, but, on the one hand, to win access for that communication by the clearness and beauty of the vehicle, and on the other hand, to take advan tage of every pause or stage in that communication to interpose some characteristic & restful beauty in its own art. We thus have
10/12

The whole duty of typography, *as with calligraphy,* is to communicate to the imagination, without loss by the way, the thought or image intended to be commu nicated by the author. And the whole duty of beautiful typography is not to substitute for the beauty or inter est of the thing thought and intended to be conveyed by the symbol, a beauty or interest of its own, but, on the one hand, to win access for that communication
12/14

The whole duty of typography, *as with calligraphy,* is to communicate to the imagination, without loss by the way, the thought or image intended to be com municated by the author. And the whole duty of beautiful typography is not to substitute for the beauty or interest of the thing thought and intended to be conveyed by the symbol, a beauty or interest of its own, but, on the one hand, to win access for that communication by the clearness and beauty of the vehicle, and on the other hand, to take advantage of every pause or stage in that commu nication to interpose some characteristic & restful beauty in its own art. We thus have a reason for the clearness and beauty of the first and introductory page and of the title, and for the especial beauty of the headings of chapters, capital or
8/12

The whole duty of typography, *as with calligraphy,* is to communicate to the imagination, without loss by the way, the thought or image intended to be communicated by the author. And the whole duty of beautiful typography is not to substitute for the beauty or interest of the thing thought and intended to be conveyed by the symbol, a beauty or interest of its own, but, on the one hand, to win access for that communication by the clearness and beauty of the vehicle, and on the other hand, to take advantage of every pause or stage in that communication to interpose some characteristic & restful beauty in its own art. We thus have a reason
9/13

The whole duty of typography, *as with calligraphy,* is to commu nicate to the imagination, without loss by the way, the thought or image intended to be communicated by the author. And the whole duty of beautiful typography is not to substitute for the beauty or interest of the thing thought and intended to be con veyed by the symbol, a beauty or interest of its own, but, on the one hand, to win access for that communication by the clearness and beauty of the vehicle, and on the other hand, to take advan tage of every pause or stage in that communication to interpose
10/14

The whole duty of typography, *as with calligraphy,* is to communicate to the imagination, without loss by the way, the thought or image intended to be commu nicated by the author. And the whole duty of beautiful typography is not to substitute for the beauty or inter est of the thing thought and intended to be conveyed by the symbol, a beauty or interest of its own, but, on
12/16

Caslon Regular

abcdefghijklmnopqrstuvwxyz
ABCDEFGHIJKLMNOPQRSTUV
WXYZ$1234567890(.,'"-;:)!?&

Caslon Bold

**abcdefghijklmnopqrstuvwxyz
ABCDEFGHIJKLMNOPQRSTUV
WXYZ$1234567890(.,'"-;:)!?&**

Centaur

abcdefghijklmnopqrstuvwxyz
ABCDEFGHIJKLMNOPQRSTUVWX
YZ$1234567890(.,'"-;:)!?&

Centaur Bold

abcdefghijklmnopqrstuvwxyz
ABCDEFGHIJKLMNOPQRSTUVW
XYZ$1234567890(.,'"-;:)!?&

Goudy Old Style

abcdefghijklmnopqrstuvwxyz
ABCDEFGHIJKLMNOPQRSTUVW
XYZ$1234567890(.,'"-;:)!?&

abcdefghijklmnopqrstuvwxyz
ABCDEFGHIJKLMNOPQRSTUV
WXYZ$1234567890(.,'"-;:)!?&

abcdefghijklmnopqrstuvwxyz
ABCDEFGHIJKLMNOPQRSTUV
WXYZ$1234567890(.,'"-;:)!?&

abcdefghijklmnopqrstuvwxyz
ABCDEFGHIJKLMNOPQRSTUV
WXYZ$1234567890(.,'"-;:)!?&

abcdefghijklmnopqrstuvwxyz
ABCDEFGHIJKLMNOPQRSTUV
WXYZ$1234567890(.,'"-;:)!?&

abcdefghijklmnopqrstuvwxyz
ABCDEFGHIJKLMNOPQRSTVW
XYZ$1234567890(.,'"-;:)!?&

Im VERLAG DES BILDUNGSVERBANDES der Deutschen Buchdrucker,
Berlin SW 61, Dreibundstr. 5, erscheint demnächst:

JAN TSCHICHOLD
Lehrer an der Meisterschule für Deutschlands Buchdrucker in München

DIE NEUE TYPOGRAPHIE

**Handbuch für die gesamte Fachwelt
und die drucksachenverbrauchenden Kreise**

Das Problem der neuen gestaltenden Typographie hat eine lebhafte
Diskussion bei allen Beteiligten hervorgerufen. Wir glauben dem Bedürf-
nis, die aufgeworfenen Fragen ausführlich behandelt zu sehen, zu ent-
sprechen, wenn wir jetzt ein Handbuch der **NEUEN TYPOGRAPHIE**
herausbringen.

Es kam dem Verfasser, einem ihrer bekanntesten Vertreter, in diesem
Buche zunächst darauf an, den engen Zusammenhang der neuen
Typographie mit dem **Gesamtkomplex heutigen Lebens** aufzuzei-
gen und zu beweisen, daß die neue Typographie ein ebenso notwendi-
ger Ausdruck einer neuen Gesinnung ist wie die neue Baukunst und
alles Neue, das mit unserer Zeit anbricht. Diese geschichtliche Notwen-
digkeit der neuen Typographie belegt weiterhin eine kritische Dar-
stellung der **alten Typographie**. Die Entwicklung der **neuen Male-
rei**, die für alles Neue unserer Zeit geistig bahnbrechend gewesen ist,
wird in einem reich illustrierten Aufsatz des Buches leicht faßlich dar-
gestellt. Ein kurzer Abschnitt „**Zur Geschichte der neuen Typographie**" leitet zu dem wichtigsten Teile des Buches, den **Grundbegriffen
der neuen Typographie** über. Diese werden klar herausgeschält,
richtige und falsche Beispiele einander gegenübergestellt. Zwei wei-
tere Artikel behandeln „**Photographie und Typographie**" und
„**Neue Typographie und Normung**".

Der Hauptwert des Buches für den Praktiker besteht in dem zweiten
Teil „**Typographische Hauptformen**" (siehe das nebenstehende
Inhaltsverzeichnis). Es fehlte bisher an einem Werke, das wie dieses Buch
die schon bei einfachen Satzaufgaben auftauchenden gestalterischen
Fragen in gebührender Ausführlichkeit behandelte. Jeder Teilabschnitt
enthält neben **allgemeinen typographischen Regeln** vor allem die
Abbildungen aller in Betracht kommenden **Normblätter** des Deutschen
Normenausschusses, alle andern (z. B. postalischen) **Vorschriften** und
zahlreiche Beispiele, Gegenbeispiele und Schemen.

Für jeden Buchdrucker, insbesondere jeden Akzidenzsetzer, wird „Die
neue Typographie" ein **unentbehrliches Handbuch** sein. Von nicht
geringerer Bedeutung ist es für Reklamefachleute, Gebrauchsgraphiker,
Kaufleute, Photographen, Architekten, Ingenieure und Schriftsteller,
also für alle, die mit dem Buchdruck in Berührung kommen.

INHALT DES BUCHES

Werden und Wesen der neuen Typographie
Das neue Weltbild
Die alte Typographie (Rückblick und Kritik)
Die neue Kunst
Zur Geschichte der neuen Typographie
Die Grundbegriffe der neuen Typographie
Photographie und Typographie
Neue Typographie und Normung

Typographische Hauptformen
Das Typosignet
Der Geschäftsbrief
Der Halbbrief
Briefhüllen ohne Fenster
Fensterbriefhüllen
Die Postkarte
Die Postkarte mit Klappe
Die Geschäftskarte
Die Besuchskarte
Werbsachen (Karten, Blätter, Prospekte, Kataloge)
Das Typoplakat
Das Bildplakat
Schildformate, Tafeln und Rahmen
Inserate
Die Zeitschrift
Die Tageszeitung
Die illustrierte Zeitung
Tabellensatz
Das neue Buch

Bibliographie
Verzeichnis der Abbildungen
Register

typ. tschichold

Das Buch enthält über 125 Abbildungen, von
denen etwa ein Viertel **zweifarbig** gedruckt ist,
und umfaßt gegen **200** Seiten auf gutem Kunst-
druckpapier. Es erscheint im Format DIN A 5 (148×
210 mm) und ist biegsam in Ganzleinen gebunden.

Preis bei Vorbestellung bis 1. Juni 1928:　　　**5.00** RM
durch den Buchhandel nur zum Preise von　　　**6.50** RM

Bestellschein umstehend ➡

Sans Serif

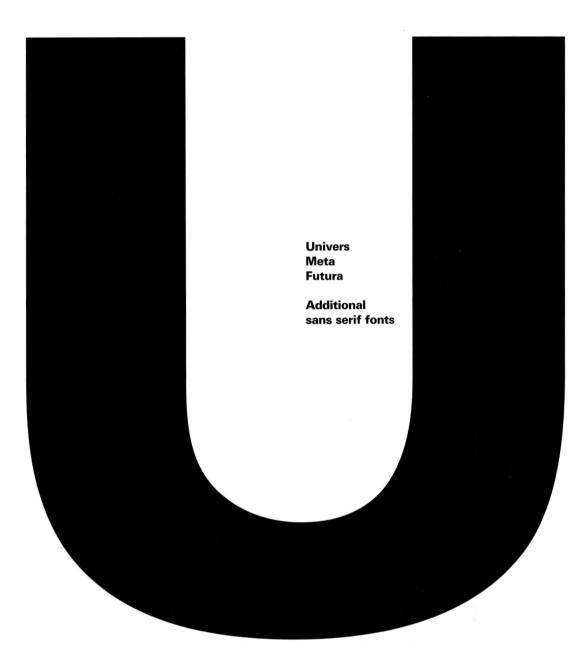

**Univers
Meta
Futura**

**Additional
sans serif fonts**

2.

Prospectus designed by Jan
Tschichold for his book *Die
neue Typographie,* 1928.

Sans serif typefaces have elemental letterforms
stripped of serifs and decorations. Although sans
serifs first appeared early in the nineteenth
century, their use accelerated during the 1920s.
"Form follows function" became the design
dictum, and the functional simplicity of sans serif
typefaces led many designers to look upon them
as the ideal typographic expression of a scientific
and technological century.

In Jan Tschichold's influential book *Die neue
Typographie,* he advocated a new functional style
for a rational era. In the prospectus for the book,
he used sans serif type as an expression of the
age (Fig. **2**). The page also demonstrates
asymmetrical balancing of elements on a grid

system, visual contrasts of type size and weight,
and the importance of spatial intervals and white
space as design elements.

During the 1950s, Univers and Helvetica were both
designed as more contemporary versions of
Akzidenz Grotesque, a German turn-of-the-century
sans serif. Compare the text setting and the
display specimens of Helvetica with their Univers
counterparts. There are subtle differences in the
drawing of many letterforms. The Univers family
is renowned for its remarkable graphic unity,
which enables the typographic designer to use all
twenty-one fonts together as a flexible, integrated
typographic system.

251

Univers was designed by
Adrian Frutiger and released
in 1957.

abcdefgh
ijklmnop
qrstuvwx
yz$12345
67890!?

124 point

ABCDEF
GHIJKLM
NOPQRS
TUVWX
YZ&(.,'"":)

abcdefghijklmnopqrstuv
wxyzABCDEFGHIJKLMN
OPQRSTUVWXYZ$12345
67890(.,'"-;:)!?&

26 point

abcdefghijklmn
opqrstuvwxyz
ABCDEFGHIJKL
MNOPQRSTUV
WXYZ$1234567
890(.,'"-;:)!?&

72 point

256

Univers 55

The whole duty of typography, *as with calligraphy,* is to communicate to the imagination, without loss by the way, the thought or image intended to be communicated by the author. And the whole duty of beautiful typography is not to substitute for the beauty or interest of the thing thought and intended to be conveyed by the symbol, a beauty or interest of its own, but, on the one hand, to win access for that communication by the clearness and beauty of the vehicle, and on the other hand, to take advantage of every pause or stage in that communication to interpose some characteristic & restful beauty in its own art. We thus have a reason for the clearness and beauty of the first and introductory page and of the title, and for the especial beauty of the headings of chapters, capital or initial letters, and so on, and an opening for the illustrator as
8/10

The whole duty of typography, *as with calligraphy,* is to communicate to the imagination, without loss by the way, the thought or image intended to be communicated by the author. And the whole duty of beautiful typography is not to substitute for the beauty or interest of the thing thought and intended to be conveyed by the symbol, a beauty or interest of its own, but, on the one hand, to win access for that communication by the clearness and beauty of the vehicle, and on the other hand, to take advantage of every pause or stage in that communication to interpose some characteristic & restful beauty in its own art. We thus have a reason for the clearness and beauty of the first and introductory page and of the
8/12

The whole duty of typography, *as with calligraphy,* is to communicate to the imagination, without loss by the way, the thought or image intended to be communicated by the author. And the whole duty of beautiful typography is not to substitute for the beauty or interest of the thing thought and intended to be conveyed by the symbol, a beauty or interest of its own, but, on the one hand, to win access for that communication by the clearness and beauty of the vehicle, and on the other hand, to take advantage of every pause or stage in that communication to interpose some characteristic & restful beauty in its own art. We thus have a reason for the clearness and beauty of the first
9/11

The whole duty of typography, *as with calligraphy,* is to communicate to the imagination, without loss by the way, the thought or image intended to be communicated by the author. And the whole duty of beautiful typography is not to substitute for the beauty or interest of the thing thought and intended to be conveyed by the symbol, a beauty or interest of its own, but, on the one hand, to win access for that communication by the clearness and beauty of the vehicle, and on the other hand, to take advantage of every pause or stage in that communication to
9/13

The whole duty of typography, *as with calligraphy,* is to communicate to the imagination, without loss by the way, the thought or image intended to be communicated by the author. And the whole duty of beautiful typography is not to substitute for the beauty or interest of the thing thought and intended to be conveyed by the symbol, a beauty or interest of its own, but, on the one hand, to win access for that communication by the clearness and beauty of the vehicle, and on the other hand, to take advantage of every pause or stage in that communication
10/12

The whole duty of typography, *as with calligraphy,* is to communicate to the imagination, without loss by the way, the thought or image intended to be communicated by the author. And the whole duty of beautiful typography is not to substitute for the beauty or interest of the thing thought and intended to be conveyed by the symbol, a beauty or interest of its own, but, on the one hand, to win access for that communication by the clearness and beauty of the vehicle, and on the other hand, to take advantage of every
10/14

The whole duty of typography, *as with calligraphy,* is to communicate to the imagination, without loss by the way, the thought or image intended to be communicated by the author. And the whole duty of beautiful typography is not to substitute for the beauty or interest of the thing thought and intended to be conveyed by the symbol, a beauty or interest of its own, but, on the one hand, to win
12/14

The whole duty of typography, *as with calligraphy,* is to communicate to the imagination, without loss by the way, the thought or image intended to be communicated by the author. And the whole duty of beautiful typography is not to substitute for the beauty or interest of the thing thought and intended to be conveyed by the symbol, a beauty
12/16

Meta was designed by Erik Spiekermann and released by Fontshop in 1991.

abcdefghij
klmnopq
rstuvwxyz
$1234567
890!?

ABCDEF
GHIJKLMN
OPQRSTU
VWXYZ&
(,'',, -;:)

abcdefghijklmnopqrstuvwxy
zABCDFGHIJKLMNOPQRS
TUVWXYZ$1234567890
(.,'"-;:)!?&

abcdefghijklmnop
qrstuvwxyzABCDE
FGHIJKLMNOPQRS
TUVWXYZ$123456
7890(.,'"-;:)!?&

abcdefghijklmnopqrstuvwxy
zABCDFGHIJKLMNOPQRS
TUVWXYZ1234567890
(.,'"-;:)!?&

26 point

abcdefghijklmnop
qrstuvwxyzABCDE
FGHIJKLMNOPQRS
TUVWXYZ$123456
7890(.,'"-;:)!?&

72 point

abcdefghijklmnopqrstuvw
xyzABCDEFGHIJKLMNOPQRS
TUVWXYZ$1234567890
(.,'"-;:)!?&

26 point

abcdefghijklmnop
qrstuvwxyzABCD
EFGHIJKLMNOPQ
RSTUVWXYZ$123
4567890(.,'";:)!?&

72 point

Meta Normal

abcdefghijklmnopqrstuvwxyz
ABCDEFGHIJKLMNOPQRSTUVWXYZ
$1234567890(.,'"-;:)!?&
abcdefghijklmnopqrstuvwxyz
ABCDEFGHIJKLMNOPQRSTUVWXYZ
$1234567890(.,'"-;:)!?&

8 point

abcdefghijklmnopqrstuvwxyz
ABCDEFGHIJKLMNOPQRSTUVWXYZ
$1234567890(.,'"-;:)!?&
abcdefghijklmnopqrstuvwxyz
ABCDEFGHIJKLMNOPQRSTUVWXYZ
$1234567890(.,'"-;:)!?&

9 point

abcdefghijklmnopqrstuvwxyz
ABCDEFGHIJKLMNOPQRSTUVWXYZ
$1234567890(.,'"-;:)!?&
abcdefghijklmnopqrstuvwxyz
ABCDEFGHIJKLMNOPQRSTUVWXYZ
$1234567890(.,'"-;:)!?&

10 point

abcdefghijklmnopqrstuvwxyz
ABCDEFGHIJKLMNOPQRSTUVWXYZ
$1234567890(.,'"-;:)!?&
abcdefghijklmnopqrstuvwxyz
ABCDEFGHIJKLMNOPQRSTUVWXYZ
$1234567890(.,'"-;:)!?&

12 point

The whole duty of typography, *as with calligraphy,* is to communicate to the imagination, without loss by the way, the thought or image intended to be communicated by the author. And the whole duty of beautiful typography is not to substitute for the beauty or interest of the thing thought and intended to be conveyed by the symbol, a beauty or interest of its own, but, on the one hand, to win access for that communication by the clearness and beauty of the vehicle, and on the other hand, to take advantage of every pause or stage in that communication to interpose some characteristic & restful beauty in its own art. We thus have a reason for the clearness and beauty of the first and introductory page and of the title, and for the especial beauty of the headings of chapters, capital or initial letters, and so on, and an opening for the illustrator as we shall see

8/10

The whole duty of typography, *as with calligraphy,* is to communicate to the imagination, without loss by the way, the thought or image intended to be communicated by the author. And the whole duty of beautiful typography is not to substitute for the beauty or interest of the thing thought and intended to be conveyed by the symbol, a beauty or interest of its own, but, on the one hand, to win access for that communication by the clearness and beauty of the vehicle, and on the other hand, to take advantage of every pause or stage in that communication to interpose some characteristic & restful beauty in its own art. We thus have a reason for the clearness and beauty of the first and introductory page and of the

8/12

The whole duty of typography, *as with calligraphy,* is to communicate to the imagination, without loss by the way, the thought or image intended to be communicated by the author. And the whole duty of beautiful typography is not to substitute for the beauty or interest of the thing thought and intended to be conveyed by the symbol, a beauty or interest of its own, but, on the one hand, to win access for that communication by the clearness and beauty of the vehicle, and on the other hand, to take advantage of every pause or stage in that communication to interpose some characteristic & restful beauty in its own art. We thus have a reason for the clearness and beauty of the first and

9/11

The whole duty of typography, *as with calligraphy,* is to communicate to the imagination, without loss by the way, the thought or image intended to be communicated by the author. And the whole duty of beautiful typography is not to substitute for the beauty or interest of the thing thought and intended to be conveyed by the symbol, a beauty or interest of its own, but, on the one hand, to win access for that communication by the clearness and beauty of the vehicle, and on the other hand, to take advantage of every pause or stage in that communication to

9/13

The whole duty of typography, as with calligraphy, is to communicate to the imagination, without loss by the way, the thought or image intended to be communicated by the author. And the whole duty of beautiful typography is not to substitute for the beauty or interest of the thing thought and intended to be conveyed by the symbol, a beauty or interest of its own, but, on the one hand, to win access for that communication by the clearness and beauty of the vehicle, and on the other hand, to take advantage of every pause or stage in that communication to interpose some

10/12

The whole duty of typography, *as with calligraphy,* is to communicate to the imagination, without loss by the way, the thought or image intended to be communicated by the author. And the whole duty of beautiful typography is not to substitute for the beauty or interest of the thing thought and intended to be conveyed by the symbol, a beauty or interest of its own, but, on the one hand, to win access for that communication by the clearness and beauty of the vehicle, and on the other hand, to take advantage of every pause or

10 /14

The whole duty of typography, *as with calligraphy,* is to communicate to the imagination, without loss by the way, the thought or image intended to be communicated by the author. And the whole duty of beautiful typography is not to substitute for the beauty or interest of the thing thought and intended to be conveyed by the symbol, a beauty or interest of its own, but, on the one hand, to win access for

12 /14

The whole duty of typography, *as with calligraphy,* is to communicate to the imagination, without loss by the way, the thought or image intended to be communicated by the author. And the whole duty of beautiful typography is not to substitute for the beauty or interest of the thing thought and intended to be conveyed by the symbol, a beauty or interest

12 /16

Futura was designed Paul
Renner; the first fonts were
released in 1927.

abcdefghi
jklmnopqr
stuvwxyz
$1234567
890!?

130 point

ABCDEF
GHIJKLM
NOPQRS
TUVWXY
Z&(.,'""-;:)

130 point

abcdefghijklmnopqrstuvwxy
zABCDFGHIJKLMNOPQRS
TUVWXYZ$1234567890
(.,'"-;:)!?&

abcdefghijklmno
pqrstuvwxyz
ABCDEFGHIJKL
MNOPQRSTUV
WXYZ$1234567
890(.,'"-;:)!?&

abcdefghijklmnopqrstuvwxy
zABCDFGHIJKLMNOPQRS
TUVWXYZ1234567890
(.,'"-;:)!?&

26 point

abcdefghijklmno
pqrstuvwxyzABC
DEFGHIJKLMNO
PQRSTUVWXYZ
$1234567890
(.,'"-;:)!?&

72 point

abcdefghijklmnopqrstu
vwxyzABCDEFGHIJKLM
NOPQRSTUVWXYZ$12
34567890(.,'"-;:)!?&

26 point

abcdefghijklmn
opqrstuvwxyz
ABCDEFGHIJKL
MNOPQRSTUV
WXYZ$123456
7890(.,'"-;:)!?&

68 point

268

Futura Regular

The whole duty of typography, *as with calligraphy,* is to communicate to the imagination, without loss by the way, the thought or image intended to be communicated by the author. And the whole duty of beautiful typography is not to substitute for the beauty or interest of the thing thought and intended to be conveyed by the symbol, a beauty or interest of its own, but, on the one hand, to win access for that communication by the clearness and beauty of the vehicle, and on the other hand, to take advantage of every pause or stage in that communication to interpose some characteristic & restful beauty in its own art. We thus have a reason for the clearness and beauty of the first and introductory page and of the title, and for the especial beauty of the headings of chapters, capital or initial letters, and so on, and an opening for the illustrator as we shall see by and by. Further, in the case of poetry, verse, in

8/10

The whole duty of typography, *as with calligraphy,* is to communicate to the imagination, without loss by the way, the thought or image intended to be communicated by the author. And the whole duty of beautiful typography is not to substitute for the beauty or interest of the thing thought and intended to be conveyed by the symbol, a beauty or interest of its own, but, on the one hand, to win access for that communication by the clearness and beauty of the vehicle, and on the other hand, to take advantage of every pause or stage in that communication to interpose some characteristic & restful beauty in its own art. We thus have a reason for the clearness and beauty of the first and introductory page and of the title, and for

9/11

The whole duty of typography, *as with calligraphy,* is to communicate to the imagination, without loss by the way, the thought or image intended to be communicated by the author. And the whole duty of beautiful typography is not to substitute for the beauty or interest of the thing thought and intended to be conveyed by the symbol, a beauty or interest of its own, but, on the one hand, to win access for that communication by the clearness and beauty of the vehicle, and on the other hand, to take advantage of every pause or stage in that communication to interpose some characteristic

10/12

The whole duty of typography, *as with calligraphy,* is to communicate to the imagination, without loss by the way, the thought or image intended to be communicated by the author. And the whole duty of beautiful typography is not to substitute for the beauty or interest of the thing thought and intended to be conveyed by the symbol, a beauty or interest of its own, but, on the one hand,

12/14

The whole duty of typography, *as with calligraphy,* is to communicate to the imagination, without loss by the way, the thought or image intended to be communicated by the author. And the whole duty of beautiful typography is not to substitute for the beauty or interest of the thing thought and intended to be conveyed by the symbol, a beauty or interest of its own, but, on the one hand, to win access for that communication by the clearness and beauty of the vehicle, and on the other hand, to take advantage of every pause or stage in that communication to interpose some characteristic & restful beauty in its own art. We thus have a reason for the clearness and beauty of the first and introductory page and of the title, and for the especial beauty of the headings

8/12

The whole duty of typography, *as with calligraphy,* is to communicate to the imagination, without loss by the way, the thought or image intended to be communicated by the author. And the whole duty of beautiful typography is not to substitute for the beauty or interest of the thing thought and intended to be conveyed by the symbol, a beauty or interest of its own, but, on the one hand, to win access for that communication by the clearness and beauty of the vehicle, and on the other hand, to take advantage of every pause or stage in that communication to interpose some characteristic & restful

9/13

The whole duty of typography, *as with calligraphy,* is to communicate to the imagination, without loss by the way, the thought or image intended to be communicated by the author. And the whole duty of beautiful typography is not to substitute for the beauty or interest of the thing thought and intended to be conveyed by the symbol, a beauty or interest of its own, but, on the one hand, to win access for that communication by the clearness and beauty of the vehicle, and on the other hand, to take advantage of every pause or

10/14

The whole duty of typography, *as with calligraphy,* is to communicate to the imagination, without loss by the way, the thought or image intended to be communicated by the author. And the whole duty of beautiful typography is not to substitute for the beauty or interest of the thing thought and intended to be conveyed by the symbol, a beauty or

12/16

Akzidenz Grotesk

abcdefghijklmnopqrstuvwxyz
ABCDEFGHIJKLMNOPQRSTUVW
XYZ$1234567890(.,'"-;:)!?&

Akzidenz Grotesk Bold

abcdefghijklmnopqrstuvwxyz
ABCDEFGHIJKLMNOPQRSTUV
WXYZ$1234567890(.,'"-;:)!?&

Din Regular

abcdefghijklmnopqrstuvwxyz
ABCDEFGHIJKLMNOPQRSTUVWXY
Z$1234567890(.,'"-;:)!?&

Din Bold

abcdefghijklmnopqrstuvwxyz
ABCDEFGHIJKLMNOPQRSTUVWXY
Z$1234567890(.,'"-;:)!?&

Franklin Gothic Book

abcdefghijklmnopqrstuvwxyz
ABCDEFGHIJKLMNOPQRSTUVWXYZ
$1234567890(.,'"-;:)!?&

abcdefghijklmnopqrstuvwxyz
ABCDEFGHIJKLMNOPQRSTUVWXY
Z$1234567890(.,'"-;:)!?&

abcdefghijklmnopqrstuvwxyz
ABCDEFGHIJKLMNOPQRSTUVWX
YZ$1234567890(.,' "-;:)!?&

abcdefghijklmnopqrstuvwxyz
ABCDEFGHIJKLMNOPQRSTUV
WXYZ$1234567890(.,'"-;:)!?&

abcdefghijklmnopqrstuvwxyz
ABCDEFGHIJKLMNOPQRSTUVWXY
Z$1234567890(.,'"-;:)!?&

abcdefghijklmnopqrstuvwxyz
ABCDEFGHIJKLMNOPQRSTVWXY
Z$1234567890(.,'"-;:)!?&

P. VIRGILII MARONIS

GEORGICON.

LIBER SECUNDUS.

HACTENUS arvorum cultus, et fidera cœli:
Nunc te, Bacche, canam, nec non filveftria tecum
Virgulta, et prolem tarde crefcentis olivæ.
Huc, pater o Lenæe; (tuis hic omnia plena
5 Muneribus: tibi pampineo gravidus autumno
Floret ager; fpumat plenis vindemia labris)
Huc, pater o Lenæe, veni; nudataque mufto
Tinge novo mecum direptis crura cothurnis.
   Principio arboribus varia eft natura creandis:
10 Namque aliæ, nullis hominum cogentibus, ipfæ
Sponte fua veniunt, campofque et flumina late
Curva tenent: ut molle filer, lentæque geniftæ,
Populus, et glauca canentia fronde falicta.
Pars autem pofito furgunt de femine: ut altæ
15 Caftaneæ, nemorumque Jovi quæ maxima frondet
Aefculus, atque habitæ Graiis oracula quercus.
Pullulat ab radice aliis denfiffima filva:
Ut cerafis, ulmifque: etiam Parnaffia laurus
Parva fub ingenti matris fe fubjicit umbra.
20 Hos natura modos primum dedit: his genus omne
Silvarum, fruticumque viret, nemorumque facrorum.
Sunt alii, quos ipfe via fibi repperit ufus.
Hic plantas tenero abfcindens de corpore matrum

Depofuit

abcdefghijklmnopqrstuvwxyz
ABCDEFGHIJKLMNOPQ
RSTUVWXYZ$123456
7890(.,'''-;:)!?&

abcdefghijklmnop

qrstuvwxyz

ABCDEFGHIJKL

MNOPQRSTU

VWXYZ$123456

7890(.,'''-;:)!?&

Bookman Light

abcdefghijklmnopqrstuvwxyz
ABCDEFGHIJKLMNOPQRSTUVWXYZ
$1234567890(.,'"-;:)!?&

Bookman Demi

**abcdefghijklmnopqrstuvwxyz
ABCDEFGHIJKLMNOPQRSTUV
WXYZ$1234567890(.,'"-;:)!?&**

Cheltenham

abcdefghijklmnopqrstuvwxyz
ABCDEFGHIJKLMNOPQRSTUVWX
YZ$1234567890(.,'"-;:)!?&

Cheltenham Bold

**abcdefghijklmnopqrstuvwxyz
ABCDEFGHIJKLMNOPQRSTUVW
XYZ$1234567890(.,'"-;:)!?&**

Mrs Eaves Roman

abcdefghijklmnopqrstuvwxyz
ABCDEFGHIJKLMNOPQRSTUVWX
YZ$1234567890(.,'"-;:)!?&

Mrs Eaves Bold

Mrs Eaves Bold

abcdefghijklmnopqrstuvwxyz
ABCDEFGHIJKLMNOPQRSTUVW
XYZ$1234567890(.,'"-;:)!?&

Melior

abcdefghijklmnopqrstuvwxyz
ABCDEFGHIJKLMNOPQRSTUVW
XYZ$1234567890(.,' "-;:)!?&

Melior Bold

abcdefghijklmnopqrstuvwxyz
ABCDEFGHIJKLMNOPQRSTUV
WXYZ$1234567890(.,'"-;:)!?&

Plantin

abcdefghijklmnopqrstuvwxyz
ABCDEFGHIJKLMNOPQRSTU
VWXYZ$1234567890(.,'"-;:)!?&

Plantin Bold

abcdefghijklmnopqrstuvwxyz
ABCDEFGHIJKLMNOPQRS
TVWXYZ$1234567890(.,'"-

63.

Modern

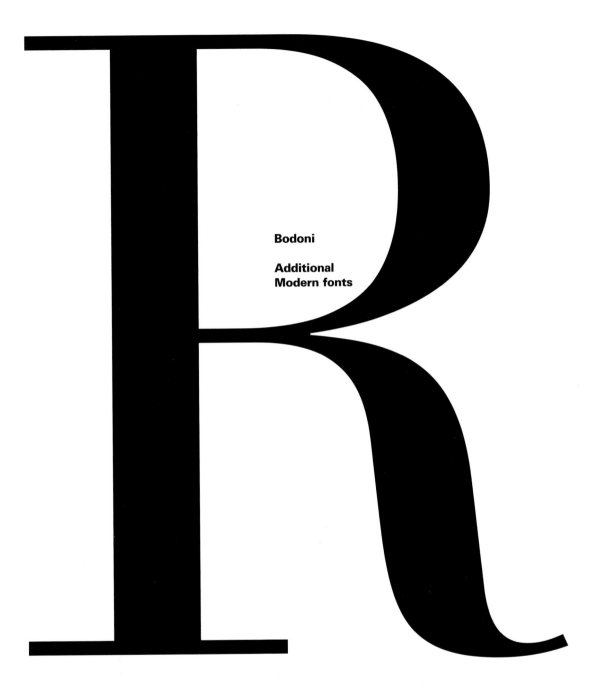

Bodoni

**Additional
Modern fonts**

4.
Page 250 from the *Manuale
Tipographico*, 1818.

The word *modern* is a relative term. Often, we use it interchangeably with the term *contemporary;* sometimes it is used to identify movements in the arts representing a radical break with tradition. In typographic design, *Modern* identifies typefaces of the late 1700s with flat, unbracketed serifs, extreme contrasts between thick-and-thin strokes, and geometric construction. The influence of writing and calligraphy upon type design was replaced by mathematical measurement and the use of mechanical instruments to construct letterforms.

After the death of type designer and printer Giambattista Bodoni, his widow and foreman published the *Manuale Tipographico,* displaying specimens of the approximately three hundred

type fonts designed by Bodoni. The page reproduced here in its actual size shows the dazzling contrasts and vigorous proportions found in Modern-style typefaces (Fig. **4**). Thick-and-thin oxford or scotch rules (see Fig. **17**, Chapter 3) echo and complement the letters' stroke weight.

Modern-style typefaces were widely used for book text type during the nineteenth century and have enjoyed continued acceptance for more than two centuries. Numerous variations – from extreme fineline versions to ultrabolds; and from very narrow, condensed fonts to wide, expanded letterforms – have been designed. Many contemporary fonts bear the names of eighteenth-century designers: Bodoni, Didot, and Walbaum.

283

This version was released
by the Bauer type foundry
in Germany in 1926.

abcdefghij

klmnopq

rstuvwxyz

$1234567

890(.,'''-;:)!?

130 point

ABCDEF
GHIJKL
MNOPQR
STUV
WXYZ&

130 point

285

abcdefghijklmnopqrstuvw
xyzABCDFGHIJKLMNO
PQRSTUVWXYZ$12345
67890(.,'"-;:)!?&

abcdefghijklmn

opqrstuvwxyz

ABCDEFGHIJK

LMNOPQRSTU

VWXYZ$1234

567890(.,'"-;:)!?&

abcdefghijklmnopqrstuvw
xyzABCDEFGHIJKLMNO
PQRSTUVWXYZ1234567
890(.,'"-;:)!?&

27 point

abcdefghijklmno

pqrstuvwxyz

ABCDEFGHIJK

LMNOPQRSTU

VWXYZ$12345

67890(.,'"-;:)!?&

81 point

abcdefghijklmnopqrstuvw
xyzABCDFGHIJKLMNOP
QRSTUVWXYZ$12345678
90(.,'"-;:)!?&

abcdefghijklmn
opqrstuvwxyz
ABCDEFGHIJK
LMNOPQRSTU
VWXYZ$12345
67890(.,'"-;:!)?&

Bauer Bodoni
Regular

abcdefghijklmnopqrstuvwxyz
ABCDEFGHIJKLMNOPQRSTUVWXYZ
$1234567890(.,'"-:;!)?&
abcdefghijklmnopqrstuvwxyz
ABCDEFGHIJKLMNOPQRSTUVWXYZ
$1234567890(.,'"-:;)!?&

8 point

abcdefghijklmnopqrstuvwxyz
ABCDEFGHIJKLMNOPQRSTUVWXYZ
$1234567890(.,'"-:;)!?&
abcdefghijklmnopqrstuvwxyz
ABCDEFGHIJKLMNOPQRSTUVWXYZ
$1234567890(.,'"-:;)!?&

9 point

abcdefghijklmnopqrstuvwxyz
ABCDEFGHIJKLMNOPQRSTUVWXYZ
$1234567890(.,'"-:;)!?&
abcdefghijklmnopqrstuvwxyz
ABCDEFGHIJKLMNOPQRSTUVWXYZ
$1234567890(.,'"-:;)!?&

10 point

abcdefghijklmnopqrstuvwxyz
ABCDEFGHIJKLMNOPQRSTUVWXYZ
$1234567890(.,'"-:;)!?&
abcdefghijklmnopqrstuvwxyz
ABCDEFGHIJKLMNOPQRSTUVWXYZ
$1234567890(.,'"-:;)!?&

12 point

The whole duty of typography, *as with calligraphy,* is to communicate to the imagination, without loss by the way, the thought or image intended to be communicated by the author. And the whole duty of beautiful typography is not to substitute for the beauty or interest of the thing thought and intended to be conveyed by the symbol, a beauty or interest of its own, but, on the one hand, to win access for that communication by the clearness and beauty of the vehicle, and on the other hand, to take advantage of every pause or stage in that communication to interpose some characteristic & restful beauty in its own art. We thus have a reason for the clearness and beauty of the first and introductory page and of the title, and for the especial beauty of the headings of chapters, capital or initial letters, and so on, and an opening for the illustrator as we shall see by and by.
8/10

The whole duty of typography, *as with calligraphy,* is to communicate to the imagination, without loss by the way, the thought or image intended to be communicated by the author. And the whole duty of beautiful typography is not to substitute for the beauty or interest of the thing thought and intended to be conveyed by the symbol, a beauty or interest of its own, but, on the one hand, to win access for that communication by the clearness and beauty of the vehicle, and on the other hand, to take advantage of every pause or stage in that communication to interpose some characteristic & restful beauty in its own art. We thus have a reason for the clearness and beauty of the first and introductory page and of the title, and for the especial
8/12

The whole duty of typography, *as with calligraphy,* is to commu nicate to the imagination, without loss by the way, the thought or image intended to be communicated by the author. And the whole duty of beautiful typography is not to substitute for the beauty or interest of the thing thought and intended to be conveyed by the symbol, a beauty or interest of its own, but, on the one hand, to win access for that communication by the clearness and beauty of the vehicle, and on the other hand, to take advantage of every pause or stage in that communication to interpose some characteristic & restful beauty in its own art. We thus have a reason for the clearness and beauty of the first and introductory page and of the title, and
9/11

The whole duty of typography, *as with calligraphy,* is to commu nicate to the imagination, without loss by the way, the thought or image intended to be communicated by the author. And the whole duty of beautiful typography is not to substitute for the beauty or interest of the thing thought and intended to be conveyed by the symbol, a beauty or interest of its own, but, on the one hand, to win access for that communication by the clearness and beauty of the vehicle, and on the other hand, to take advantage of every pause or stage in that communication to interpose some characteristic &
9/13

The whole duty of typography, *as with calligraphy,* is to communicate to the imagination, without loss by the way, the thought or image intended to be communicated by the author. And the whole duty of beautiful typography is not to substitute for the beauty or interest of the thing thought and intended to be conveyed by the symbol, a beauty or interest of its own, but, on the one hand, to win access for that communication by the clearness and beauty of the vehicle, and on the other hand, to take advantage of every pause or stage in that communication to interpose some characteristic
10/12

The whole duty of typography, *as with calligraphy,* is to communicate to the imagination, without loss by the way, the thought or image intended to be communicated by the author. And the whole duty of beautiful typography is not to substitute for the beauty or interest of the thing thought and intended to be conveyed by the symbol, a beauty or interest of its own, but, on the one hand, to win access for that communication by the clearness and beauty of the vehicle, and on the other hand, to take advantage of every pause or
10/14

The whole duty of typography, *as with calligraphy,* is to communicate to the imagination, without loss by the way, the thought or image intended to be com municated by the author. And the whole duty of beautiful typography is not to substitute for the beau ty or interest of the thing thought and intended to be conveyed by the symbol, a beauty or interest of its own, but, on the one hand, to win access for that
12/14

The whole duty of typography, *as with calligraphy,* is to communicate to the imagination, without loss by the way, the thought or image intended to be com municated by the author. And the whole duty of beautiful typography is not to substitute for the beau ty or interest of the thing thought and intended to be conveyed by the symbol, a beauty or interest of its own, but, on the one hand, to win access for that
12/16

289

Bodoni Book

abcdefghijklmnopqrstuvwxyz
ABCDEFGHIJKLMNOPQRSTUVWXYZ$
1234567890(.,'"-;:)!?&

Bodoni Bold

abcdefghijklmnopqrstuvwxyz
ABCDEFGHIJKLMNOPQRSTUVW
XYZ$1234567890(.,'"-;:)!?&

Bodoni Poster

abcdefghijklmnopqrstuvwxyzA
BCDEFGHIJKLMNOPQRSTUVW
XYZ$1234567890(.,'"-;:)!?&

ITC Century Light

abcdefghijklmnopqrstuvwxyz
ABCDEFGHIJKLMNOPQRSTUVW
XYZ$1234567890(.,'"-;:)!?&

ITC Century Book

abcdefghijklmnopqrstuvwxyz
ABCDEFGHIJKLMNOPQRSTUVWXYZ
$1234567890(.,'"-;:)!?&

abcdefghijklmnopqrstuvwxyz
ABCDEFGHIJKLMNOPQRSTUV
WXYZ$1234567890(.,' "-;:)!?&

abcdefghijklmnopqrstuvwxyz
ABCDEFGHIJKLMNOPQRSTUV
WXYZ$1234567890(.,'"-;:)!?&

abcdefghijklmnopqrstuvwxyz
ABCDEFGHIJKLMNOPQRSTUV
WXYZ$1234567890(.,'"-;:)!?&

abcdefghijklmnopqrstuvwxyz
ABCDEFGHIJKLMNOPQRSTUVWXYZ$123456
7890(.,'"-;:)!?&

abcdefghijklmnopqrstuvwxyz
ABCDEFGHIJKLMNOPQRSTVWXYZ
$1234567890(.,'"-;:)!?&

NEW LINE BETWEEN
ALBANY & NEWBURG

LANDING AT

Hamburgh, Marlborough, Milton, Poughkeepsie, Hyde Park, Kingston, Rhinebeck, Barrytown, Redhook, Bristol, Westcamp Catskill, Hudson, Coxsackie, Stuyvesant, Baltimore & Coeymans.

On and after MONDAY, October 15th,

The Superior Low Pressure Steamer

ST. NICHOLAS

CAPTAIN WILSON,

Will run as a Passage and Freight Boat between Newburgh and Albany, leaving Newburgh

MONDAYS, WEDNESDAYS & FRIDAYS

AT SEVEN O'CLOCK A.M.,

And ALBANY on Tuesdays, Thursdays & Saturdays, at half-past 9 o'clock A.M.

Albany, Oct. 9th, 1849.

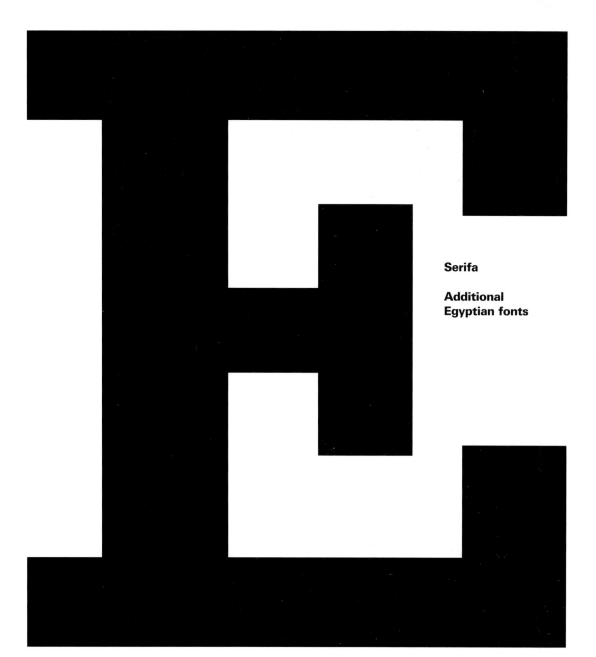

Egyptian

Serifa

**Additional
Egyptian fonts**

5.
Broadsheet, 1849. This slab-serif display type has been lightly inked, and the textured grain of the wooden type is clearly visible, as in the words *St. Nicholas.*

Egyptian or slab-serif typefaces first appeared in the early nineteenth century and enjoyed great popularity. Their bold, machinelike qualities offered a dynamic expression of the industrial age. During the Industrial Revolution, letterpress printers delighted in using bold slab-serif display fonts to give their messages graphic impact (Fig. **5**). Rectangular serifs, uniform or almost uniform stroke weight, and geometric letterform construction give Egyptian typefaces a bold, abstract quality. Egyptian styles whose abrupt right-angle joinery is tempered by curved bracketing include the Clarendon, Century, and Cheltenham type families.

Serifa was designed Adrian
Frutiger in 1966.

abcdefghi

jklmnopqr

stuvwxyz

$12345678

90(.,'"-;:)!?

ABCDEF
GHIJKL
MNOPQR
STUVWX
YZ&

abcdefghijklmnopqrstu
vwxyzABCDEFGHIJKL
MNOPQRSTUVWXYZ
$1234567890(.,'''-;:)!?&

abcdefghijklmn

opqrstuvwxyz

ABCDEFGHIJK

LMNOPQRSTU

VWXYZ$123456

7890(.,'''-;:)!?&

Serifa Roman

abcdefghijklmnopqrstuvwxyz
ABCDEFGHIJKLMNOPQRSTUVWXYZ
$1234567890(.,'"-;:)!?&
abcdefghijklmnopqrstuvwxyz
ABCDEFGHIJKLMNOPQRSTUVWXYZ
$1234567890(.,'"-;:)!?&

abcdefghijklmnopqrstuvwxyz
ABCDEFGHIJKLMNOPQRSTUVWXYZ
$1234567890(.,'"-;:)!?&
abcdefghijklmnopqrstuvwxyz
ABCDEFGHIJKLMNOPQRSTUVWXYZ
$1234567890(.,'"-;:)!?&

abcdefghijklmnopqrstuvwxyz
ABCDEFGHIJKLMNOPQRSTUVWXYZ$
1234567890(.,'"-;:)!?&
abcdefghijklmnopqrstuvwxyz
ABCDEFGHIJKLMNOPQRSTUVWXYZ$
1234567890(.,'"-;:)!?&

abcdefghijklmnopqrstuvwxyz
ABCDEFGHIJKLMNOPQRSTUVWXY
Z$1234567890(.,'"-;:)!?&
abcdefghijklmnopqrstuvwxyz
ABCDEFGHIJKLMNOPQRSTUVWXY
Z$1234567890(.,'"-;:)!?&

The whole duty of typography, *as with calligraphy,* is to communicate to the imagination, without loss by the way, the thought or image intended to be communicated by the author. And the whole duty of beautiful typography is not to substitute for the beauty or interest of the thing thought and intended to be conveyed by the symbol, a beauty or interest of its own, but, on the one hand, to win access for that communication by the clearness and beauty of the vehicle, and on the other hand, to take advantage of every pause or stage in that communication to interpose some characteristic & restful beauty in its own art. We thus have a reason for the clearness and beauty of the first and introductory page and of the title, and for the especial beauty of the headings of chapters,

8/10

The whole duty of typography, *as with calligraphy,* is to communicate to the imagination, without loss by the way, the thought or image intended to be communicated by the author. And the whole duty of beautiful typography is not to substitute for the beauty or interest of the thing thought and intended to be conveyed by the symbol, a beauty or interest of its own, but, on the one hand, to win access for that communication by the clearness and beauty of the vehicle, and on the other hand, to take advantage of every pause or stage in that communication to interpose some characteristic & restful beauty in its own art. We thus have a reason for the clearness

8/12

The whole duty of typography, *as with calligraphy,* is to communicate to the imagination, without loss by the way, the thought or image intended to be communicated by the author. And the whole duty of beautiful typography is not to substitute for the beauty or interest of the thing thought and intended to be conveyed by the symbol, a beauty or interest of its own, but, on the one hand, to win access for that communication by the clearness and beauty of the vehicle, and on the other hand, to take advantage of every pause or stage in that communication to interpose some characteristic & restful beauty in its own art. We thus have

9/11

The whole duty of typography, *as with calligraphy,* is to communicate to the imagination, without loss by the way, the thought or image intended to be communicated by the author. And the whole duty of beautiful typography is not to substitute for the beauty or interest of the thing thought and intended to be conveyed by the symbol, a beauty or interest of its own, but, on the one hand, to win access for that communication by the clearness and beauty of the vehicle, and on the other hand, to take advantage of every pause or

9/13

The whole duty of typography, *as with calligraphy,* is to communicate to the imagination, without loss by the way, the thought or image intended to be communicated by the author. And the whole duty of beautiful typography is not to substitute for the beauty or interest of the thing thought and intended to be conveyed by the symbol, a beauty or interest of its own, but, on the one hand, to win access for that communication by the clearness and beauty of the vehicle, and on the other hand, to take advantage of

10/12

The whole duty of typography, *as with calligraphy,* is to communicate to the imagination, without loss by the way, the thought or image intended to be communicated by the author. And the whole duty of beautiful typography is not to substitute for the beauty or interest of the thing thought and intended to be conveyed by the symbol, a beauty or interest of its own, but, on the one hand, to win access for that communication by the clearness and beauty of the

10/14

The whole duty of typography, *as with calligraphy,* is to communicate to the imagination, without loss by the way, the thought or image intended to be communicated by the author. And the whole duty of beautiful typography is not to substitute for the beauty or interest of the thing thought and intended to be conveyed by the symbol, a

12/14

The whole duty of typography, *as with calligraphy,* is to communicate to the imagination, without loss by the way, the thought or image intended to be communicated by the author. And the whole duty of beautiful typography is not to substitute for the beauty or interest of the

12/16

City Light

abcdefghijklmnopqrstuvwxyz
ABCDEFGHIJKLMNOPQRSTUVWXYZ$123
4567890(.,'"-;:)!?&

City Bold

abcdefghijklmnopqrstuvwxyz
ABCDEFGHIJKLMNOPQRSTUVWXYZ
$1234567890(.,'"-;:)!?&

Clarendon

abcdefghijklmnopqrstuvwxyz
ABCDEFGHIJKLMNOPQRSTU
VWXYZ$1234567890(.,'"-;:)!?&

Clarendon Bold

abcdefghijklmnopqrstuvwxyz
ABCDEFGHIJKLMNOPQRSTU
VWXYZ$1234567890(.,'"-;:)!?&

Memphis Light

abcdefghijklmnopqrstuvwxyz
ABCDEFGHIJKLMNOPQRSTUVW
XYZ$1234567890(.,'"-;:)!?&

abcdefghijklmnopqrstuvwxyz
ABCDEFGHIJKLMNOPQRSTUVW
XYZ$1234567890(.,'"-;:)!?&

abcdefghijklmnopqrstuvwxyz
ABCDEFGHIJKLMNOPQRSTUV
WXYZ$1234567890(.,'"-;:)!?&

abcdefghijklmnopqrstuvwxyz
ABCDEFGHIJKLMNOPQRSTUVWXY
Z$1234567890(.,'"-;:)!?&

abcdefghijklmnopqrstuvwxyz
ABCDEFGHIJKLMNOPQRSTUV
WXYZ$1234567890(.,'"-;:)!?&

abcdefghijklmnopqrstuvwxyz
ABCDEFGHIJKLMNOPQRSTU
VWXYZ$1234567890(.,'"-;:)!?&

Typefaces that often defy historical classification are sometimes called decorative or novelty typefaces. Most often these are used as display types or as text when appropriate. These typefaces provide context for typographic messages, adding visual accent and charisma.

Anonymous (Designer: Mark Simonson)

abcdefghijklmnopqrstuvwxyz
ABCDEFGHIJKLMNOPQRSTUVWXY
Z$1234567890(.,'"-;:)!?&

Glas (Designer: AtelierMAChauer)

abcdefghijklmnopqrstuvwxyz
ABCDEFGHIJKLMNOPQRSTUV
WXYZ$1234567890(.,-;:)!?&

Maus (Designer: James Arboghast)

ABCDEFGHIJKLMNOPQRSTUVW
XYZABCDEFGHIJKLMNOPQRSTU
VWXYZ$1234567890(.,)!?&

Montessori Script (Designer: Stefan Hattenbach)

abcdefghijklmnopqrstuvwxyz
ABCDEFGHIJKLMNOPQRSTUV
WXYZ$1234567890(.,'"-;:)!?&

Morpheus (Designer: Eric Oehler)

ABCDEFGHIJKLMNOPQRSTUVWXYZ
ABCDEFGHIJKLMNOPQRSTUV
WXYZ$1234567890(.,"'-;:)!?&

Mosaico (Designer: Alexjandro Paul)

abcdefghijklmnopqrstuvwxyz
ABCDEFGHIJKLMNOPQRSTUVWXYZ$1234
567890(.,;:)!?&

Overwork (Designer: Bagel & Co.)

abcdefghijklmnopqrstuvwxyz
ABCDEFGHIJKLMNOPQRSTUV
WXYZ$1234567890(.,—;:)!?&

Plexifont BV (Designer: Jess Latham)

ABCDEFGHIJKLMNOPQRS
TUVWXYZ
$1234567890!?

Torn Univers (Designer: Matt Gardner)

abcdefghijklmnopqrstuvwxyz
ABCDEFGHIJKLMNOPQRS
TUVWXYZ$1234567890

A.A. Abbreviation for "author's alteration," used to flag a mistake or correction by the author.

ABA form. Design principle of form interrelationships, involving repetition and contrast.

Accents. Small marks over, under, or through a letterform, indicating specific punctuation or changes in stress.

Agate. Vertical unit used to measure space in newspaper columns, originally five-and-one-half point type. Fourteen agate lines equal approximately one inch.

Alert box. A message box that appears on a computer screen with information for the user, for example, a "bomb message" when a computer crashes.

Alignment. Precise arrangement of letterforms upon an imaginary horizontal or vertical line.

Alphabet length. Horizontal measure of the lowercase alphabet in a type font, used to approximate the horizontal measure of type set in that font.

Ampersand. Typographic character (&) representing the word *and.*

Anti-aliasing. The blurring of a jagged line or edge on a screen or output device to give the appearance of a smooth line. Application program. Computer software used to create and modify documents.

Area composition. The organization of typographic and other graphic elements into their final positions by electronic means (keyboard, graphics tablets, and electronic pens, etc.), eliminating the need for hand assembly or pasteup.

Ascender. Stroke on a lowercase letter that rises above the mean-line.

ASCII code. Abbreviation for American Standard Code of Information Interchange. The numbers 0 through 127 represent the alphanumeric characters and functions on the keyboard.

Aspect ratio. The ratio of an image, screen, or other medium's height to its width. Images will become distorted if forced into a different aspect ratio during enlargement, reduction, or transfers.

Autoflow. A page-layout program setting for placing blocks of text from page to page without operator intervention.

Autopaging, Automatic pagination. A capability in computer typesetting for dividing text into pages. Advanced autopaging can add page numbers and running heads, and avoid awkward widows and orphans.

Auto-runaround, Automatic runaround. A page-layout program feature that flows text smoothly around graphics or headlines placed within the normal text area.

Base alignment. A typesetter or printer specification that the baseline for all letters should be horizontal, even in a line of mixed sizes or styles; also called baseline alignment.

Baseline. An imaginary horizontal line upon which the base of each capital letter rests.

Baud rate. The number of bits per second, often used as a measure of data transmission; for example, by a modem.

Bezier curves. A type of curve with nonuniform arcs, as opposed to curves with uniform curvature, which are called arcs. A Bezier curve is defined by specifying control points that set the shape of the curve, and are used to create letter shapes and other computer graphics.

Binary code. Number system using two digits: zero and one.

Bit. Contraction of binary digit, which is the smallest unit of information that a computer can hold. The value of a bit (1 or 0) represents a two-way choice, such as yes or no, on or off, positive or negative.

Bitmap. A computerized image made up of dots. These are "mapped" onto the screen directly from corresponding bits in memory (hence the name). Also referred to as paint format.

Bitmapped font. A font whose letters are composed of dots, such as fonts designed for dot-matrix printers. Compare *outline font* and *screen font.*

Body size. Depth of a piece of metal type, usually measured in points.

Body type. Text material, usually set in sizes from 6 to 12 points. Also called text type.

Boldface. Type with thicker, heavier strokes than the regular font. Indicated as "BF" in type specifications.

Boot. A computer's start-up procedures; coined from "pulling yourself up by your bootstraps."

Bounding box. In drawing or page-description languages, a bounding box is an imaginary box within which an image is located. It represents the rectangular area needed to create the image.

Byte. Unit of computer information. The number of bits used to represent a character. For personal computers, a byte is usually eight bits.

Backslant. Letterforms having a diagonal slant to the left.

C. and l.c. Used in marking copy, to instruct the typesetter to use capitals and lowercase.

C. and s.c. Used in marking copy, to instruct the typesetter to use capitals and small capitals.

Camera ready (or camera-ready copy). Copy and/or artwork that is ready to be photographed to make negatives, which are exposed to printing plates.

Cap height. Height of the capital letters, measured from the baseline to the capline.

Capline. Imaginary horizontal line defined by the height of the capital letters.

Capitals. Letters larger than – and often differing from – the corresponding lowercase letters. Also called uppercase.

Caps. See *Capitals.*

Caption. Title, explanation, or description accompanying an illustration or photograph.

Cascading style sheets. Web-site design software permitting the specification of type characteristics such as type size, letter-, and line-spacing.

Casting off. Determining the length of manuscript copy, enabling a calculation of the area that type will occupy when set in a given size and style of type.

Cathode ray tube (CRT). An electronic tube with a phosphorescent surface that produces a glowing image when activated by an electronic beam.

CD-ROM. An optical data storage device; initials for compact disk read-only memory.

Central processing unit (CPU). Computer component that controls all other parts, performs logical operations, and stores information.

Character. Symbol, sign, or mark in a language system.
Character count. The number of characters in a block of text. In typography, spaces are counted but other nonprinting characters usually are not. In data processing, both printing and nonprinting characters are usually counted.

Chase. Heavy metal frame into which metal type is locked for proofing or printing.

Chip. A small piece of silicon impregnated with impurities that form miniaturized computer circuits.

Chooser. Software that tells a computer which output device and connection port to use.

Cicero. European typographic unit of measure, approximately equal to the American pica.

Clipboard. A computer's "holding place," a buffer area in memory for the last material to be cut or copied from a document. Information on the clipboard can be inserted (pasted) into documents.

Cold type. Type that is set by means other than casting molten metal. A term most frequently used to indicate strike-on composition rather than photo or digital typesetting.

Colophon. Inscription, frequently placed at the end of a book, that contains facts about its production.

Column guide. Nonprinting lines that define the location of columns of type.

Command. The generic name for an order or instruction to a computer.

Command character. The combination of a command key plus character(s) used to instruct a computer to take an action.

Comp. See *Comprehensive layout.*

Compensation. In visual organization, the counter-balancing of elements.

Composing stick. Adjustable handheld metal tray, used to hold handset type as it is being composed.

Composition. Alternate term for typesetting.

Compositor. Person who sets type.

Comprehensive layout. An accurate representation of a printed piece showing all type and pictures in their size and position. Comps are used to evaluate a design before producing final type and artwork.

Computer. Electronic device that performs predefined (programmed) high-speed mathematical or logical calculations.

Condensed. Letterforms whose horizontal width has been compressed.

Consonance. In design, harmonious interaction between elements.

Copyfitting. Calculating the area that will be occupied by a given manuscript when set in a specified size and style of type.

Counter. Space enclosed by the strokes of a letterform.

Counterform. "Negative" spatial areas defined and shaped by letterforms, including both interior counters and spaces between characters.

CPS. Characters per inch.

CPU. See *Central processing unit.*

CRT. See *Cathode ray tube.*

CSS. See *Cascading style sheets.*

Cursive. Type styles that imitate handwriting, often with letters that do not connect.

Cursor. Term for the pointer or insertion point on a computer screen.

Cut and paste. To move material from one location to another within a document, or from one document to another. This is a computer's electronic equivalent to clipping something with scissors, then using glue to paste the clipping in another location.

Cutoff rules. Rules used to separate pages into various units, such as advertisements or news stories.

Daisy wheel. Strike-on printing wheel containing relief characters on spokes, radiating from a central disk. As the wheel spins, a hammer impacts the characters against an inked ribbon.

Data. Information, particularly information upon which a computer program is based.

Data bank. Mass storage of large quantities of information, indexed for rapid retrieval.

Data processing. The storing and handling of information by a computer.

Data transmission. Rapid electronic transfer of coded data via telephone or other communication links.

Dazzle. Visual effect caused by extreme contrast in the strokes of letterforms.

Default. A value, action, or setting that a computer system assumes, unless the user gives an explicit instruction to the contrary; for example, a certain point size and typeface style will be used by a page-layout program unless the user selects another size and font.

Descender. Stroke on a lowercase letterform that falls below the baseline.

Desktop. Refers to the desktop metaphor depicted on the computer screen, with a menu bar across the top, icons for applications and disk drives, and other icons, such as a trash can used to throw away unwanted material.

Desktop publishing. The popular use of this term is incorrect, because publishing encompasses writing, editing, designing, printing, and distribution activities, not just makeup and production. See *Electronic page design.*

Dialog box. A box displayed on a computer screen requesting information or a decision by the user.

Digital type. Type stored electronically as digital dot or stroke patterns rather than as photographic images.

Digitizer. A computer peripheral device that converts images or sound into a digital signal.

Directory. The contents of a computer disk or folder. Directory contents can be arranged and displayed on a screen by name, icon, date created, size, or kind, etc.

Digital computer. A device that translates data into a discrete number system to facilitate electronic processing.

Disk. Thin, flat, circular plate with a magnetic surface upon which data may be stored. See *Floppy disk* and *Hard disk.* Also, a circular grid containing the master font in some typesetting systems.

Display Postscript. A technology by Adobe Systems that allows PostScript commands (for special graphic effects) to be displayed on the screen.

Display type. Type sizes 14 points and above, used primarily for headlines and titles.

Dissonance. In design, visual tension and contrast between typographic elements.

Dithering. A technique for alternating the value of adjacent dots or pixels to create the effect of an intermediate value.

Line breaks. The relationships of line endings in a ragged-right or ragged-left setting. Rhythmic line breaks are achieved by adjusting the length of individual lines of type.

Line length. The measure of the length of a line of type, usually expressed in picas.

Linespacing. The vertical distance between two lines of type measured from baseline to baseline. For example, "10/12" indicates 10-point type with 12 points base-to-base (that is, with 2 points of leading). See *Leading, Interline spacing.*

Lining figures. Numerals identical in size to the capitals and aligned on the baseline: 1 2 3 4 5 6 7 8 9 10.

Linotype. A machine that casts an entire line of raised type on a single metal slug.

Local area network (LAN). A network of computers and peripherals, usually in the same office or building, connected by dedicated electrical cables rather than telephone lines.

Logotype. Two or more type characters that are combined as a sign or trademark.

Lowercase. The alphabet set of small letters, as opposed to capitals.

LPM. Lines per minute, a unit of measure expressing the speed of a typesetting system.

Ludlow. A typecasting machine that produces individual letters from hand-assembled matrices.

Machine composition. General term for the mechanical casting of metal type.

Majuscules. A term in calligraphy for letterforms analogous to uppercase letterforms, usually drawn between two parallel lines, the capline and the baseline. See *Minuscules.*

Makeup. The assembly of typographic matter into a page, or a sequence of pages, ready for printing.

Margin. The unprinted space surrounding type matter on a page.

Markup. The marking of typesetting specifications upon manuscript copy.

Marquee. A rectangular area, often surrounded by blinking dashed or dotted lines, used to select objects or regions in a application program.

Master page. In a page-layout program, a master page is a template providing standard columns, margins, and typographic elements that appear on a publication's individual pages.

Masthead. The visual identification of a magazine or newspaper, usually a logotype. Also a section placed near the front of a newspaper or periodical containing information such as names and titles of publishers and staff, along with addresses.

Matrix. In typesetting, the master image from which type is produced. The matrix is a brass mold in linecasting and a glass plate bearing the font negative in phototypesetting.

Meanline. An imaginary line marking the tops of lowercase letters, not including the ascenders.

Measure. See *Line length.*

Mechanical. A camera-ready pasteup of artwork including type, images showing position of color and halftone matter, line art, etc., all on one piece of artboard.

Megabyte (MB). A unit of measurement equal to 1024 kilobytes or 1,048,576 bytes.

Megahertz (MHz). A million cycles per second. Describes the speed of computer chips; used to measure of how rapidly a computer processes information.

Menu. A list of choices in a computer application, from which the user selects a desired action. In a computer's desktop interface, menus appear when you point to and click on menu titles in the menu bar. Dragging through a menu and releasing the mouse button while a command is highlighted chooses that command.

Menu bar. A horizontal band across the top of a computer screen that contains menu titles.

Message box. A box that appears on a computer screen to give the user information.

Microprocessor. A single silicon chip containing thousands of electronic components for processing information; the "brains" of a personal computer.

Minuscules. A term in calligraphy for letterforms analogous to lowercase letters and usually drawn between four parallel lines determining ascender height, x-height, baseline, and descender depth. See *Majuscules.*

Minus spacing. A reduction of interline spacing, resulting in a baseline-to-baseline measurement that is smaller than the point size of the type.

Mixing. The alignment of more than one type style or typeface on a single baseline.

Modem. Contraction of modulator/demodulator; a peripheral device to send data over telephone lines from a computer to other computers, service bureaus, and information services, etc.

Modern. Term used to describe typefaces designed at the end of the eighteenth century. Characteristics include vertical stress, hairline serifs, and pronounced contrasts between thick and thin strokes.

Monocase alphabet. A language alphabet, such as Hebrew and Indic scripts, having only capital-height letters and no lowercase letterforms.

Monochrome. Refers to material or a display consisting of a single color, typically black or white.

Monogram. Two or more letterforms interwoven, combined, or connected into a single glyph, typically used as abbreviations or initials.

Monoline. Used to describe a typeface or letterform with a uniform stroke thickness.

Monospacing. Spacing in a font with characters that all have the same set width or horizontal measure; often found in typewriter and screen fonts. See *Proportional spacing.*

Monotype. A trade name for a keyboard-operated typesetting machine that casts individual letters from matrices.

Mouse. A small computer device that controls an on-screen pointer or tool when the mouse is moved around on a flat surface by hand. The mouse-controlled pointer can select operations, move data, and draw images.

Multifinder. A computer program permitting several applications to be open at the same time, so that a designer can work back and forth between page-layout and drawing programs, for example, without having to repeatedly open and close programs.

Navigation. The act of manually moving a cursor through an on-screen page or series of pages.

Negative. The reversal of a positive photographic image.

Network. A system connecting multiple computers so they can share printers and information, etc.

Object-oriented. A method in drawing and other computer programs that produces graphics from arc and line segments that are mathematically defined by points located on the horizontal and vertical axes on the screen.

Oblique. A slanted roman character. Unlike many italics, oblique characters do not have cursive design properties.

Offset lithography. A printing method using flat photo-mechanical plates, in which the inked image is transferred or offset from the printing plate onto a rubber blanket, then onto the paper.

Old Style. Typeface styles derived from fifteenth- to eighteenth-century designs, and characterized by moderate thick-and-thin contrasts, bracketed serifs, and a handwriting influence.

Old Style figures. Numerals that exhibit a variation in size, including characters aligning with the lowercase x-height, and others with ascenders or descenders: 1 2 3 4 5 6 7 8 9 10.

Operating system. A computer program that controls a computer's operation, directing information to and from different components.

Optical adjustment. The precise visual alignment and spacing of typographic elements. In interletter spacing, the adjustment of individual characters to achieve consistent spacing.

Orphan. A single word on a line, left over at the end of a paragraph, sometimes appearing at the top of a column of text. See *Widow.*

Outline font. A font designed, not as a bitmap, but as outlines of the letter shapes that can be scaled to any size. Laser printers and imagesetters use outline fonts. See *Bitmapped font* and *Screen font.*

Outline type. Letterforms described by a contour line that encloses the entire character on all sides. The interior usually remains open.

Output. The product of a computer operation. In computerized typesetting, output is reproduction proofs of composition.

Page preview. A mode on many word-processing and page-layout programs that shows a full-page view of what the page will look like when printed, including added elements such as headers, footers, and margins.

Pagination. The sequential numbering of pages.

Paint program. A computer application that creates images as a series of bitmapped dots, which can be erased and manipulated by turning the pixels on and off. Compare *Draw program.*

Pantone Matching System (PMS). The trademarked name of a system for specifying colors and inks that is a standard in the printing industry.

Paragraph mark. Typographic elements that signal the beginning of a paragraph. For example, ¶.

Parallel construction. In typography, the use of similar typographic elements or arrangements to create a visual unity or to convey a relationship in content.

Paste. To place a copy of saved material into a computer-generated document or layout.

P.E. Abbreviation for "Printer's Error," used to flag a mistake made by the compositor rather than by the author.

Pen plotter. A printer that draws using ink-filled pens that are moved along a bar, which also moves back and forth. Many plotters have very high resolutions but have slow operation, poor text quality, and poor handling of raster images.

Peripheral. An electronic device that connects to a computer, such as a disk drive, scanner, or printer.

Photocomposition. The process of setting type by projecting light onto light-sensitive film or paper.

Photodisplay typesetting. The process of setting headline type on film or paper by photographic means.

Phototype. Type matter set on film or paper by photographic projection of type characters.

Photounit. Output component of a photocomposition system, which sets the type and exposes it to light-sensitive film or paper.

Pica. Typographic unit of measurement: 12 points equal 1 pica. 6 picas equal approximately one inch. Line lengths and column widths are measured in picas.

PICT. A computer format for encoding pictures. PICT data can be created, displayed on the screen, and printed, thus enabling applications without graphics-processing routines to incorporate PICT data generated by other software.

Pixel. Stands for picture element; the smallest dot that can be displayed on a screen.

Point. A measure of size used principally in typesetting. One point is equal to 1/12 of a pica, or approximately 1/72 of an inch. It is most often used to indicate the size of type or amount of leading added between lines.

Pointer. A graphic form that moves on a computer screen and is controlled by a pointing device; usually a symbolic icon such as an arrow, I-beam, or clock.

Pointing device. A computer input device, such as a mouse, tablet, or joystick, used to indicate where an on-screen pointer or tool should be placed or moved.

Port. An electrical socket where cables are inserted to connect computers, peripheral devices, or networks. Ports are named for the type of signal they carry, such as printer port, serial port, or SCSI port.

PostScript.™ A page-description programming language created by Adobe Systems that handles text and graphics, placing them on the page with mathematical precision.

Preview. To view the final output on a computer screen before printing. Because most screens have lower resolution than an imagesetter or laser printer, fine details are often different from the final output.

Processor. In a computer system, the general term for any device capable of carrying out operations upon data. In phototypography, the unit that automatically develops the light-sensitive paper or film.

Program. A sequence of instructions that directs the operations of a computer to execute a given task.

Proof. Traditionally, an impression from metal type for examination and correction; now applies to initial output for examination and correction before final output.

Proportional spacing. Spacing in a font adjusted to give wide letters (M) a larger set width than narrow letters (I).

Quad. In metal type, pieces of type metal shorter than type-high, which are used as spacing matter to separate elements and fill out lines.

Quoins. Wedges use to lock up metal type in the chase. These devices are tightened and loosened by a quoin key.

Ragged. See *Unjustified type.*

RAM. Abbreviation for *random access memory,* the area of a computer's memory that temporarily stores applications and documents while they are being used.

RAM cache. An area of the computer's memory set aside to hold information from a disk until it is needed again. It can be accessed much more quickly from a RAM cache than from a disk.

Raster display. A raster image is divided into scan lines, each consisting of a series of dots from a thin section of the final image. This dot pattern corresponds exactly to a bit pattern in the computer memory.

Raster image file format (RIFF). A file format for paint-style color graphics, developed by Letraset USA.

Raster image processor (RIP). A device or program that translates an image or page into the actual pattern of dots received by a printing or display system.

Raster scan. The generation of an image upon a cathode ray tube made by refreshing the display area line by line.

Recto. In publication design, the right-hand page. Page one (and all odd-numbered pages) always appears on a recto. The left-hand page is called the verso.

Resolution. The degree of detail and clarity of a display; usually specified in dots per inch (dpi). The higher the resolution, or the greater the number of dpi, the sharper the image.

Reverse. Type or image that is dropped out of a printed area, revealing the paper surface.

Reverse leading. A reduction in the amount of interline space, making it less than normal for the point size. For example, 12-point type set on an 11- point body size becomes reverse leading of 1 point.

Revival. A little-used historic typeface previously unavailable in current font formats, now released for contemporary technology.

RIFF. See *Raster Image File Format.*

River. In text type, a series of interword spaces that accidentally align vertically or diagonally, creating an objectionable flow of white space within the column.

ROM. Abbreviation for *read only memory,* which is permanently installed on a computer chip and can be read but cannot accept new or changed data; for example, some laser printers have basic fonts permanently installed in a ROM chip.

Roman. Upright letterforms, as distinguished from italics. More specifically, letters in an alphabet style based on the upright serifed letterforms of Roman inscriptions.

Rule. In handset metal type, a strip of metal that prints as a line. Generally, any line used as an element in typographic design, whether handset, photographic, digital, or hand-drawn.

Run-around. Type that is set with a shortened line measure to fit around a photograph, drawing, or other visual element inserted into the running text.

Run in. To set type without a paragraph indentation or other break. Also, to insert additional matter into the running text as part of an existing paragraph.

Running foot or running footer. A line of text that duplicates a line of text from another page but positioned at or near the bottom of a page.

Running head. Type at the head of sequential pages, providing a title or publication name.

Sans serif. Typefaces without serifs.

Saving. Transferring information – such as an electronic page design – from a computer's memory to a storage device.

Scanner. A computer peripheral device that scans pictures and converts them to digital form so they can be stored, manipulated, and output.

Scrapbook. A computer's "holding place" for permanent storage of images, text, etc.

Screen font. A bitmapped version of an outline font that is used to represent the outline font on a computer screen.

Script. Typefaces based on handwriting, usually having connecting strokes between the letters.

Scroll bar. A rectangular bar that may appear along the right or bottom of a window on a computer screen. By clicking or dragging on the scroll bar, the user can move through the document.

Scrolling. In typesetting and computer-assisted design, moving through a document to bring onto the screen portions of the document not currently displayed.

SCSI. Abbreviation for Small Computer System Interface; pronounced "scuzzy." SCSI is a computer-industry standard interface allowing very fast transfer of data.

Semantics. The science of meaning in linguistics; the study of the relationships between signs and symbols, and what they represent.

Serifs. Small elements added to the ends of the main strokes of a letterform in serifed type styles.

Set width. In metal type, the width of the body upon which a letter is cast. In phototype and digital type, the horizontal width of a letterform measured in units, including the normal space

before and after the character. This interletter space can be increased or decreased to control the tightness or looseness of the fit.

Shoulder. In metal type, the flat top of the type body that surrounds the raised printing surface of the letterform.

Sidebar. A narrow column of text, separated from the main text by a box or rule and containing a secondary article.

Side head. A title or other heading material placed to the side of a type column.

Slab serifs. Square or rectangular serifs that align horizontally and vertically to the baseline and are usually the same (or heavier) weight as the main strokes of the letterform.

Slug. A line of metal type cast on a linecasting machine, such as the Linotype. Also, strips of metal spacing material in thicknesses of 6 points or more.

Small capitals. A set of capital letters having the same height as the lowercase x-height, frequently used for cross-reference and abbreviations. Also called small caps and abbreviated "s.c."

Smoothing. The electronic process of eliminating jaggies (the uneven staircase effect on diagonal or curved lines).

Software. Components of a computer system consisting of the programs or instructions that control the behavior of the computer hardware.

Solid. Lines of type that are set without additional interline space. Also called *set solid.*

Sorts. In metal type, material that is not part of a regular font, such as symbols, piece fractions, and spaces. Also, individual characters used to replace worn-out type in a font.

Stand-alone typesetting system. A typesetting system that is completely self-contained, including editing terminal, memory, and character generation.

Startup disk. The computer disk drive containing the system software used to operate the computer.

Stet. A proofreader's mark meaning that copy marked for correction should not be changed; rather, any instructions for changes should be ignored and the text should be left as originally set.

Storage. In computer typesetting, a device (such as a disk, drum, or tape) that can receive information and retain it for future use.

Straight matter. Text material set in continuous columns with limited deviation from the basic typographic specifications.

Stress. The gradual variation in the thickness of a curved character part or stroke; often used for any variation in the thickness of a character part or stroke.

Style sheets. In several word-processing and page-layout programs, style sheets are special files containing formatting instructions for creating standardized documents.

Subscript. A small character beneath (or adjacent to and slightly below) another character.

Superscript. A small character above (or adjacent to and slightly above) another character.

Swash letters. Letters ornamented with flourishes or flowing tails.

Syntax. In grammar, the way in which words or phrases are put together to form sentences. In design, the connecting or ordering of typographic elements into a visual unity.

System. A related group of interdependent design elements forming a whole. In computer science, a complete computing operation including software and hardware (Central Processing Unit, memory, input/output devices, and peripherals or devices required for the intended functions).

System software. Computer files containing the operating system program and its supporting programs needed to make the computer work, interface with peripherals, and run applications.

Tag Image File Format (TIFF). A computer format for encoding pictures as high-resolution bitmapped images, such as those created by scanners.

Telecommunications. Sending messages to distant locations; usually refers to communicating by telephone lines.

Terminal. See *Video display terminal.*

Text. The main body of written or printed material, as opposed to display matter, footnotes, appendices, etc.

Text type. See *Body type.*

Thumbnail. A miniature image of a page, either a small planning sketch made by a designer or a reduction in a page-layout program.

TIFF. See *Tag Image File Format.*

Tracking. The overall tightness or looseness of the spacing between all characters in a line or block of text. Sometimes used interchangeably with *kerning,* which more precisely is the reduction in spacing between a specific pair of letters.

Transitional. Classification of type styles combining aspects of both Old Style and Modern typefaces; for example, Baskerville.

Type family. The complete range of variations of a typeface design, including roman, italic, bold, expanded, condensed, and other versions.

Typeface. The design of alphabetical and numerical characters unified by consistent visual properties.

Type-high. The standard foot-to-face height of metal types; 0.9186 inches in English-speaking countries.

Typescript. Typewritten manuscript material used as copy for typesetting.

Typesetting. The composing of type by any method or process, also called *composition.*

Type specimen. A typeset sample produced to show the visual properties of a typeface.

Typo. See *Typographical error.*

Typographer. A firm specializing in typesetting. Sometimes used to denote a compositor or typesetter.

Typographical error. A mistake in typesetting, typing, or writing.

Typography. Originally the composition of printed matter from movable type. Now the art and process of typesetting by any system or method.

U.C. and l.c. Abbreviation for *uppercase and lowercase,* used to specify typesetting that combines capitals with lowercase letters.

Undo. A standard computer command that "undoes," or reverses, the last command or operation executed.

Uniform Resource Locator (URL). A location pointer name used to identify the location of a file on a server connected to the World Wide Web.

Unit. A subdivision of the em, used in measuring and counting characters in photo- and digital typesetting systems.

Unitization. The process of designing a typeface so that the individual character widths conform to a typesetter's unit system.

Unitized font. A font with character widths conforming to a typesetter's unit system.

Unit system. A counting system first developed for Monotype, used by most typesetting machines. The width of characters and spaces are measured in units. This data is used to control line breaks, justification, and interword and interletter spacing.

Unit value. The established width, in units, of a typographic character.

Unjustified type. Lines of type set with equal interword spacing, resulting in irregular line lengths. Also called *ragged.*

Uploading. Sending information from your computer to a distant computer. See *Downloading.*

Uppercase. See *Capitals.*

URL. See *Uniform Resource Locator.*

User interface. The way a computer system communicates with its user; the "look and feel" of the machine as experienced by the user.

Vector-based software. Software using computer instructions that specify shapes by defining linear elements by specifying starting and ending locations.

Verso. In publication design, the left-hand page. Page two (and all even-numbered pages) always appear on a verso. The right-hand page is called the recto.

Virus. A computer program that invades computers and modifies data, usually in a destructive manner.

Visual display terminal. A computer input/output device utilizing a cathode ray tube to display data on a screen. Information from memory, storage, or a keyboard can be displayed.

Web browser. A utility viewer used to display documents on the World Wide Web, which are usually written in HTML.

Web page. A document written in HTML, typically stored on a Web site and accessible through a Web browser.

Web site. A collection of files on a Web server computer system that are accessible to a Web browser or by Web TV.

Weight. The lightness or heaviness of a typeface, which is determined by ratio of the stroke thickness to character height.

White space. The "negative" area surrounding a letterform. See *Counter* and *Counterform.*

White-space reduction. A decrease in the amount of interletter space, achieved in typesetting by reducing the unit value of typeset characters. See *tracking.*

Widow. A very short line that appears at the end of a paragraph, column, or page, or at the top of a column or page. These awkward typographic configurations should be corrected editorially.

Width tables. Collections of information about how much horizontal room each character in a font should occupy, often accompanied by information about special kerning pairs or other exceptions.

Windows. An area of a computer screen in which a single document is displayed.

Woodtype. Hand-set types cut from wood by a mechanical router. Formerly used for large display sizes that were not practical for metal casting, woodtype has been virtually eliminated by display photographic typesetting.

Word. In computer systems, a logical unit of information, composed of a predetermined number of bits.

Word-processing program. A computer application used to type in text, then edit, correct, move, or remove it.

Wordspacing. The spatial interval between words. In setting justified body type, space is added between words to extend each line to achieve flush left and right edges. See *Interword spacing.*

World Wide Web. A global graphic media system used to exchange data between computer users.

WORM. Acronym for "Write Once Read Many," usually applied to storage media such as CD-ROMs, which can only be written once but read many times.

WYSIWYG. Abbreviation for "what you see is what you get"; pronounced Wizzywig. This means the image on the screen is identical to the image that will be produced as final output.

x-height. The height of lowercase letters in a font, excluding characters with ascenders and descenders. This is most easily measured on the lowercase *x.*

A chronology of typeface designs

The dates of design, production, and release of a typeface often differ, and additional fonts in a type family frequently follow later; therefore, many dates listed here are approximate.

[1] Revivals of many typefaces are often named after early designers or authors. These faces were not so named during their epoch; however, their contemporary names are used here for identification purposes.

c. 1450: First Textura-style type, Johann Gutenberg

1467: First Roman-style type, Sweynheym and Pannartz

1470: Jenson,[1] Nicolas Jenson

1495: Bembo, Francesco Griffo

1499: Poliphilus, Francesco Griffo

1501: First italic type, Francesco Griffo

1514: Fraktur, Hans Schoensperger

1532: Garamond, Claude Garamond

1557: Civilité, Robert Granjon

c. 1570: Plantin, Anonymous

c. 1570: Canon d'Espagne, the Plantin Office

c. 1582: Flemish bold Roman, the Plantin Office

1616: Typi Academiae, Jean Jannon

c. 1670: Fell Roman, Peter Walpergen

1690: Janson, Nicholas Kis

1702: Romain du Roi, Philippe Grandjean

1722: Caslon Old Style, William Caslon

c. 1743: Early transitional types, Pierre Simon Fournier le Jeune

c. 1746: Fournier decorated letters, Pierre Simon Fournier le Jeune

1757: Baskerville, John Baskerville

c. 1764: Italique Moderne and Ancienne, Pierre Simon Fournier le Jeune

1768: Fry's Baskerville, Isaac Moore

c. 1780: Bodoni, Giambattista Bodoni

1784: Didot, Firmin Didot

c. 1795: Bulmer, William Martin

1796: Fry's Ornamented, Richard Austin

c. 1800: Walbaum, J. E. Walbaum

c. 1810: Scotch Roman, Richard Austin

1815: Two Lines Pica, Antique (first Egyptian style), Vincent Figgins

1815: Five Lines Pica, In Shade (first perspective font), Vincent Figgins

1816: Two-line English Egyptian (first sans serif), William Caslon IV

1820: Lettres Ornées, Fonds de Gille

1828: Roman, Darius Wells

1830: Two-line great primer sans serif, Vincent Figgins

1832: Grotesque, William Thorowgood

1838: Sans serryphs ornamented, Blake and Stephenson

1844: Ionic, Henry Caslon

1845: Clarendon, Robert Besley and Company

1845: Rustic, V. and J. Figgins

1845: Zig-Zag, V. and J. Figgins

1850: Scroll, Henry Caslon

1859: Antique Tuscan Outlined, William Page

1856: National, Philadelphia Type Foundry

c. 1860: P. T. Barnum, Barnhart Brothers and Spindler

c. 1865: French Antique (later called Playbill), Miller and Richard

c. 1865: Old Style Antique (called Bookman in the U.S.), Miller and Richard

c. 1869: Runic, Reed and Fox

c. 1870: Figgins Condensed No. 2, Stevens Shanks

c. 1870: Bank Gothic, Bardhart Brothers and Spindler

1878: Circlet, Barnhart Brothers and Spindler

1878: Glyphic, MacKellar, Smiths and Jordan

c. 1885: Geometric, Central Type Foundry

c. 1890: Ringlet, Marr Typefounding

c. 1890: Gothic Outline No. 61, American Typefounders

c. 1890: Rubens, Marr Typefounding

c. 1890: Karnac, Marr Typefounding

1890: Century, L. B. Benton

1890: Golden, William Morris

1892: Troy, William Morris

1893: Chaucer, William Morris

1894: Bradley, Will Bradley

1895: Merrymount Type, Bertram Goodhue

1895: Century Roman, Theodore Low DeVinne and L. B. Benton

1896: Cheltenham, Bertram Goodhue

1896: Vale Type, Charles Ricketts

1898: Grasset, Eugène Grasset

c. 1898: Paris Metro Lettering, Hector Guimard

1898–1906: Akzidenz Grotesque (Standard), Berthold Foundry

1900: Eckmann-Schrift, Otto Eckmann

1900: Century Expanded, Morris F. Benton

1900: Doves Roman, T. J. Cobden-Sanderson and Emery Walker

1901: Endeavor, Charles R. Ashbee

1901: Copperplate Gothic, Frederic W. Goudy

1901–4: Auriol, Georges Auriol

1902: Behrens-Schrift, Peter Behrens

1902: Subiaco, C. H. St. John Hornby

1903: Brook Type, Lucien Pissarro

1904: Korinna, H. Berthold

1904: Franklin Gothic, Morris F. Benton

1904: Arnold Böcklin, O. Weisert

1904: Linoscript, Morris F. Benton

1907: Behrens-Kursiv, Peter Behrens

1907: Clearface Bold, Morris F. Benton

1907–13: Venus, Bauer Foundry

1908: Behrens-Antiqua, Peter Behrens

1908: News Gothic, Morris F. Benton

1909: Aurora, Wagner and Schmidt Foundry

1910: Kochschrift, Rudolf Koch

1910–15: Hobo, Morris F. Benton

1911: Kennerly Old Style, Frederic W. Goudy

1912: Nicolas Cochin, G. Peignot

1913: Belwe, Georg Belwe

1914: Souvenir, Morris F. Benton

1914: Cloister Old Style, Morris F. Benton

1915: Century Schoolbook, Morris F. Benton

1915–16: Goudy Old Style, Frederic W. Goudy

1916: Centaur, Bruce Rogers

1916: Johnston's Railway Type, Edward Johnston

1919–24: Cooper Old Style, Oswald Cooper

1921: Cooper Black, Oswald Cooper

1922: Locarno (Eve), Rudolf Koch

1923: Windsor, Stephenson Blake Foundry

1923: Tiemann, Walter Tiemann

1923: Neuland, Rudolf Koch

1925: Perpetua, Eric Gill

1926: Weiss Roman, E. R. Weiss

1926: Bauer Bodoni, Bauer typefoundry

1927–29: Futura, Paul Renner

1927–29: Kabel, Rudolf Koch

1928: Ultra Bodoni, Morris F. Benton

1928–30: Gill Sans, Eric Gill

1928: Modernique, Morris F. Benton

1929: Zeppelin, Rudolf Koch

1929: Golden Cockerel, Eric Gill

1929–30: Metro, William A. Dwiggins

1929: Bernhard Fashion, Lucien Bernhard

1929: Bifur, A. M. Cassandre

1929: Broadway, Morris F. Benton

1929: Novel Gothic, H. Becker

1929: Bembo, Monotype Corporation

1929: Lux, Josef Erbar

1929: Memphis, Rudolf Weiss

1929–30: Perpetua, Eric Gill

1929–34: Corvinus, Imre Reiner

1930: City, Georg Trump

1930: Joanna, Eric Gill

1930: Dynamo, Ludwig and Mayer Foundry

1930: Metro, William A. Dwiggins

1931: Prisma, Rudolf Koch

1931: Times New Roman, Stanley Morison and Victor Lardent

1931: Stymie, Morris F. Benton

1931–36: Beton, Heinrich Jost

1932–40: Albertus, Berthold Wolpe

1933: Agency Gothic, Morris F. Benton

1933: Atlas, K. H. Schaefer

1934: Rockwell, H. F. Pierpont

1935: Electra, William A. Dwiggins

1935: Huxley Vertical, Walter Huxley

1936: Acier Noir, A. M. Cassandre

1937: Peignot, A. M. Cassandre

1937: Stencil, Robert H. Middleton

1937: Onyx, Gerry Powell

1938: Caledonia, William A. Dwiggins

1938: Libra, S. H. De Roos

1938: Lydian, Warren Chappell

1938: Empire, American Typefounders

1939: Chisel, Stephenson Blake Foundry

1940: Trajanus, Warren Chappell

1940: Tempo, Robert H. Middleton

1945: Stradivarius, Imre Reiner

1945: Courier, Bud Kettler

1946: Profil, Eugen and Max Lenz

1948: Trade Gothic, Mergenthaler Linotype

c. 1950: Brush, Harold Brodersen

1950: Michelangelo, Hermann Zapf

1950: Palatino, Hermann Zapf

1951: Sistina, Hermann Zapf

1952: Horizon, K. F. Bauer and Walter Baum

1952: Melior, Hermann Zapf

1952: Microgramma, A. Butti

1953: Mistral, Roger Excoffon

1954: Trump Mediaeval, Georg Trump

1955: Columna, Max Caflisch

1955: Egizio, Aldo Novarese

1955–56: Egyptienne, Adrian Frutiger

1956: Craw Clarendon, Freeman Craw

1956: Murry Hill, E. J. Klumpp

1957: Meridien, Adrian Frutiger

1957: Univers, Adrian Frutiger

c. 1957: Helvetica, Max Miedinger

1960: Aurora, Jackson Burke

1961: Octavian, Will Carter and David Kindersley

1962: Eurostile, Aldo Novarese

1962–66: Antique Olive, Roger Excoffon

1964: Sabon, Jan Tschichold

1965: Americana, Richard Isbell

1965: Snell Roundhand, Matthew Carter

1965: Friz Quadrata, Ernest Friz

1966: Egyptian 505, André Gürtler

1966: Vladimir, Vladimir Andrich

1966: Sabon, Jan Tschichold

1967: Serifa, Adrian Frutiger

1967: Americana, Richard Isbell

1967: Cartier, Carl Dair

1967: Avant Garde Gothic, Herb Lubalin and Tom Carnase

1967: Poppl-Antiqua, Friedrich Poppl

1968: Syntax, Hans E. Meier

1969: Aachen, Colin Brignall

1970: Olympian, Matthew Carter

1970: Machine, Tom Carnase and Ron Bonder

1970: ITC Souvenir, Edward Benguiat

1972: Iridium, Adrian Frutiger

1972: Times Europa, Walter Tracy

1972: University, Mike Daines

1974: American Typewriter, Joel Kadan

1974: ITC Tiffany, Edward Benguiat

1974: Newtext, Ray Baker

1974: Korinna, Ed Benguiat and Vic Caruso

1974: American Typewriter, Joel Kaden and Tony Stan

1974: Serif Gothic, Herb Lubalin and Tony DiSpigna

1974: Lubalin Graph, Herb Lubalin, Tony DiSpigna, and Joe Sundwall

1975: ITC Bauhaus, based on Bayer's universal alphabet

1975: ITC Bookman, Ed Benguiat

1975: ITC Century, Tony Stan

1975: ITC Cheltenham, Tony Stan

1975: Concorde Nova, Gunter Gerhard Lange

1975: ITC Garamond, Tony Stan

1975: Marconi, Hermann Zapf

1976: Eras, Albert Hollenstein and Albert Boton

1976: Poppl-Pontiflex, Friedrich Poppl

1976: Zapf Book, Hermann Zapf

1976: Frutiger, Adrian Frutiger

1977: Quorum, Ray Baker

1977: Korinna Kursiv, Edward Benguiat

1977: Italia, Colin Brignall

1977: Benguiat, Edward Benguiat

1977: Zapf International, Hermann Zapf

1977: Fenice, Also Novarese

1978: Basilia, André Gürtler

1978: Bell Centennial, Matthew Carter

1978: Galliard, Matthew Carter

1979: Benguiat Gothic, Edward Benguiat

1979: Glypha, Adrian Frutiger

1979: Zapf Chancery, Hermann Zapf

1980: Fenice, Aldo Novarese

1980: Novarese, Aldo Novarese

1980: Icone, Adrian Frutiger

1980: Marconi, Hermann Zapf

1980: Edison, Hermann Zapf

1981: Adroit, Phil Martin

1981: Barcelonia, Edward Benguiat

1981: Isbell, Dick Isbell and Jerry Campbell

1982: Cushing, Vincent Pacella

1983: ITC Berkeley Old Style, Tony Stan

1983: Weidemann, Kurt Weidemann and Kurt Strecker

1983: Neue Helvetica, Linotype (Stempel) staff designers

1984: Macintosh screen fonts, Susan Kare

1984: Osiris, Gustav Jaeger

1984: Usherwood, Les Usherwood

1984: Veljovic, Jovica Veljovic

1985: Aurelia, Hermann Zapf

1985: Elan, Albert Boton

1985: Emigre, Zuzana Licko

1985: Kis-Janson, Autologic staff designers

1985: Lucida, Charles Bigelow and Kris Holmes

1985: Mixage, Aldo Novarese

1985: Oakland, Zuzana Licko

1986: Linotype Centennial, Matthew Carter

1986: Matrix, Zuzana Licko

1986: Centennial, Adrian Frutiger

1987: Amerigo, Gerard Unger

1987: Charter, Matthew Carter

1987: Gerstner Original, Karl Gerstner

1987: Glyphia, Adrian Frutiger

1987: Neufont, David Weinz

1987: Stone Informal, Sans and Serif, Sumner Stone

1987: Charlemagne, Carol Twombly

1987: Belizio, David Berlow

1987: Zapf Renaissance, Hermann Zapf

1988: Visigoth, Arthur Baker

1988: Avenir, Adrian Frutiger

c. 1989: FF Meta, Erik Spiekermann

1989: Adobe Garamond, Robert Slimbach

1989: Giovanni, Robert Slimbach

1989: Helicon, David Quay

1989: Lithos, Carol Twombly

1989: Rotis, Otl Aicher

1989: Trajan, Carol Twombly

1989: Keedy Sans, Jeffery Keedy

1989: Phaistos, David Berlow

1989: Commerce, Greg Thompson and Rick Valicenti

1989–90: Bronzo, Rick Valicenti

1990: Bodega Sans, Greg Thompson

1990: Journal, Zuzana Licko

1990: Adobe Caslon, Carol Twombly

1990: Quay, David Quay

1990: Tekton, David Siegel

1990: Template Gothic, Barry Deck

1990: Dead History, Scott Makela

1990: Myriad, Robert Slimbach and Carol Twombly

1990: Minion, Robert Slimbach

1990: Arcadia, Industria, and Insignia, Neville Brody

1991: Print, Sumner Stone

1991: Exocet, Jonathan Barnbrook

1991: Adobe Caslon, Carol Twombly

1991: Remedy, Frank Heine

1992: Syndor, Hans Edward Meier

1992: Mason: Jonathan Barnbrook

1992: Poetica, Robert Slimbach

1993: Mantinia and Sofia, Matthew Carter

1993: Agenda, Greg Thompson

1994: Barcode, Brian Lucid

1994: Dogma, Zuzana Licko

1994: Big Caslon CC, Matthew Carter

1995: DIN, Albert-Jan Pool

1995: Walker, Matthew Carter

1995: Shogun, Richard Lipton

1996: Filosofia, Zuzana Licko

1996: Mrs Eaves, Zuzano Licko

1997: Vendetta, John Downer

1997–2000: Poynter Old Style, Tobias Frere-Jones

1999: Council, John Downer

1999: Spira, Andy Stockley

1999: Acropolis, Jonathan Hoefler

1999: Leviathan, Jonathan Hoefler

1999: Dispatch, Cyrus Highsmith

1999: Scala, Martin Majoor

2000: Verdana, Matthew Carter

2000: Georgia, Matthew Carter

2000: Seria, Martin Majoor

2001: Atma Serif Book, Alan Greene

2001: Dalliance, Frank Heine

2001: Vesta, Gerard Unger

2002: Bau, Christian Schwartz

2002: Gotham, Tobias Frere-Jones

2003: Benton Sans, Tobias Frere-Jones and Cyrus Highsmith

2003: Max, Morten Rostgaart Olson

2003: Page Sans and Serif, Albert Boton

2004: Amira, Cyrus Highsmith

2004: Nexus, Martin Majoor

2005: Dederon Sans, Tomas Brousil

2005: Minah, Jacqueline Sakwa

2005: Titling Gothic, David Berlow

2005: Truth, David Berlow

(Frontispiece) *Saint. Barbara,* 15th-Century German or French polychromed walnut sculpture. (50"H x 23"W x 13"D) 127.0 cm x 58.4 cm x 33.0 cm. The Virginia Museum of Fine Arts, Richmond. The Williams Fund, 1968.

Chapter One.

1. Impressed tablet from Godin Tepe, Iran. West Asian Department, Royal Ontario Museum, Toronto.
2. Facsimile of the cuneiform impression on a clay tablet, after Hansard.
3. The Pyramids at Giza, from *The Iconographic Encyclopaedia of Science, Literature, and Art* by Johann Georg Heck, 1851.
4. Egyptian Old Kingdom *False Door Stele,* limestone. The Virginia Museum of Fine Arts, Richmond. Museum Purchase: The Williams Fund.
5. Cuneiform tablet. Sumero-Akkadian. The Metropolitan Museum of Art, New York. Acquired by exchange with J. Pierpont Morgan Library, 1911.
6. Photograph of Stonehenge; courtesy of the British Tourist Authority.
7. Egyptian Polychromed Wood Sculpture, XVIII–XIX Dynasty. Ushabti. The Virginia Museum of Fine Arts, Richmond. Museum Purchase: The Williams Fund, 1955.
8. *The Book of the Dead of Tuthmosis III.* Museum of Fine Arts, Boston. Gift of Horace L. Meyer.
10. Phoenician inscription. The Metropolitan Museum of Art, New York. The Cesnola Collection. Purchased by subscription, 1874–76.
12. Photograph of the Parthenon; courtesy of the Greek National Tourist Office.
13. Photograph of Greek record of sale; Agora Excavations, American School of Classical Studies, Athens.
15. Photograph of a wall in Pompeii, by James Mosley.
17. Photographer anonymous; c. 1895. Private collection.
18. *Funerary inscription of Lollia Genialis.* Marble. The Metropolitan Museum of Art, New York.
19. Photographer anonymous; c. 1895. Private collection.
20. Photograph; courtesy of the Italian Government Travel Office.
24. Detail, "Christ attended by angels," from *The Book of Kells,* fol. 32v; photograph; courtesy of the Irish Tourist Board.
25 and 26. Photographs; courtesy of the Irish Tourist Board.
28. Photograph; courtesy of the French Government Tourist Office.
30. Bronze and copper *Crucifix.* The Virginia Museum of Fine Art, Richmond. Museum Purchase: The Williams Fund, 1968.
32. *Madonna and Child on a Curved Throne.* Wood, 0.815 x 0.490m (32 1/8 x 19 3/8 in.) National Gallery of Art, Washington. Andrew W. Mellon Collection, 1937.
34. Lippo Memmi; Sienese, active 1317–47. *Saint John the Baptist.* Wood, 0.95 x 0.46m (37 1/4 x 18 in.). National Gallery of Art, Washington. Samuel H. Kress Collection, 1939.
35. Photograph courtesy of the Italian Government Tourist Office.
37. Fra Filippo Lippi; Florentine c. 1406–69. *Madonna and Child.* Wood, 0.80 x 0.51m (31 3/8 x 20 1/8 in.). National Gallery of Art, Washington. Samuel H. Kress Collection, 1939.
38. The Rosenwald Collection; The Library of Congress, Washington, DC.
39. Woodcut illustration from *Standebuch* by Jost Amman, 1568.
40. Photographer anonymous; c. 1895. Private collection.
42. Typography from *Lactantu . . . .* Printed by Sweynheym and Pannartz; Rome, 1468. The Library of Congress Rare Book and Special Collections Division, Washington, DC.

43. From *De evangelica praeparatione* by Eusebius Pamphilii. Printed by Nicolas Jenson; Venice, 1470.
44. From *The Recuyell of the Historyes of Troye* by Raoul Le Fevre. Printed by William Caxton and Colard Mansion; Burges, c. 1475.
45. Filippino Lippi; *Portrait of a Youth.* Wood, 0.510 x 0.355 m (20 x 13 7/8 in.). National Gallery of Art, Washington, DC. Andrew Mellon Collection, 1937.
46. Erhard Ratdolt, earliest extant type specimen sheet. Published April 1, 1486, in Augsburg, Germany. Bayerische Staatsbibliothek, Munich.
47. Woodcut portrait of Aldus Manutius. Published by Antoine Lafrery; Rome, 16th century.
48. From *De aetna* by Pietro Bembo. Published by Aldus Manutius, Venice, 1495.
49. Page from *Virgil.* Published by Aldus Manutius; Venice, 1501.
50. Photograph by Rommler and Jonas; 1892. Private collection.
53. From *Underweisung der Messung* by Albrecht Durer; Nuremburg, 1525.
54. From *Champ Fleury* by Geoffroy Tory; Paris, 1529.
55. Photograph; courtesy of the French Government Tourist Office.
57. Titian; Venetian c. 1477–1565. *Cardinal Pietro Bembo.* Canvas, 0.945 x 0.765m (37 1/8 x 30 1/8 in.). National Gallery of Art, Washington, DC. Samuel H. Kress Collection, 1952.
58. Title page for *Elementary Geometry* by Oronce Fine. Printed by Simone de Colines; Paris, 1544.
59. From *Hypnerotomachia Poliphili* by Fra Francesco Colonna. Printed by Jacque Kerver; Paris, 1546.
60. El Greco; Spanish 1541–1614. *Saint Martin and the Beggar.* Canvas, 1.935 x 1.030m (76 1/8 x 40 1/2 in.). National Gallery of Art, Washington, DC. Widener Collection, 1942.
61. From *Nejw Kunstliches Alphabet* by Johann Theodor de Bry; Germany, 1595.
62. Photographer anonymous; c. 1895. Private collection.
63. Detail, typographic specimens of Jean Jannon; Sedan, 1621.
64. Page from *Stamperia Vaticana Specimen;* Rome, 1628.
65. Photograph; courtesy of the Government of India Tourist Office.
66. Sir Anthony van Dyck; Flemish, 1599–1641. *Henri II de Lorraine, Duc de Guise.* Canvas, 2.046 x 1.238m (80 5/8 x 48 5/8 in.). National Gallery of Art, Washington, DC. Gift of Cornelius Vanderbilt Whitney, 1947.
67. Jan Vermeer; Dutch 1632–75. *Woman Holding a Balance,* c. 1664. Canvas, 0.425 x 0.380m (16 3/4 x 15 in.). National Gallery of Art, Washington, DC. Widener Collection, 1942.
69. Photograph; courtesy of the British Tourist Authority.
71. Photographer anonymous; 1896. Private collection.
72. From the 1764 specimen book of W. Caslon and Son, London.
73. Photograph; courtesy of the Irish Tourist Board.
74. Title page for *Cato Major, or His Discourse on Old Age* by M. T. Cicero. Printed by Benjamin Franklin; Philadelphia, 1744.
75. Francois Boucher; French 1703–70. *The Love Letter,* 1750. Canvas, 0.813 x 0.741m (32 x 29 1/8 in.). National Gallery of Art, Washington, DC. Timken Collection, 1959.
76. Anonymous; engraved portrait of John Baskerville.
77. From the specimen book of Thomas Cottrell, English typefounder; London, c. 1765.
78. Detail, title page of *Historie de Louis de Bourbon . . . ,* using types and ornaments designed by Pierre Simon Fournier le Jeune. Published by Lottin; Paris, 1768.

Picture Credits

79. Johann David Steingruber, 1702–1787. Engraved letter *A* from *Architectonishes Alphabet,* Schwabach, 1773. The Metropolitan Museum of Art. The Elisha Whittelsey Collection, 1955. The Elisha Whittelsey Fund.

80. Photograph; courtesy of the Library of Congress, Washington, DC.

82. Detail, title page using type designed by Bodoni. Dante's *Divine Comedy;* Pisa, 1804.

83. From Thorowgood's *New Specimen of Printing Types, late R. Thorne's, No. 2;* London, 1821.

84. Jacques-Louis David; French 1748–1825. *Napoleon in his Study,* 1812. Canvas, 2.039 x 1.251m (80 1/4 x 49 1/4 in.). National Gallery of Art, Washington, DC. Samuel H. Kress Collection, 1961.

85–6. From *Specimen of Printing Types* by Vincent Figgins; London, 1815.

87. From *Specimen of Printing Types* by William Caslon IV; London, 1816.

88. From *Manuale Typographico.* Published by Signora Bodoni and Luigi Orsi; Parma, Italy, 1818.

89. From Thorowgood's *New Specimen of Printing Types, late R. Thorne's, No. 2;* London, 1821.

90. Photograph; courtesy of the Virginia State Travel Service.

91. From *Bower, Bacon & Bower's Specimen of Printing Types;* Sheffield, c. 1825.

92. Wood engraving of Darius Wells, from *The Inland Printer;* Chicago, July 1888.

93. From *Specimen of Printing Types* by Vincent Figgins; London, 1833.

94. Poster by the Davy & Berry Printing Office; Albion, England, 1836.

95. From *Specimen of Printing Types by V. & J. Figgins, successors to Vincent Figgins, Letter-Founder;* London, 1836.

96. Courtesy of the Library of Congress Rare Book and Special Collections Division, Washington, DC.

97. Photograph; courtesy of the British Tourist Authority.

98. From *The Specimen Book of Types Cast at the Austin Foundry by Wood & Sharwoods;* London, c. 1841.

99. From *A General Specimen of Printing Types.* Published by W. Thorowgood and Company; London, 1848.

100. Photograph; The Library of Congress Rare Book and Special Collections Division, Washington, DC.

101. Photograph; The Library of Congress Rare Book and Special Collections Division, Washington, DC.

102. From the wood type specimen book of William H. Page & Company; Greenville, Connecticut, 1859.

103. Private collection.

104. Honoré Daumier; French 1808–79. *The Third-Class Carriage.* Oil on canvas, 65.4 x 90.2m (25 3/4 x 35 1/2 in.). The Metropolitan Museum of Art, New York. Bequest of Mrs. H. O. Havemeyer, 1929. The H. O. Havemeyer Collection.

105. Private collection.

106. Private collection.

107. Courtesy of The New York Convention and Visitors Bureau.

108. Private collection.

109. Private collection.

110. Wood engraving from *The Inland Printer;* Chicago, December 1889.

112. Courtesy of the French Government Tourist Office.

113. Photograph; courtesy of the Archives: The Coca-Cola Company.

114. Paul Gauguin; French 1848–1903. *Fatata Te Miti (By the Sea),* 1892. Canvas, 0.679 x 0.915m (26 3/4 x 36 in.). National Gallery of Art, Washington, DC. The Chester Dale Collection, 1962.

117. William Morris. *News from Nowhere.* Published by Kelmscott Press; London, 1892.

118. Title page from *Van nu en Straks.* Designed by Henri van de Velde, 1893.

119. Title page from *Limbes de Lumieres* by Gustave Kahn; Brussels, 1897.

120. From *The Inland Printer;* Chicago, June 1900.

121. Title page from *A Lady of Quality* by Francis Hodgson Burnett. Published by Charles Scribner's Sons; New York, 1897.

122. Cover for Vienna Secession Catalog No. 5; Vienna, 1899.

123. Photograph; courtesy of the French Government Tourist Office.

124. Dedication page from *Feste des Lebens und der Kunst: Ein Betrachtung des Theaters als hochsten Kultursymbols (Celebrations of Life and Art: A Consideration of the Theater as the Highest Cultural Symbol)* by Peter Behrens; Darmstadt, 1900.

125. Filippo Marinetti, Futurist poem, S.T.F., 1914.

126. Cover, *Delikatessen Haus Erich Fromm, Haupt-List 2;* Cologne, c. 1910.

127. Wassily Kandinsky. *Improvisation 31 (Sea Battle),* 1913. National Gallery of Art, Washington, DC. Ailsa Mellon Bruce Fund.

128. War Bond Fund Drive poster for the British government by Bert Thomas, c. 1916.

129. Advertisement for the *Kleine Grosz Mappe (Small Grosz Portfolio)* from *Die Neue Jugend.* Designed by John Heartfield. Published by Der Malik-Verlag, Berlin, June 1917.

130. First cover for *De Stijl,* the journal of the de Stijl movement. Designed by Vilmos Huszar. Published/edited by Theo van Doesburg, The Netherlands; October 1917.

131. Raoul Hausmann. *Poème Phonetique,* 1919.

132. Piet Mondrian; Dutch 1872–1944. *Diamond Painting in Red, Yellow, and Blue.* Oil on canvas, 40 x 40 in. National Gallery of Art, Washington, DC. Gift of Herbert and Nannette Rothschild, 1971.

133. Poster announcing availability of books, by Alexander Rodchenko; Moscow, c. 1923. Private collection.

134. Illustration by Mike Fanizza.

135. Title page from *Die Kunstismen* by El Lissitzky and Hans Arp. Published by Eugen Rentsch Verlag; Zurich, 1925.

136. Proposed universal alphabet. Designed by Herbert Bayer as a student at the Bauhaus.

137. Constantin Brancusi; Romanian 1876–1957. *Bird in Space.* Marble, stone, and wood, hgt. 3.446m (136 1/2 in.). National Gallery of Art, Washington, DC. Gift of Eugene and Agnes Meyer, 1967.

138. Title page for special insert, "Elementare Typographie" from *Typographische Mitteilungen;* Leipzig, October 1925.

139–40. Advertisements by Piet Zwart; courtesy of N. V. Nederlandsche Kabelfabriek, Delft.

141. Trial setting using Futura. Designed by Paul Renner. Published by Bauersche Giesserei; Frankfurt am Main, 1930.

142. Photograph; courtesy of New York Convention and Visitors Bureau.

143. Max Bill. Poster for an exhibition of African Art at the Kunstgewerbemuseum, Zurich.

144. Alexey Brodovitch. Poster for an industrial design exhibition at the Philadelphia Museum of Art.

145. Walker Evans. Photograph, "Fields family, sharecroppers," Hale County, Alabama. The Library of Congress, Washington, DC.

146. Jean Carlu. Advertisement for Container Corporation of America, December 21, 1942.

147. Max Bill. Poster for an exhibition of Art Concrete at the Kunsthalle, Basle.

148. Paul Rand. Title page for *On My Way* by Hans Arp. Published by Wittenborn, Schultz Inc.; New York, 1948.

149. Willem de Kooning. *Painting,* 1948. Enamel and oil on canvas, 42 5/8 x 56 1/8 in. Collection; Museum of Modern Art, New York. Purchase.

150. Ladislav Sutnar. Cover for *Catalog Design Progress* by K. Lonberg-Holm and Ladislav Sutnar. Published by Sweet's Catalog Service; New York, 1950.

151. Illustration by Stephen Chovanec.

152. Henri Matisse; French 1869–1954. *Woman with Amphora and Pomegranates.* Paper on canvas (collage), 2.436 x 0.963m (96 x 37 7/8 in.). National Gallery of Art, Washington, DC. Ailsa Mellon Bruce Fund, 1973.

153. Josef Müller-Brockmann. Poster for a musical concert; Zürich, January 1955.

154. Saul Bass. Advertisement from the Great Ideas of Western Man series, Container Corporation of America.

155. Willem Sandberg. Back and front covers for *Experimenta Typographica.* Published by Verlag Galerie der Spiegel; Cologne, 1956.

156. Saul Bass, designer. Film title for *Anatomy of a Murder.* Produced and directed by Otto Preminger, 1959.

157. Photograph; courtesy of the New York Convention and Visitors Bureau.

158. Carlo L. Vivarelli. Cover for *Neue Grafik.* Published by Verlag Otto Walter AG; Olten, Switzerland, 1959.

159. Henry Wolf. Cover for *Harper's Bazaar* magazine, December 1959.

160. Gerald Holton. Symbol for the Campaign for Nuclear Disarmament; Great Britain, c. 1959.

161. Otto Storch. Typography from *McCall's* magazine; July 1959.

162. Karl Gerstner. Poster for the newspaper *National Zeitung;* Zürich, 1960.

163. Herb Lubalin. Advertisement for Sudler and Hennessey Advertising Inc.; New York.

164. George Lois. Advertisement for A. H. Robins Company Incorporated.

165. Photograph; courtesy of the Virginia State Travel Service.

166. Seymour Chwast and Milton Glaser, Push Pin Studios Inc. Poster for the Lincoln Center for the Performing Arts, New York.

167. George Lois. Cover for *Esquire* magazine, October 1966.

168. Seymour Chwast and Milton Glaser, Push Pin Studios Inc. Poster for Filmsense, New York.

169. Photograph; courtesy of the Public Relations Department, City of Montreal, Canada.

170. Designer not known. Symbol widely used in the environmental movement.

171. Photograph; courtesy of the National Aeronautics and Space Administration.

172. Wolfgang Weingart. Experimental interpretation of a poem by Elsbeth Bornoz; Basel, Switzerland.

173. Herb Lubalin. Volume 1, Number 1, of *U&lc.* Published by the International Typeface Corporation, New York.

174. Cook and Shanosky, commissioned by the American Institute of Graphic Arts under contract to the U.S. Department of Transportation. From *Symbol Signs,* a series of thirty-four passenger-oriented symbols for use in transportation facilities.

175. Bruce Blackburn, then of Chermayeff and Geismar Associates. Symbol for the U.S. Bicentennial Commission and stamp for the U.S. Postal Service, first released in 1971.

176. Photograph; courtesy of the French Government Tourist Office.

177. Trademark reproduced by permission of Frederic Ryder Company; Chicago, Illinois.

178. Willi Kuntz. Poster for an exhibition of photographs by Fredrich Cantor, FOTO Gallery, New York.

179. Title film for *All That Jazz,* Twentieth Century-Fox. Director/designer Richard Greenberg, R/Greenberg Associates Inc., New York.

180. MTV logo courtesy of Pat Gorman, Manhattan Design, New York.

181. Photograph; courtesy of the Office of the Mayor, Portland, Oregon.

182. Warren Lehrer, designer. Published by ear/say, Purchase, NY, and Visual Studies Workshop, Rochester, NY.

183. Emperor 8, 10, 15 & 19 designed by Zuzana Licko in 1985. Courtesy of Emigre Inc., Sacramento, CA.

184. David Carson, designer; Art Brewer, photographer. *Beach Culture* next issue page, 1990.

185. Ted Mader and Tom Draper, designers. Ted Mader + Associates, Seattle, WA. Published by Peachpit Press Inc., Berkeley, CA.

186. Template Gothic designed by Barry Deck in 1990. Courtesy of Emigre Inc., Sacramento, CA.

187. Exocet Heavy designed by Jonathan Barnbrook in 1991. Courtesy of Emigre Inc., Sacramento, CA.

188. Fetish typeface designed by Jonathan Hoefler. Copyright 1994, The Hoefler Type Foundry Inc.

189. Meta typeface designed by Erik Spiekerman and released by FontShop, c. 1991.

190. Robert Slimbach and Carol Twombly, designers. Myriad Multiple Master typeface designed by courtesy of Adobe Systems Inc., San Jose, CA.

191. Ron Kellum, designer. Courtesy of Kellum McClain, Inc., New York.

192. James Victore, designer. Racism poster, 1993.

193. Registered logo of Netscape, used by permission of America Online Inc.

194. Matthew Carter, designer. Walker typefaces, 1994.

195. Landor Associates, designers. Courtesy of Xerox/The Document Company.

196. Stefan Sagmeister, designer. Courtesy of Sagmeister Inc.

197. Frank Gehry, architect. Guggenheim Museum in Bilbao, Spain, 1997. Photograph courtesy of the Tourist Office of Spain, New York.

198. Paula Scher and Keith Daigle, designers. Courtesy of Pentagram Design Inc., New York.

199. Robert Slimbach, designer. Adobe Garamond, 1989. Courtesy of Adobe Systems Inc., San Jose, CA.

200. Janice Fishman, Holly Goldsmith, Jim Parkinson, and Sumner Stone, designers. ITC Bodoni, 1994–95.

201. Mrs Eaves Roman designed by Zuzana Licko in 1996. Courtesy of Emigre Inc., Sacramento, CA.

202. Neville Brody, designer. Fuse 98: Beyond Typography poster, 1998.

203. Wolfgang Weingart, designer.

204. Jennifer Sterling, designer. Fox River Paper Company calendar, 2001.

205. Art Director and Designer: Mirko Ilić. Creative Directors: Nada Raiicic and Stanislav Shorpe. Courtesy of Mirko Ilić Corp.

206. Jim Sherraden. Courtesy of Hatch Show Print, a division of the Country Music Foundation, Inc.

207. Irma Boom, designer.

208. Philippe Apeloig, designer.

209. Max Kisman, designer.

210. Jianping He, designer. Courtesy of Hesign International, GmbH

211. Lawrence Weiner, designer/artist. Courtesy of Anderson Gallery.

212. Mevis & Van Deursen, designers. Courtesy of Mevis & Van Deursen.

213. Jean Benoît-Lévy, designer. Courtesy of AND Trafic Grafic.

Chapter Three

4. Willi Kunz, designer. Poster; 14 x 16 1/2 in.

9. Walter Ballmer, designer. Courtesy of Olivetti.

30. Designer: Frank Armstrong; photograph by Sally Anderson-Bruce

57. Designer: Danne and Blackburn. Courtesy of NASA.

Chapter Four

36. Matthew Carter, designer. Copyright Microsoft.

37. Matthew Carter, photographer.

38. Emperor 8, 10, 15 & 19 designed by Zuzana Licko in 1985. Courtesy of Emigre Inc., Sacramento, CA.

Chapter Five

1. Designer: Jan Tschichold. Title page for special insert, "Elementare Typographie" from *Typographische Mitteilungen;* Leipzig, October 1925.

7. Psalterium, 12th century. Spencer Collection, The New York Public Library, Astor, Lenox and Tilden Foundations.

10. Paul Rand, designer. Courtesy of the Estate of Paul Rand.

11. Courtesy of type-ø-tone.

15. Cover and spread from *Die Weise von Liebe und Tod des Cornets Christoph Rilke* (Insel-Bucherei Nr. 1) 1957. Courtesy of Insel Verlag, Frankfurt.

16. Designer: Rob Carter; photographer: Leo Divendal.

17. Photograph; courtesy of Trickett & Webb Limited, London.

18. Victor Levie, designer. Courtesy of Anne Frank House, Amsterdam.

25. Creative Director: Christian Beckwith; designer: Sam Serebin. Courtesy of *Alpinist.*

26. Designer: Typography, Interiority & Other Serious Matters. Courtesy of Stichting De Best Verzorgde Boeken.

27. Photograph; courtesy of the Burdick Group.

29. Josef Müller-Brockmann, designer. Courtesy of Verlag Niggli AG, Switzerland.

33. Photograph; courtesy of Graphic Thought Facility, London.

34. Photograph; courtesy of Main Street Design, Boston.

35. Web site design: Juan Benedit. Courtesy of Demographik.

36. Web site design: Virtual Identity AG; Graphic design: Uli Weidner. Courtesy of Vitra.

Chapter Six

1. Eugen Gomringer. "ping pong," from *Concrete Poetry: A World View.* Edited by Mary Ellen Solt, Indiana University Press, 1970.

15. Herb Lubalin, designer. Courtesy of *Reader's Digest.*

20. Photograph; courtesy of Olivetti.

25. Gerrit Rietveld, designer. Red/blue chair, 1918. Collection Stedelijk Museum, Amsterdam.

26. Stephen Coates, designer. Masthead for *eye, The International Review of Graphic Design.* Courtesy of *eye* magazine.

29. J. Abbott Miller, James Hicks, Paul Carlos, and Scott Davendorf, designers. Courtesy of Pentagram Design Inc., New York.

Chapter Seven

4, 5, and 6. Photographs; courtesy of Mergenthaler Linotype Company.

9. George Nan, photographer.

18. Courtesy of Autologic Inc., Newbury Park, CA.

26. Photograph; courtesy of Mergenthaler Linotype Company.

34. Microphotographs courtesy of Mike Cody, Virginia Commonwealth University, Richmond, VA.

Chapter Eight

1–7. Courtesy of Jean Benoît-Lévy, designer.

8–11. Courtesy of United States National Park Service.

13–20. Courtesy of *Interiors* magazine.

21–25. Courtesy of Richard Greenberg, designer.

26–38. Courtesy of Sussman/Prejza, designers.

39–50. Courtesy of MetaDesign/San Francisco.

51–60. Courtesy of Maureen Kringen, Kringenmedia, Sebastopol, CA.

61–69. Courtesy of Frankfurt, Gips, Balkind, New York.

70-79. Courtesy of John Malinoski, designer.

80-86. Liselore Kamping, photographer.

Chapter Ten

18. Courtesy of Holland Fonts.

19. Brad Rhodes, designer. Courtesy of eudesCo.

25-32. Courtesy of Heather Boone, designer.

33-43. Courtesy of Matt Gardner, designer.

44-49. Courtesy of Benjamin Gaydos, designer.

50-56. Courtesy of Justin Howard, designer.

57-71. Courtesy of Matt Klimas, designer.

72-90. Courtesy of Chris Malven, designer.

91-107. Courtesy of Thirada Raungpaka, designer.

108-118. Courtesy of Karen Stein, designer.

119-128. Courtesy of Todd Timney, designer.

129-140. Courtesy of Shuangshuang Wu, designer.

Chapter Eleven

5. From *American Advertising Posters of the Nineteenth Century* by Mary Black; courtesy of Dover Publications Inc., New York.

Sources for specimen quotations

Pages i, 241, 247, 257, 263, 269, 279, 289, and 299. From *The Book Beautiful* by Thomas James Cobden-Sanderson. Hammersmith: Hammersmith Publishing Society, 1902.

Page 137, from *The Alphabet and Elements of Lettering* by Frederic W. Goudy, courtesy of Dover Publications Inc., New York.

Printing:	R.R. Donnelley and Sons, Willard, Ohio
Binding:	R.R. Donnelley and Sons, Willard, Ohio
Cover printing:	Brady Palmer Printing Co., Carmel, New York
Typography:	9/11 Univers 55 text with 7/11 Univers 55 captions and 9/11 Univers 75 headings
Design:	First edition: Rob Carter, Stephen Chovanec, Ben Day, and Philip Meggs; Second edition: Rob Carter and Philip Meggs; Third edition: Rob Carter, Philip Meggs, and Sandra Wheeler; Fourth edition: Rob Carter and Sandra Wheeler
Web site design:	Chris Malven
Design Assistance:	First edition: Tina Brubaker Chovanec, Justin Deister, John Demao, Akira Ouchi, Tim Priddy, Anne Riker, Joel Sadagursky, and Jennifer Mugford Weiland; Second edition: Linda Johnson, Jeff Price, and Brenda Zaczek
Photography and digital imaging:	First and second edition: George Nan; Third edition: Rob Carter, Philip Meggs, George Nan, North Market Street Graphics, and Sandra Wheeler; Fourth edition: Rob Carter and Sandra Wheeler

The authors wish to thank the following people for their contributions to this book. At John Wiley & Sons, Senior Editor Margaret Cummins, Production Director Diana Cisek, Senior Production Editor David Sassian, and Manufacturing Manager Tom Hyland guided this book through the editorial and production phases. Libby Phillips Meggs contributed ongoing consultation and advice. Jerry Bates, Margaret Bates, Tina Brubaker Chovanec, and Diana Lively have provided logistical support. At Virginia Commonwealth University, Matt Woolman, and Dr. Richard Toscan offered encouragement.